GRANDPARENTING
IN
BRITAIN:

A baseline study

Geoff Dench   &   Jim Ogg

INSTITUTE OF COMMUNITY STUDIES

First published in 2002
by the *Institute of Community Studies*

18 Victoria Park Square
London
E2 9PF
UK

tel. 020 8980 6263

fax. 020 8981 6719

ISBN 0 95368037 4 7

Printed in UK by
Antony Rowe Ltd, Eastbourne

This report is dedicated to

Michael Young

and his last brainchild

Grandparents Plus

Contents:

Tables:

Figures:

GRANDPARENTING IN BRITAIN: SUMMARY

1   Setting a baseline

This report presents some of the findings of the Grandparenting module included in the 1998 *British Social Attitudes* Survey. It is the first national survey of the subject undertaken in Britain, and represents one of the most extensive studies of three-generational family life carried out for several decades. Information was collected from members of over 2000 families, with sample members responding as grandparents, teenage and adult grandchildren, and 'linking-parents'.

2   The place of grandparents

Prior to the emergence of the modern welfare state there used to be a generalised assumption in British society of continuing mutual support within extended families. During the twentieth century, however, as state welfare provisions developed, grandparents came to be seen by progressive opinion as unduly conservative influences in families and then, over the last quarter of the century, were played down or ignored completely by official institutions. The BSA98 survey found much more positive public attitudes than expected towards grandparental involvement in family life. In the absence of preceding research though it is hard to tell how far this may represent a *revival* of extended family ties, or how far it indicates that these may have *continued* to be active all along in spite of official neglect.

3   Outline of survey and findings

One of the key features of this survey is that it provides a range of complementary perspectives on family life, from people in different kinship positions in three family generations. Grandparents themselves display the most enthusiasm for their role. They express the greatest satisfaction in family relationships, feel the most 'closeness' to kin, and claim the highest rates of contact. Survey data cover frequency and types of contact, a range of shared activities within and outside of the home, grandparental assistance with childcare, giving and receiving money, advice and various practical supports, and the part played by grandparents when parents are not together.

x

4 Demography

Inclusion of questions on grandparenting in the BSA survey creates an opportunity to explore the changing demography of extended family life. The shape of families has changed considerably over the last century, due to declining fertility and increasing longevity. Women born in the late 1930s and early 1940s show a low proportion of childlessness, and those having their first children in the late 1960s and 1970s had them at a younger age than preceding cohorts. So there are many young grandparents at the moment – with more than half of the British population now grandparents by the age of 54, when they still have several decades of life ahead of them. However, women are also having *fewer* children. So most people now are living in 'bean-pole' families, which stretch across several generations while having few members in any one of them. Nearly two-thirds of grandparents currently are not the senior generation in their families.

5 Changes in domestic life

The narrowing of descent groups is to some extent offset by the reduction in conjugal stability. Increasing proportions of parents (each year) are splitting and recombining, so that more people now have a range of step- and half-relations too. The breakdown of parental relationships has a very marked effect though on ties between grandparents and grandchildren. On the one hand, those grandparents who are linked to the parent with the main care of grandchildren are liable to find themselves much more heavily depended upon. The other grandparents however may well find that it is hard even to maintain contact with them. So there is a polarisation which is taking place of involvement and 'closeness' with grandchildren.

6 Emergence of lineage

This polarisation is very largely structured by the descent line through which grandparental relationships are traced. We can see a clear tendency at the moment for matrilineal ties (through the mother) to become the more active, while patrilineal, through the father, may often be very tenuous or even non-existent. While parents are living together there is more or less equal contact and interaction with grandparents in both lines. But where they are not, differences emerge between maternal and paternal grandparents, on top of those already there between grandmothers and grandfathers. Thus where breakdown has occurred, maternal grandmothers are by far the most involved in their offspring's lives, and paternal grandfathers by far the *least* involved. Maternal grandfathers and paternal grandmothers both fall between the two extremes – though they vary a good deal between themselves according to the particular grandparental activities under consideration.

7   The family development cycle

The principal overall source of variability in grandparenting behaviour is the age of grandchildren. Birth of a grandchild, above all a first grandchild, is followed by a period of intense contact and interest in the role. This then gradually tails off and changes its nature as the grandchild grows older – leading eventually to a reversal of the direction of main support. Being a grandparent should also be seen as a late stage in *parenting* – in which adult children are launched as parents themselves. There is a right time for this to happen in terms of grandparents' own personal development, in that becoming a grandparent too soon – much under fifty, or while still occupied with dependent children at home – appears to be a less satisfying experience.

8   Caring and paid employment

One of the dominant public perceptions of grandparents is as providers of childcare support, enabling mothers to participate more easily in the labour force. The survey contained a number of measures of direct care, as well as of activities producing indirect help for working mothers. The findings suggest that the relationship between family childcare supply and demand is not straightforward. It is mothers working part rather than full-time who get the highest rates of direct support, as well as greater indirect help. Part-time work seems generally more compatible with family life – and is linked also with higher levels of agreement over the upbringing of grandchildren, and closeness in relationships, than full-time. There are also indications that the work status of grand*mothers* is important too – with working grannies doing *less* formal childcare than others, but having greater informal involvement, providing more financial support, and deriving greater role satisfaction.

9   Patterns of involvement in upbringing

Much of the variation in grandparental involvement that is not linked to age and family development can be understood in terms of lineage differences in relationships. As earlier chapters have shown, where parents are apart there is a gravitation towards maternal ties, through a child's mother. This gravitation points to qualitative differences in lines of parenting, which are examined here. Even where parents are living together, and the rates of contact and activity are the same for maternal and paternal relations, those on the maternal side have considerably more say. Maternal grandmothers in particular are intimately involved, while paternal grandmothers are relatively excluded – and accordingly have much lower levels of satisfaction in the role. The reactions of grand*fathers* to differential participation follow a contrary pattern – with maternal possibly *more* involved than appears to suit them, and paternal grandfathers comparatively happy *not* to be very active.

10   Effects of social class

We would expect the different lifestyles associated with 'class' to be related to variations in grandparenting, as in terms of both demographic and economic characteristics there are many factors linked with class that impinge on family life. But the class differences found in grandparenting behaviour in this survey are not in fact very clear. Middle-class families do stand out as different. Perhaps because they are more often geographically-dispersed, they record the least frequent contact and shared activity rates – though they make up for this with more economic transfers, gifts and shared holidays, not to mention sharing of values across generations. Beyond this there is not much pattern though. The highest rates of interaction and childcare support appear to occur not in the working class, but among *intermediate* class groups. This may reflect that an active family life requires both resources *and* time, which may be best combined in this middling portion of the social structure. But the pattern of findings may *not* indicate very much at all. One of the main problems in this analysis is that in modern, open society family networks may cut across class groupings so much that no measures of individuals' class (especially those of women) can give us more than a very tentative guide to the lifestyle of their wider family group.

11   Step-relationships

Only very small numbers of step-ties crop up in each of the sub-samples of respondents. But the pattern of behaviour they point to is remarkably consistent. What the findings all suggest is that new family life is becoming increasingly organised around female descent groupings, with men (much more readily than women) able to move between families. Thus on most measures, on data collected from all sub-samples, step-grand*fathers* are as active as natural grandfathers, or even more so. It seems to be men's relationships with their current partners (rather than directly with offspring) which mainly influence their family behaviour and feelings. So a step-grandfather, moving into a new relationship, may be much more involved with step-children and step-grandchildren than with his natural offspring. Step-grand*mothers* on the other hand are on most measures much less active than natural grandmothers (and even than natural grandfathers). This is presumably because they tend to remain more involved with any natural offspring of their own (and also may not want to compete with the natural mothers and grandmothers of their step-offspring). Step-grandmothers can be seen as in a sort of extreme 'paternal grandmother' situation.

12   Grandparents in changing family life

Much of what seems to be happening to grandparenting does not really make sense in isolation from general changes in family life – in particular the growing frailty of ties between parents. The overall trend here, as just suggested in relation to step-relationships, appears to be an increasing marginalisation of men, and of ties traced through men, and a stronger focusing of families around women. This also entails a growing *de facto* domestic sexual division of labour. For whereas (grand)fathers can and do move on to become active step (grand)fathers in other families, men who live alone seem to remain relatively detached from their offspring, and to hold less family-oriented attitudes. On the other hand (grand)mothers who live alone remain *no less* involved with their offspring, and express *pro*-family values. It seems possible that this continuity and durability in the family orientation of women may be an important underlying factor in the apparent rehabilitation of grandparents and extended family life in contemporary Britain.

xiv

ACKNOWLEDGEMENTS

The *Institute of Community Studies* is grateful to the *Robert Gavron Charitable Trust* and the *Nuffield Foundation* for funding the research on which this report is based, to the *National Centre for Social Research* for carrying out the survey and collaborating in its analysis, and to the *Direction des Recherches sur le Vieillissement* of the *Caisse Nationale d'Assurance Vieillesse* in Paris for valued support during the analysis.

1

Setting a Baseline

Over the last few years there has been a dramatic surge of interest in Britain in grandparents. For most of the previous two or three decades older people had been treated by the state merely as senior citizens, with a largely dependent role in the general community. Beyond that they had little importance. But as the family form favoured by the modern state, the nuclear family, becomes increasingly unstable and difficult for the state apparatus to uphold, there has been a change of official attitudes. Grandparents, so often represented by influential thinkers throughout the twentieth century as enemies of progress and personal freedom, have been rehabilitated as guardians of family life and children's well-being (Uhlenberg and Kirby, 1998; Home Office, 2000).

This rediscovery of grandparents has prompted a welter of commentaries on how their role has changed. But the truth is that we simply do not know what part they now play. We can safely presume that grandparenting these days *is* different. Society in general is very different. Compared with a generation or two ago, more women are staying in employment after having children and pursuing long-term careers. This change is especially marked for middle-class women, who are more likely to have access to interesting work leading to a career. Many women are having children before their mid-twenties; but more are delaying their first child until their mid-thirties. So generation spans are diversifying. Virtually all older people are living separately from their children, and commonly in single-person households. More parents themselves are living in single-parent households, and three-generational co-residence is now very rare. Altogether there is so much that is different that it is inconceivable that the nature of grandparenting has not changed too. But precisely how we cannot really say. Policy-makers eager to understand how best to incorporate grandparents into new family policies have been obliged to rely for guidance on personal experience, casual anecdotes and journalists' fancies or brain-storms.

It was against this background of mounting speculation and conjecture that the *Institute of Community Studies* (ICS) planned with the *National Centre for*

Social Research (at that time *Social and Community Planning Research*) to include some questions on grandparenting in the 1998 British Social Attitudes (BSA) survey. Our sponsors (the Robert Gavron Charitable Trust and the Nuffield Foundation) responded very quickly to our research proposal, as they felt it was important to start collecting data as quickly as possible. No survey on any reasonable scale had been carried out in Britain before on grandparents. Consequently there was no immediate prospect of being able to show, reliably, how their position had already changed. However, the sooner that research was implemented, the sooner we could get beyond anecdote, map out the current situation, and start the process of charting the direction in which it was moving. Studies of grandparenting had already been undertaken in several other countries. In the US especially there had been extensive and sustained research for well over a decade (Bengston and Robertson, 1985; Kornhaber, 1996). So there were leads that we could follow, and indeed a considerable literature available to guide us. But as far as Britain was concerned, the 1998 BSA grandparenting survey was inevitably a 'baseline' study, in that while there were no earlier studies with which to compare its own findings, it could itself hope to lay down some firm points of reference for later work.

Key findings from this survey have already been presented in the 16th BSA Report (Dench et al., 1999). The appendices to that volume also contain full sets of questions asked with details of responses to them. In addition to this, the raw data from the survey is now accessible electronically via the ESRC Data Archive at the University of Essex. However, given the information void surrounding British grandparents, we felt that it would be useful to publish a fuller analysis of the data, to help speed its dissemination and spread it as widely as possible. Interpretation of the findings has also been assisted by our involvement in a parallel, qualitative follow-on study looking in detail at grandparenting in the lives of a sub-sample of BSA respondents (recently reported in Arthur et al., 2002). Completion of our own fuller analysis has also, very happily, coincided with the establishment of Grandparents Plus[1] - thereby giving a further point to this present volume.

Structure of the sample

The grandparenting component of the BSA survey was rather complex in its nature, and a brief explanation of its structure is necessary at the outset if the tables in the report are to be read correctly.[2] All respondents in the BSA sample were asked to indicate which categories of lineal relatives they had alive. Those with a grandchild were put into a **grandparent** sub-sample (sometimes

---

[1] Set up recently to promote grandparenting within the context of wider family & kin groupings.
[2] A fuller description of it than given here is included in Appendix B.

abbreviated to 'GPs') and were then asked to comment on their relationship with a selected grandchild. Those with a grandparent were placed in an **adult grandchild** sub-sample (GCs) and as such were then asked about their relationship with a selected grandparent. Those without either grandchildren or grandparents, but with a dependent child living with them who did have a grandparent alive, were put in a '**linking parent**' sub-sample. These respondents reported on the relationship between (one of) their child(ren) and one of that child's grandparents. Eleven respondents had both a grandchild and a grandparent alive. These were allocated to the grandparent group.

Of the 3,146 BSA respondents, 933 were thus enlisted as grandparents, 584 as adult grandchildren, and 674 as linking parents; so two-thirds of the whole sample came into one of these groups. These three groups are occasionally referred to as samples A, B and C. In addition to the main survey, BSA98 also surveyed young people living in the households of respondents. This resulted in a Young People sample of 11-17 year olds, of whom 88% had at least one grandparent alive. These respondents were defined by us as a '**teenage grandchild**' sample – or sample D. Full technical details of the main selection procedure are given at the end of the BSA Report (Jowell et al., 1999).

Table 1.1 Structure of the sample

A	B	C	D
GRANDPARENTS	**ADULT GRANDCHILDREN**	**LINKING PARENTS**	**TEENAGE GRANDCHILDREN**
answer questions about their relationship with a selected grandchild (*n=933*)	answer questions about their relationship with a selected grandparent (*n=584*)	answer questions about the relationship between one of their children and a selected grandparent (*n=674*)	answer questions about their relationship with a selected grandparent (*n=474*)

When designing the grandparenting survey, we decided that in order to be able to analyse grandparenting relationships fully and reliably we should concentrate on exploring the behaviour of sub-sample members regarding one relevant family member (or family relationship). Thus each member of the grandparent group, for example, would be asked in detail about their ties with a particular grandchild, each grandchild about one grandparent, and each linking-parent about one grandparent-grandchild pair which they mediated. Of course, most respondents had more than one eligible relative. But it was not possible to ask detailed questions about each family member in turn, since this would have extended the length of the interview considerably. In designing the research procedure therefore, we had to find a way to select a relevant family member so that we could draw valid and reliable conclusions about that type of relationship in general.

There were different ways in which this selection could be made. We had to choose between these, and in the event we did not select all relationships in the same way. We decided that it was essential to pick some pairs of relatives at random - so that the data generated by them could be taken as directly representative of that relationship in the general population. Others however were identified on a most-contact basis, in order to give us a fuller set of findings relating to the most active and intensive relationships.

To this end, all sub-sample members were assigned to one of two streams, on the basis of their serial number in the survey. For those respondents with an *even* serial number, a relevant family member was selected randomly by the interviewer from those available. If there was only one, this person was automatically selected. The other respondents, with *odd* serial numbers, were asked if there was a particular family member with whom they had more contact than others.

In the event, this second procedure led to a number of outcomes other than the simple identification of a most-contact pairing. Around one quarter of grandparent respondents with odd serial numbers had only one grandchild, and so had no choice to make. For analytic purposes these were no different to grandparents in the random stream with only one grandchild - and indeed could be effectively included with them. On top of this, some of the grandparents with more than one grandchild pointed out that they always saw several as a group, and so could not really say that they had more contact with one than with others. Such cases were therefore transferred to the group with even serial numbers, and a *random* selection was made. (Note that because of weighting procedures, base figures for tabulated data do not add up to the actual numbers of respondents. See Appendix B for fuller discussion of this.)

Table 1.2 Random and most-contact streams of sample

A		B		C		D	
GRANDPARENTS		**ADULT GRANDCHILDREN**		**LINKING PARENTS**		**TEENAGE GRANDCHILDREN**	
Random (*n=715*)	Most contact (*n=350*)	Random (*n=489*)	Most contact (*n=389*)	Random (*n=467*)	Most contact (*n=307*)	(All random) (*n=474*)	

Use of different sample streams in the analysis

As a result of this selection procedure the random groups in each sub-sample ended up considerably larger than the most-contact. For the purpose of the original BSA chapter, we confined ourselves to analysing the random component when dealing with specific grandparent/grandchild ties. But for the present report we have also drawn on the most-contact sets of data as well.

We do this in two distinct ways. Firstly we refer to most-contact figures in several places where we want to contrast them with the random figures - in order to illuminate more clearly the range of behaviour surveyed. On most of the variables, the random and most contact groups produce very similar profiles though. So in a few places we have combined the two groups of figures together into a single set – or occasionally added an additional column of data for reference. We do either of these things where we are making detailed breakdowns which require as many cases in cells as we can muster. When we do them, we refer to the pooled data as being unweighted.[3]

We are reasonably confident that where pooling of random and most-contact groups has been carried out it has not seriously influenced any of the patterns that are found when the groups are examined separately. There are obviously differences between the random and most-contact sets of data, which render them unequally representative. For instance, 'matrilineal' pairings of kin - that is where grandparent and grandchild are linked through a female parent - tend to involve more frequent contact. As a result, all of the most-contact sub-sets of data contain higher proportions of matrilineal kin pairs than do the random groups - as indeed they do of any other characteristic closely related to contact rates. Because of this, any direct estimation from the survey data to the general population needs to be based on the random sets of data only.

However, when we move to analysing patterns of association between respondent characteristics, or kin-pair measures, many of these seem to be broadly similar regardless of whether the pairs of kin have been selected on a random or most-contact basis. Clearly this is least true where measures involved in an analysis are themselves linked with frequency of contact. And we avoid using pooled data in these situations. But in some detailed analyses of responses - as opposed to estimation of general population values - it does appear to us to be reasonably safe to increase the size of tabulation bases by pooling the random and most-contact cases. The distributions of variable association for unweighted data are very similar to those for the random data, but – because numbers are larger – they have higher levels of significance.

---

[3] See Appendix B for further discussion of the procedures followed.

These points will be discussed again at relevant places in the text, and are also developed further in the appendices. They do need to be given a first airing here, though, because unless the complex nature of the sample is made evident at the outset then the meaning and reference of many of the tabulations which follow here may be more difficult to work out.

2

THE PLACE OF GRANDPARENTS

Grandparents in the past

Although there has never been an extensive study of grandparenting in Britain, and virtually no research at all on extended families for some decades, we do of course have a reasonable idea of the nature of family relations in Britain prior to this research gap, and we could bear this mind when planning and analysing our own research.

Much of this understanding dates from the first two reports on research in Bethnal Green published by the new Institute of Community Studies in the 1950s. That is, Michael Young and Peter Willmott's *Family and Kinship in East London*, and Peter Townsend's *Family Life of Old People*. It was *Family and Kinship* which had the greater initial impact at the time, as it shattered a whole host of academic and political myths by revealing the continuing importance and positive character of lifelong kinship ties in British society. The study was all the more influential because it was written from within a left-progressive milieu, so that the authors were particularly well placed to argue that elite opinion was out of touch with ordinary people's views. Little was actually known about how families lived in the past, as so much was taken for granted that very little had been written down. Only when informed commentators started assuming that three-generational family ties were dead, as happened in the middle of the twentieth century, was there much point in bothering to check, and finding that it wasn't true.

Family and Kinship had tremendous effect by showing how, among people widely regarded at the time by intellectuals and policy-makers as living on the edge of social disorganisation, and even brutishness (see e.g. Orwell, 1937), most adults were in frequent contact with a wide range of kin and were deeply immersed in mutual supports with them. At the heart of it all was the relationship between mothers and their own mothers, often living very nearby, which involved a constant exchange of services informed by a spirit of reciprocity that evolved in character according to its participants' ages and changing needs.

> And so it goes on – the daughter's labours are in a hundred little ways shared with the older woman whose days of child-bearing (but not of child-rearing) are over. When the time comes for the mother to need assistance, the daughter reciprocates, as reported elsewhere, by returning the care which she has herself received (Young & Willmott, 1957, p.39).

The report by Townsend gave even greater weight to grandparenting as such because it focused more specifically on older people, following the work of Sheldon (1948). *Family Life of Old People* documents meticulously the intensive interactions between pensioners and their children, and shows the part which older people – in particular women - continued to play in family life long after they had lost their public roles and importance as workers. Nearly three out of five old people belonged to what Peter Townsend defined as three-generational extended families, by virtue of both seeing members of two succeeding generations every day and sharing much of their lives with them (Townsend, 1957, p.110). Grandparents were at the very hub of family life.

> We found old people getting a great deal of help, regularly and in emergencies, from their female relatives, particularly their daughters, living in neighbouring streets. The remarkable thing was how often this help was reciprocated – through provision of midday meals, care of grandchildren and other services. The major function of the grandparent is perhaps the most important fact to emerge from this book (1957, p. 205).

Townsend concluded, very tellingly as it has turned out, that this private role was valuable to the state, and should be protected by it. *'So far at least as the old are concerned, therefore, there is no justification for an attempt to supplant the family with State services. Their job is to support the family and provide substitute help when it no longer exists'* (ibid, p.203). These studies in the East End were followed by an explosion of family research in the 1960s, which documented the nature of current family exchanges and also tried to reconstruct what had gone on in the past.

These family supports were grounded in shared neighbourhood rather than co-residence, as there is not much tradition in British society of grandparents living as part of an extended family household (Laslett, 1977; Wall, 1984, 1995). However, the importance of mutual aid could overcome this preference for separate residence at times, as for example when migration took young parents away from ready access to grandparents. Michael Anderson (1972) has shown how the value of grandparents within families, and their roles in the family structure complementary to those of parents, led to the adoption of shared households as a means of keeping extended families together during the industrial revolution. He argued in his study of nineteenth century Lancashire that the exchange of services between generations was a key factor leading to co-residence of married children and their parents as workers were pulled from villages into urban settings. Most women who worked outside of the home while having young children had a co-resident grandmother who looked after the children in return for her own keep. Parish records of household composition show that the granny would move to the town with the migrating workers, or join them when needed. Both generations had something to gain from this and, Anderson suggests, this exercise of kinship reciprocity also meant that there were very few older women on relief under the poor law - though plenty of older men.

The logic of this exchange was explicitly understood by participants. Anderson quotes a contemporary account:

> Many (aged persons), especially aged females, afford a service very appropriate to their condition, and of not inconsiderable value, by keeping house and taking care of the youngest children, while the working part of the family are absent at their work.

The mutual benefits were so obvious that where an actual granny was not available, then non-family members might be incorporated. The account goes on:

> It is not uncommon for aged females to become domesticated for the purpose of affording service of this nature in the families of those who have no elderly relatives to support (Anderson, 1972, p.143).

At times of population stability the preference in Britain seems to have been for living *near* grandmothers rather than co-residing with them.[1] So the element of exchange in their relationships is not immediately obvious from official records, and only becomes evident when actually probed by social researchers. During the period of widespread research after Townsend's pioneering work there were many references to trading of childcare by grandparents for material services and assistance, as being part of normal extended family life. Rosser and Harris wrote in 1965 that a fifth of households in Swansea were three-generational, and that a majority of children lived in one at some point in their childhood.[2]

---

[1] This preference seems to go back to at least the Middle Ages; see McFarlane, 1978 & Hibbert, 1987.
[2] *Family and Social Change*, pp. 167/8

Such references disappear however during the 1970s, as the effects of growing state involvement in providing personal security filtered through into family values and behaviour. The postwar introduction of universal state pensions, followed by gradual individualisation of other welfare supports, eventually diverted commentators' attention away from family support systems while also helping to feed a presumption that such exchanges had become less necessary. An important aspect of this was growing resistance among women to caring for elderly relatives. This meant that the state was required to take on more responsibility for care of the elderly, including through payment of carer's allowances to kin giving up work to look after them. Perhaps the weakest component of extended family life at this point was the expectation of the old for care from their children, as this was placing an increasing burden on younger women during a period when more of them were working and had less need themselves of personal help from relatives. Older women were living longer, and needing care for longer. Younger women on the other hand were having fewer children, and could if they wanted postpone this for career reasons – often to a point where their own mothers were no longer likely to be active and useful. A growing problem was that, as people were living longer, many elderly women did not need support until their daughters were themselves young grannies - and pulled between the needs of their own daughters and grandchildren, their elderly kin, and often a job as well.[3]

So the balance of interests underlying traditional female reciprocity was coming under strain. *Family and Kinship* and its successor *Family and Class* were criticised from the mid-sixties onwards by feminists who felt that the studies romanticised social arrangements which trapped (younger) women in domesticity. Quotations from old ladies affirming that '*With a daughter you've always got someone to ask,*' (Willmott & Young, 1960, p.72) were instantly translated by them into, '*As a daughter you can never say no*', confirming that women lived in bondage.

This unravelling of mutual dependence within the family as a framework for reciprocity increased the pressure on government departments to provide more care for the old, and support for their carers. Consistent with this, research documenting and above all celebrating family reciprocity was attacked as an impediment to women's liberation (Platt, 1971). Michael Young responded by pointing out in several publications over the next few years that extended family exchanges provided security for women in their old age. '*Women out at work who do not have much time to spare for their mothers will, when they are old themselves, suffer likewise when their daughters follow their example*' (1977, p.351).

---

[3] The issue of this 'sandwich generation' is considered at the end of chapter 7.

But he was writing against the trend, and during the seventies and eighties the state took on more care of the elderly and grandparents became officially invisible. Virtually all research among older people was concerned about their position and needs as individual citizens. The main arguments revolved not round family roles – which by convention had become inadmissible issues - but around whether or not, as members of a lifestyle cohort or generational interest group, they were taking more out of a *national* intergenerational exchange than they (had) put in (Thomson, 1989; Kotlikoff, 1992). This paved the way for a number of campaigning studies attempting to chart or organise the interests of older people (Bosanquet et al., 1989; Peace, 1990; Askham et al., 1992; Midwinter, 1992), which led in turn to some alarmist models of growing conflict between polarised age-groups of citizens (e.g. Mulgan & Wilkinson, 1995).

Such fears might not have arisen if researchers had *not* detached older people from their family networks. A study carried out in the mid-nineties by ICS discovered that when encouraged to discuss their lives in terms of their own preoccupations most older people, especially older women, still did so in the context of their families. They did not regard themselves as isolated social units, or members of age-specific categories, but as links in multi-generational families. And the needs of their children and grandchildren were of great significance in their lives (Dench, 1997). Far from being passive recipients of state care and support, they saw themselves as centrally and actively involved in continuing give-and-take within family networks.

Other work in the 1990s revealed a gradual rekindling of interest in the social context of older citizens' lives, and the place of grandparenting activities in this (Arber & Ginn, 1995; Kosberg, 1992; Marsh & Arber, 1992; Phillipson, 1996, etc.). But this did not produce any systematic analysis in Britain of the nature of the relationships between three-generation family members. In the absence of such research it is very hard to know how much has actually changed, and how far family activities had just become less visible.

On the one hand, recent social change appears to be making grandparenting more salient; but on the other it may also be making it more problematic and difficult to sustain. As the collectivist supports promised by the burgeoning welfare state a generation ago fail to materialise, or get cut back, family ties may be seen again as extremely valuable - even by many people who would prefer state provisions. However, the framework of family solidarity of which grandparenting formed part in the old days may have been weakened through the growth of informal partnerships and short-term relationships less attuned to interpersonal reciprocity. In that case, routine exchanges involving grandparents as understood in the past may have become rather more difficult to operate. More may now be done by grandparents in crisis mode, which could be detrimental to family moral economies in the long term (Bengtsen and Robertson, 1985; Troll,

1985; Johnson and Barer, 1987; Chalfie, 1994). So to help establish a general picture of what British society now does feel grandparents ought to be doing, we asked *all* BSA respondents a few very broad questions about the role.

Current expectations

All sample members were invited to consider a number of general propositions relating to the place of grandparents in British society. These responses represent an essentially public view of what contemporary grandparents do or are expected to do. This is perhaps their main value. At the same time, we are able to make some analytic connections for those respondents who do fall into one of the grandparenting samples between their public evaluations of the role and their personal views and involvement.

The following table summarises levels of agreement with these propositions. They are listed in the order of overall percentages of respondents expressing agreement with them. The table gives both overall levels of agreement, and that for each family status grouping, as defined by allocation to one or other sub-sample in the grandparenting section of the survey.[4]

Table 2.1 Attitudes towards grandparenting

			Respondent is:-			
% agreeing with proposition:-	GP	Adult GC	Linking parent	*Not* in extnded family	[*All* Adult]	Teen-age GC
a. With so many working mothers, families need grandparents to help more and more	80	72	74	72	74	-
b. People today don't place enough value on the part grandparents play in family life	50	50	51	55	51	47
c. Many parents today do not appreciate the help that grandparents give	40	31	41	49	41	31
d. In most families, grandparents should be closely involved in deciding how their grandchildren are brought up	24	19	16	21	20	33
e. Grandparents tend to interfere too much with how their grandchildren are brought up	9	10	8	16	11	14
f. Grandparents have little to teach the grandchildren of today	13	7	6	10	9	13
Base	*735*	*462*	*570*	*764*	*2531*	*474*

Note: Questions [A.11.a-f] [190-5].[5]

---

[4] Numbers are smaller than for the total membership of these sub-samples, as this set of questions formed part of a self-completion questionnaire which not all respondents completed.
[5] For a listing of BSA questions see Appendix A. For conventions regarding the use of measures of association see Appendix B.

The profile of attitudes produced in this table is immediately very striking, in two major respects. Firstly it shows a remarkable level of homogeneity across all of the very diverse sub-samples - ranging from teenage grandchildren to grandparents themselves. Close attention to the detailed distribution of responses does reveal variations in perceptions. But the divergences are minor compared with the evident broad consensus running throughout the BSA sample as a whole on the place of grandparents. Manifestly there is a grandparenting culture which is shared by the majority of people in British society.

Secondly, when we come to the content of that culture, there is obviously a high level of belief in the value and importance of grandparents. In spite of decades of official neglect of extended family life in Britain, most members of British society do evidently regard it very positively. The propositions at the top of the table, attracting high levels of agreement, turn out to be those which offer favourable views. Those at the bottom, eliciting little favour, are the ones offering negative evaluations.[6]

Behind this broadly consensual public picture it is possible to identify minority viewpoints linked to personal circumstances. Some of that analysis though cannot be presented until the broad pattern of grandparenting behaviour and attitudes has been spelt out. However, there are some interesting variations in responses to these propositions which are related to the main family status categories and so can be mentioned from the outset. The main pattern of responses to each proposition is accordingly sketched out here in the light of family status differences, elaborated by reference to some basic measures of personal status - that is age and sex - and social class.

Variations in perspective

The proposition attracting the greatest support is the one asserting that grandparents can provide valuable help for working mothers. This is an idea which is frequently put forward at the moment by social commentators and policy-makers. It represents an area where state, community and family concerns are widely seen as convergent; so high levels of endorsement are hardly surprising. What does stand out from the survey results though is just how much consensus there is on this. Very few respondents actively rejected the idea, and most of those not actually agreeing offered neutral rather than negative responses.

There are, moreover, only minor variations in response. Grandparents themselves record the top rates of agreement - presumably reflecting their

---

[6] For the *order* in which the propositions were actually presented, and other details, see the outline survey questionnaire in Appendix A.

approval of a positive image in which they are represented as useful to both their offspring and the wider community. Consistent with this, there is a slightly higher rate of agreement among women, with grand*mothers* accordingly reporting the highest assent of all. In terms of both age and sex, much of this difference comes down to the greater tendency of younger people (and men) to express neutral opinions. This is documented later on here. It presumably reflects a generally *weaker* evaluation of the importance of family life by people who are less involved in it, more than with any real disagreement over whether grandparents do play a useful role within families.

The two next propositions, stating that grandparents are not sufficiently valued by society nor (more specifically) appreciated by the parents they assist, receive lower levels of support. This may not mean however that respondents do not themselves value grandparents; for in retrospect, and after controlling them against other responses, it seems to us likely that both of these questions contain elements of ambiguity. They may not just indicate the value attached by respondents to grandparents. What they really measure perhaps is the feeling that there are discrepancies between the respect which is merited, and that which is actually given. In those cases where respondents do feel that grandparents are actually receiving the respect that they deserve, we can expect them to disagree with the proposition. So while agreement with the proposition certainly entails a high evaluation of grandparenting, disagreement with it does not necessarily mean low evaluation.

This element of ambiguity makes variations in response trickier to interpret. For example, grandparents themselves record only average levels of agreement with these two views, even though their response to the first proposition would suggest that they are keen to see their contributions emphasised. This could be because many of them do actually feel, from their own involvement, that what they do *is* appreciated. Equally, though, it could just be that they do not want to grumble, or prefer to be modest about their value. Diplomacy may govern their responses here.

Although public opinion evidently does assume a role for grandparents, it also clearly sees limits to what they do or should do. Proposition d regarding closer involvement in child-rearing, for example, receives only lukewarm approval – possibly highlighting a dimension in which the role may have changed over recent decades. Some loosening of extended family ties may be indicated. Grandparents are hardly more enthusiastic here than parents, and it is teenage grandchildren still living with their parents who offer the warmest support of any of family status category. Perhaps grandparents are seen by them as allies against the common foe - parents. The proportion of respondents selecting neutral responses here is however greater than that agreeing with the proposition. This includes grandparents themselves, who may have found this particular question especially difficult to deal with.

The factor which produces caution in responses here may be a desire to avoid the appearance of grandparental interference. The idea that childrearing belongs to parents, and not grandparents, is widely seen as a defining characteristic of modern family culture (Thompson et al., 1991; Kornhaber, 1996). So parents will be alert to the dangers of interference, and grandparents themselves will be fearful of giving the wrong impression. But in view of the existence of some support for grandparental involvement in child-rearing, situations are bound to arise where grandparents do overstep the mark. What is perhaps surprising here is the small proportion of respondents asserting this - only 11%. This was also true among parents, who might be expected to be the most sensitive to such behaviour.

It was in fact outsiders - respondents not themselves belonging to three-generational families, and who were commenting as external observers of extended family life, with little personal experience, who were the most attracted to this dramatic portrayal. Sixteen percent of them supported it, compared with 11% for all respondents, with only 36% rejecting it, compared with 50% for all respondents. By contrast, it was respondents with the greater experience of family life who most rejected the stereotype of interfering grandparent. Women (53%) as opposed to men (47%) and older people (55% of over-55s) as opposed to younger (48% of 18-34s) were the leaders in rejecting it. When age, sex and family status are all taken into account it is grandmothers (65%) who rate the highest in rejecting this criticism.[7]

Notably the most negative attitudes to grandparenting were found among childless people who were themselves old enough to be grandparents – a special category of outsiders. Thus for example 24% of childless women over 55 (and 28% of childless men) agreed that grandparents tend to interfere too much. This compares with 9% of women over 55 with children (or grandchildren) and 13% of older (grand)fathers. Lack of personal experience of parenting seems to be an important factor influencing views generally in later life, and perhaps leading to an alternative life-cycle progression.

This overwhelmingly positive view of the role of grandparents is then confirmed, indirectly, by the very limited support given to the remaining suggestion here, that grandparents have little to teach grandchildren. Grandparents themselves, perhaps being modest again, offer higher levels of agreement here than do parents and grown-up grandchildren.

---

[7] Teenage respondents possibly deviate slightly from the general rule linking close personal experience of family life with a positive view of grandparents. This arises perhaps because they are themselves at the stage in life where all family relationships are liable to be seen as interference.

Diplomacy or modesty is detectable in several of the responses of grandparents. But any such tendency does not seem to prevent them from expressing more diverse reactions to these propositions than members of other family status categories. In addition to recording average levels of agreement on most of these questions, they also show higher than average levels of disagreement. And not only are their views more scattered; they are also stronger. For proposition b, 17% of grandparents either agreed or disagreed strongly, compared with 11% of parents and 12% of adult grandchildren. A similar distribution of responses is found to a greater or lesser degree for all these propositions. It presumably reflects both the greater interest of older people (and grandparents especially) in family life generally - and particularly in questions relating to their own place in it - and also their more extensive personal experience, on which to base firm views. Grandchildren (and indeed younger people as a whole) were rather more likely to register neutral views on all of these propositions.

This pattern is shown in table 2.2, where the family status of respondents is cross-tabulated with the strength of their responses. People who agreed or disagreed strongly are counted as having *strong* views; those who just agreed or disagreed counted as having *moderate* views, and those who could not choose, or did not know, are counted as having *neutral* views. Only the strong and neutral categories are included in this table.

Table 2.2 Strength of feeling about grandparent role by family position

	PROPOSITION:-						
	a	b	c	d	e	f	Base
% Holding strong view							
Teenage GC	n/a	17	**7**	5	7	**20**	*474*
Adult GC	16	12	**10**	8	**10**	**23**	*462*
Linking parent	15	11	**11**	11	**10**	**24**	*570*
GP	21	17	**14**	9	**13**	**26**	*764*
Not in extended family	15	16	9	10	8	25	*735*
% Holding neutral view							
Teenage GC	n/a	38	29	32	34	19	*474*
Adult GC	**21**	37	**37**	37	**42**	19	*462*
Linking parent	**17**	**33**	29	30	**35**	**13**	*570*
GP	**15**	**25**	**22**	36	**30**	**12**	*764*
Not in extended family	23	34	34	35	48	17	*735*

Note: Figures in bold highlight where views appear to progress as family status develops.

The distributions in table 2.2 show that the percentage of respondents registering strong views tends to rise with progress through the family life-cycle, while that of respondents with neutral views goes down. The latter effect is more consistent than the former. Teenage grandchildren do not fit the pattern neatly. This presumably reflects both the formative stage of their development and also the fact that, as dependent residents in the households of a different family status-group (their parents) they are probably more subject than other respondents to competing influences.[8] The residue of respondents not currently part of a three-generation family is even more of a mixed bag, and could not be expected to form a part of a coherent pattern. But it is worth noting that these respondents show a profile of responses very similar to that of adult grandchildren. However, whereas no adult grandchildren are aged above 47, the majority (51%) of this category are childless people of 50 and above. This perhaps shows that progression in views is less related to ageing as such, than to the taking on of family responsibilities for dependants etc.

The pattern of progression *is* followed by the three main family 'status groupings' of adult grandchildren (some of whom would be parents too), linking-parents and grandparents. The only exception to the broad pattern occurs in relation to proposition d, the one suggesting that grandparents should be closely involved in decisions about how grandchildren are brought up. This proposition identifies a nub issue in relations between parents and grandparents, as it raises the spectre of interference by grandparents. Response figures to it show that it clearly rings alarm bells for parents, strengthening their views and lifting more out of neutrality. For similar reasons it may have numbed some *grand*parents into diplomatic neutrality. This is the only view on which grandparents score rates of neutrality approaching those of other family status categories.

In addition to the intensification of responses with movement to senior family status there is also evidence of slightly stronger reactions by women than men. This is the case for all of the propositions except 'd'.

The class factor

There is also a class dimension to the distribution of responses and this possibly helps to clarify the bifurcation of attitudes found among grandparents. Table 2.3 displays the links between class and responses on the most relevant propositions, revealing how the experience of grandparents at opposite ends of the social spectrum may be rather different.

---

[8] Young peoples' views on a number of attitudes generally tend to be closer to those of parents than of young childless adults. In fact there also seems to be some linking of young peoples' views on an individual basis with their parents', as we hope to explore in a future report.

Table 2.3 Views on grandparent role by social class[9]

Propositions	Salariat	Inter-mediate	Working class	DK	All
		Respondent's social class:-			
GPs should be closely involved					
Agree	15	19	27	24	20
Neutral	33	34	36	42	34
Disagree	52	46	37	35	45
People don't value GPs					
Agree	48	50	56	74	51
Neutral	34	32	29	20	32
Disagree	18	18	14	6	17
Parents don't appreciate GPs					
Agree	36	41	45	51	41
Neutral	33	28	29	27	30
Disagree	31	30	25	21	29
GPs have little to teach GC's					
Agree	6	8	15	16	9
Neutral	13	16	17	19	15
Disagree	81	76	69	65	76
Base	*784*	*1103*	*580*	*64*	*2531*

Note: Questions [A.11.a-f] [class] $p<0.05$ for each proposition

What stand out most in this table are some of the contradictions of feelings. There is thus a stronger feeling among respondents in lower social class groups that grandparents ought to be closely involved in rearing children. But alongside this view there is also a widespread belief among them that society does not value grandparents, and that parents do not sufficiently appreciate the help that they receive from them. The more ambitious view of grandparenting held among the working class appears therefore to entail greater disappointment with the role. Understandably, part of this class-view seems to be a greater propensity to feel that grandparents do not in fact have much that they can teach grandchildren. Such a sentiment may be linked to the fact that working-class people exercise less authority in wider society, and also may tend to be less in tune than middle-class elders with contemporary social and moral values.[10]

---

[9] Social class categories follow the Goldthorpe convention, grouped here into three main sections. See Appendix F.

[10] See for example discussion by Evans, in BSA 2000 report.

3

OUTLINE OF SURVEY & FINDINGS

In this section we are presenting the main findings of the survey in outline form, before analysing the results in more detail. This will provide a general map of topics covered, and give an indication of the range (and meaning) of responses to questions, as a background context for the fuller examination of particular issues.

General feelings about role

Before identifying specific relationships to probe in depth, we put some general questions to grandparents and grandchildren to sum up their attitudes towards their role. The results of these questions are shown in the first two tables here. It is important to remember that all of these responses refer to respondents' overall sentiments. Where they have more than one tie with that category of relative, then the general sentiments recorded in these preliminary questions cannot be assumed to relate directly to the particular relationship which is selected and explored in detail.

Most respondents in both groups appeared to attach a high value to three-generational family life. This came out more strongly for grandparents, as is shown in table 3.1. Altogether, nine in ten of them agreed that grandparenting was a very rewarding part of their life, with nearly two-thirds agreeing *strongly*. Only a minority felt that they wanted a life free from family duties now their own children were grown up, and a half of grandparents rejected that proposition. Three-quarters of all grandparents agreed that they had often put themselves out to help look after their grandchildren. Barely one in twenty had actually cut down on or given up work for this reason, though, so this was clearly not seen as appropriate or necessary behaviour.

Replies to these general questions give us some broad measures of *satisfaction* with family roles. The responses for 'finding the role rewarding' correlate very closely with those for 'feeling very close' to specific grandchildren, in particular when analysis is restricted to grandparents with one grandchild only. So this offers a very good measure of positive role evaluation. The responses on 'wanting a free life' are similarly useful as an index of *dis*satisfaction. As will be seen later in the report, though, this second measure does not fit in all that reliably with other measures of satisfaction, largely because of the way that it interacts with frequency of grandparental activity. There is some ambiguity in the proposition, which in full reads "Now my own children have grown up I want a life that is free from too many family duties." What is not clear here, we now appreciate, is how far agreement with this means that respondents do or do *not* feel free. Agreement is linked both with high rates of contact and activity, suggesting *failure* to achieve freedom, and also with very low rates, suggesting *success*. Overall, looking at how agreement on this question is linked with other responses, the former meaning seems to be the more common. But it is not the only one.

The third general proposition here is perhaps even more ambiguous, as it is not clear whether to put yourself out entails a negative feeling about the effect of having grandchildren. We expected it to pick up grandparents' experience of being burdened. But many grandparents agreeing with it also recorded positive feelings elsewhere, indicating that 'putting themselves out' might in fact be for them a sign of commitment, and valuing the role, rather than of discontent. Responses to the fourth question have been mainly useful as descriptive of the behavioural consequences of being a grandparent rather than for assessing respondents' feelings about the role.

Table 3.1 Grandparents' evaluation of their role

% GPs responding to proposition:	Agree strongly	Agree	Neutral	Disagree	Disagree strongly
Grandchildren are very rewarding	63	28	5	2	1
Would like life free from family	8	29	14	36	13
Have put themselves out to help GC	31	43	8	14	3
Have given up/reduced work to help	1	6	4	52	36

Note: Group A, [198-201], *Base:715.*

The responses of grandchildren were also largely positive, though less powerfully so. Two-thirds said that their grandparents were an important part of their lives, with one-third of these agreeing strongly. And this is a good indication of positive feelings towards this role. But around one fifth did not consider them important, and one in ten agreed that they would not see them as often if they did not have to. Against this, most grandchildren recognised that they were important to their grandparents, in that less than a fifth felt that their grandparents might not be interested in them, and over two-thirds agreed that their grandparents would like to see more of them than they do.

Table 3.2 Grandchildrens' evaluation of their role

a.   Adult GCs

% GCs responding to proposition:	Agree strongly	Agree	Neutral	Disagree	Disagree strongly
GPs are important part of their lives	35	35	12	14	4
Wouldn't see GPs often if didn't have to	2	9	12	47	30
GPs not very interested in their lives	7	11	6	42	34
Don't see as much of GPs as GPs would like	17	53	10	13	7

Note: Group B, [276-279], *Base: 489.*

b.   Teenage GCs

% GCs responding to proposition:	Agree strongly	Agree	Neutral	Disagree	Disagree strongly
GPs are important part of their lives	37	44	8	5	1
Wouldn't see GPs often if didn't have to	2	9	10	50	23
GPs not very interested in their lives	2	6	8	40	38

Note: Group D, [47.a-c], *Base: 474.*

Teenage grandchildrens' responses reveal slightly stronger sentiments towards their grandparents than those of their older counterparts, and reflect the positive attitudes of the grandparents. Eight in ten reported that their grandparents were an important part of their lives and fewer than one in ten thought that their grandparents were not very interested in them. The greater closeness to grandparents could either be due to their younger age and continuing co-residence with their parents, or might be a cohort effect reflecting the changing quality of relationships between generations.

Contact and closeness

After particular relationships had been identified for detailed investigation, respondents were first of all asked a number of questions about rates of contact and how close they felt to the selected relatives. The table which follows here summarises answers to these questions from the three main samples. The first two columns refer to information given by grandparents in relation to grandchildren (with random stream 'R' on the left and most-contact 'MC' on the right). The middle two columns refer to information given by adult grandchildren in relation to grandparents - again with random stream on the left. The two right-hand columns are based on responses made by parents of dependent grandchildren on their behalf, and give those parents' observations from *outside* of the relationship with the selected grandparent.

Table 3.3 Contact with selected relative, and 'closeness'

| | | | Respondent is:- | | | |
| | GP | | Adult GC | | Linking-Parent | |
% where GP (or GC):-	R	MC	R	MC	R	MC
Has seen GC/GP within 2 years	96	98	88	92	94	97
Sees GC/GP several times a week	30	47	9	11	21	34
Sees GC/GP *less than* once month	32	16	56	49	36	21
Often spends day with GC/GP without parents	35	50	24	31	27	39
Has *not* within year spent day with GC/GP without parents	28	13	41	32	34	23
Has stayed overnight within year with GC/GP without parents	38	50	11	13	30	37
Lives within 15 mins of GC/GP*	33	49	34	33	37	50
Lives 1 hr + from GC/GP*	32	18	38	38	30	18
Feels 'very close' to GC/GP*	68	81	32	37	45	60
Feels very *or* 'fairly' close to GC/GP*	91	97	73	80	82	91
Base	*715*	*350*	*489*	*389*	*467*	*307*
Base relationships where contact within last 2 years*	*681*	*341*	*424*	*348*	*438*	*299*

Note: Group A, [232.234.238.239.241.242]; Group B, [301.303.305.306.308.309]; Group C, [374.376.380. 381.383.384]. List of questions given in Appendix A.

The figures given in these six columns vary in two general ways. Firstly the figures for most-contact relationships all show somewhat greater contact, and closeness, than those in the random columns. This is obviously consistent with the manner of selection. It is interesting though how little difference there is in the case of adult grandchildren respondents, presumably because contact rates are low even for those grandparents seen relatively more often than others.

(Rates of contact are lower overall for this sub-sample. If we select even *less* frequent values for these variables than those used in this table, then more differential between random and most-contact does emerge).

The second type of variation is between estimates given by grandparents on one hand, and those by or for grandchildren on the other, with the latter generally lower. In the case of adult grandchildren this is partly an effect of age. All responding grandchildren here are over the age of eighteen, meaning that the age of their selected grandparents is considerably above the average for that of *responding* grandparents. So the data collected for this sub-sample relates to a stage in the family development cycle where contacts are generally low, and the behavioural measures given *are* compatible with those for the older grandparents, with grown-up grandchildren, in the grandparents sample.

In the case of the linking-parents, though, the differences are more likely to do with factors of reporting. Parents are responding on behalf of grandchildren. They may be unaware of some contacts that grandchildren have had or, and perhaps more generally, they may disregard as unimportant events which grandparents are likely to value and remember. Given the indirect nature of the data collection via parents the results are in fact remarkably consistent with those collected from grandparents themselves.

This broad similarity extends to the ratio between random and most-contact rates. For example, 30% of grandparents in the random stream reported seeing the selected grandchild several times a week, with a figure of 47% in the most-contact stream. The responses from parents run from 21% to 34%. The rates are lower. But the proportional difference for most-contact is very similar, on this and on many other measures.

When it comes to the measure of sentiment or felt closeness there is less correspondence between the sets. Grandparents clearly felt closer towards grandchildren than (adult) grandchildren felt to them; this holds, strongly, even when we look only at those grandparents whose selected grandchildren are adult too. So it is a matter of differences between attitudes to ascending and descending generations. The responses of linking parents are intriguingly pitched mid-way between the two other sets, suggesting that they are managing in their assessments to pool both participants' sentiments. But it is also possible that on a very intangible question like this they are influenced mainly by their personal views. In later parts of the report, especially chapters 6 and 7, there is discussion of the effect that parents' own feelings seem to have on responses to some behavioural questions too.

The table does not contain figures for teenage grandchildren, as not all of the questions were put to them. Where we do have data, though, this shows that rates of contact and activity tend to lie between those given by adult grandchildren and those given by parents for dependent grandchildren, suggesting that age is the main determinant. Thus 18% of teenagers reported seeing grandparents at least several times a week (compared with 9% adult grandchildren and 21% parental responses) 25% often spent time with them during the day without parents (compared with 24% and 25%), and 78% felt very or fairly close to them (compared with 73% and 82%).

Pattern of shared activities

In the next section of the questionnaire, respondents were asked a battery of questions about things they did with the selected relative.[1] Some of the main activities are considered here. Frequency ranges offered in the questionnaire were from once a week or more often, to never in the past year. We have chosen frequency levels to display here which both collect a reasonable volume of positive responses while also helping to illustrate differences between streams and sub-samples. In most cases, by moving to the highest rates of activity we can accentuate differences, but at the cost of reducing the volume of positive responses to rather low levels.

The overall finding in this section of data is again one of considerable similarity of responses by the different sub-samples. The figures in the next table are self-explanatory on the whole, and require little comment at this stage - except perhaps for the last two measures relating to shared holidays. Here the relationship between random and most-contact responses becomes rather different, for all categories of respondents, with rates for random streams as high or higher than those for most-contact. This invites some interpretation.

The most probable explanation for this is that it points to different styles of relationship. Although grandparents do go on holiday with those grandchildren whom they see often, this is *also* something commonly done by those grandparents who do *not* manage to see their grandchildren often. It seems to be a type of high-intensity contact which may be pursued in some families as a way of *compensating* for not normally having much time together. The figures do include grandchildren going to stay at the homes of those grandparents who live too far away to be seen very often. Hence the bipolar distributions. Another point of interest here is just *how* close the grandparental and parental estimates are on the shared holiday questions. This may arise because it is a type of activity which almost by definition has to be carried out with a good deal of planning, so that there are clear, shared reference points for both sets of respondents.

---

[1] See Appendix A below for a full list of questions *asked*, and Appendix III in the BSA98 report, that is Jowell et al., 1999, for details of *response categories and rates*.

Table 3.4 Shared activities with selected relative

	Respondent is:-					
	GP		**Adult GC**		**Linking parent**	
	R	**MC**	**R**	**MC**	**R**	**MC**
% where GP (& GC):-						
Give or receive presents at least monthly	42	49	10	18	32	45
Go to park or playground at least monthly w/o parents	24	27	n/a	n/a	n/a	n/a
Go shopping etc. at least monthly w/o parents	21	33	8	12	15	29
Play watch video/TV etc. at least monthly w/o parents	40	55	18	32	36	48
Visit relatives or friends together at least monthly w/o parents	14	23	7	12	10	19
Has in past year gone away together for holiday w/o parents	7	9	3	5	8	6
Has in past year gone away together for holiday with parents	17	19	4	5	17	22
Base	*681*	*341*	*424*	*348*	*438*	*299*

Note: Group A, [243-249]; Group B, [310-315]; Group C, [385-390].

Looking after children

Next we asked grandparents with younger grandchildren (also linking parents) some questions about activities that could be regarded as direct participation in childcare. Within a family context there is obviously a thin line, and inevitably some overlap, between socialising with grandchildren and sharing some responsibility for their care. This issue is considered in chapter 8, which examines these variables in more detail. Here we just summarise responses regarding activities where grandparents explicitly have some responsibility delegated to them.

We also explored how far grandparents and parents agreed on the upbringing of children, and what say grandparents had in it all. Grandparents tended to report more say than parents, while both reported the same amount of agreement. But again, this shifts a bit according to the strength of a measure that is considered. These issues are looked at in some detail in chapter nine.

In table 3.5 we summarise the findings on these variables. Because of the focus on grandparents with younger grandchildren, the bases are smaller for childcare as such. Again we find a reasonable overall correspondence between parental and grandparental responses, though the tendency for grandparents to give higher estimates than parents is slightly stronger for these variables than for those dealing simply with shared activities.

Table 3.5 Childcare role of grandparents

| | Respondent is: | | | | | |
| | GP | | Adult GC | | Linking parent | |
% where GP has:-	R	MC	R	MC	R	MC
Helped with daytime childcare weekly or more*	22	32	n/a	n/a	11	27
Helped with daytime childcare at least monthly*	53	66	n/a	n/a	39	51
Helped with evening childcare at least monthly	42	58	n/a	n/a	31	47
Taken GC to or from school/nursery at least monthly*	18	25	n/a	n/a	16	31
Looked after GC when sick during last year*	17	26	n/a	n/a	16	22
Had at least a little say in decisions affecting GC**	59	62	n/a	n/a	46	59
At least some agreement with parents on how to bring up GC**	73	79	72	76	72	82
*Base** - Where selected GC under 12	422	213			229	168
*Base*** - All	681	341	424	348	438	299

Note: Group A, [250-54.273-5]; Group B, [336]; Group C, [395-99.414-16].

Advice and financial help

We also asked about types of support which do not require close and frequent contact, or even any direct contact at all, plus some which grand*children* can give to grand*parents*. These activities bring in adult grandchildren much more, and often refer to events in which parents may not be involved at all, and perhaps do not even know about. Grandparents were not themselves asked about help given to them by grandchildren, so on those measures we do not have any data offering their perspective.

In most cases the level of correspondence between complementary accounts is good. On financial help direct to grandchildren, parents give estimates rather similar to grandparents – particularly among the most-contact group. But this is largely a matter of needing to identify matching age groups. Where data from grandparents is restricted to ties with selected grandchildren up to 18, the grandparental figures on money direct to grandchildren (R= 33%, MC = 30%) do correspond very closely with those given by parents. With adult grandchildren, differences are sharper – 14% having received money in the last year among the random group compared to 40% among the most-contact. Differences were also apparent for receiving advice (R=24% , MC=30%).

Regarding help to grandparents, there are obviously certain types of support (like providing transport) where adult grandchildren are bound to be more active than younger. So rates given by adult grandchildren for these will be higher than those reported by parents. More detailed commentary on the pattern of support according to grandchild age is given in chapter seven.

Table 3.6 Other (and mutual) supports given in past year

| | GP | | Adult GC | | Linking parent | |
	R	MC	R	MC	R	MC
% where GP has:-						
Helped parent with money for GC	26	27	n/a	n/a	18	25
Helped grandchild direct with money	28	29	n/a	n/a	23	28
Given GC advice	37	52	n/a	n/a	n/a	n/a
Base	*681*	*341*			*438*	*299*
% where GC has helped GP:-						
With shopping	n/a	n/a	29	31	26	34
With house or garden work	n/a	n/a	28	37	32	38
With transportation	n/a	n/a	23	33	7	11
By looking after when sick	n/a	n/a	9	10	14	7
Base			*424*	*348*	*438*	*299*

Note: Group A, [257-62]; Group B, [316-19.322-25]; Group C, [391-4.402-5].

State of parental relationship

The final section of the questionnaire looked at whether the *parents* of grandchildren were living together or not, as we felt that this might be a key factor influencing not only the style of grandparental involvement but also their opportunity to play any part at all. We asked whether parents (if both alive) were still together, how long those who were apart had been, and how closely (specified) grandparents had been involved at the time of a split. The basic findings are summarised in table 3.7.

Table 3.7 Relationship of grandchild's parents

	GP R	GP MC	Adult GC R	Adult GC MC	Linking parent R	Linking parent MC
Respondent is:						
% where GC parents are:-						
Still together	75	69	62	63	83	86
Now separated*	10	15	4	4	6	6
Now divorced*	11	11	23	19	9	8
Now widowed	3	4	13	14	1	0
DK	1	1	0	0	1	0
Base	*715*	*350*	*426*	*334*	*467*	*307*
where apart (separated or divorced:						
% GC parents have been:-						
Separated/divorced < 5 years	57	53	15	9	72	79
Base	*156*	*96*	*125*	*91*	*112*	*69*
% where GC:-						
Stayed with GP at time of parental split	29	39	22	26	10	13
Had more contact with GP at time of split	44	53	33	39	19	29
Had less contact with GP at time of split	12	9	13	11	12	9
Base	*156*	*96*	*125*	*91*	*112*	*69*
% where GP:-						
Had difficulty keeping in touch with GC at time of split	21	11	9	9	12	11
Base	*156*	*96*	*125*	*91*	*112*	*69*

Note: Group A, [264-272]; Group B, [327-335]; Group C, [406-413].
* Perhaps not too much should be made of the distinction between separation and divorce here when looking for differences or trends. Some (older) respondents may have selected separation as a euphemism for divorce; against that, as smaller proportions of parents are actually getting married then fewer of them become eligible for it.

A fuller analysis of parenting breakdown and its consequences is made in chapter 5. We do however at this point want to consider briefly the variability in responses to these breakdown questions between different samples of respondents, as much of this boils down to technical (including demographic) differences between the samples which are bound to generate diverse reporting. The sets of figures given here may not be so incompatible as they appear at first.

Thus at first sight it may appear odd, given that so much is written about increasing instability of relationships, that it is the linking parents who (referring to their own partnerships) report the lowest levels of breakdown, and the adult grandchildren (whose parents are bound to be among the oldest considered here) who report the *highest*. An important reason for this is of course that breakdown rates are cumulative over the life-time of a cohort, so that high rates reported for parents of adult grandchildren represent much nearer the final level likely to be achieved than is the case for the parental groups in the other samples. Many parents in that generation will, moreover, have stayed together until their children were grown up. So, for many of the adult grandchildren, parenting breakdown will have occurred fairly late in their personal development – long after they would have had time to forge strong ties with grandparents, certainly – and may have had relatively little influence on them. On top of this, even where splits did occur during these respondents' childhood, they have now had more time (as autonomous adults) to seek out lost grandparents and establish a relationship. So although the proportion of breakdowns in this group is high it may have had relatively *less* influence on current grandparenting relationships for this sub-sample than a similar rate would for the others.

Conversely, the low breakdown rates reported by linking parents (who constitute the youngest sub-sample of parents in the study, and include many who have only just *become* parents) represent only an early point in that cohort's accumulation of broken relationships. It may for some purposes even constitute an unrealistically low proportion, as there are bound to be within this sample a number of couples in a latent breakdown state – that is still actually together but heading towards separation in the not-too-distant future, and already displaying behaviour in terms of family contacts and shared activities which is more like parents who are *not* together.

Parents referred to in the grandparents' data (sample A) cover a wider age-span than either of the other groups, and accordingly show an intermediate (or average) level of breakdown.

There are even sharper variations between samples when we look at details of those cases where parenting breakdown has taken place. Regarding *duration* of separation, the low proportion of recent breakdowns reported by adult grandchildren is understandable. But there are also large differences in the accounts of grandparental involvement at the time of breakdown. Again, this is quite easy to understand for adult grandchildren, as many of these will have been grown-up when their parents separated, and so not have needed much help from grandparents. But the differences between sample A and sample C responses cannot be explained in this way. Almost certainly, these differences are related to the fact that in sample C, the linking parents, it is the respondents *own* breakdown that is being probed here. This could well have made them much less forthcoming (and interviewers less confident to probe) on matters of grandparental involvement, compared with respondents in the other sub-samples.

In relation to the data collected from linking parents, we have to remember more generally that only those parents currently *co-resident* with children identified as participants in a grandchild/grandparent relationship were included in this sub-sample and interviewed as parents. Where parents are not together, the bulk of children are living with their mothers. This means that there are many more separated mothers in this sub-sample (plus occasional step-fathers) than there are separated fathers (or step-mothers).[2] Very few of the separated fathers will be represented. All of this will surely have influenced the volume and content of data collected on the circumstances surrounding parental separations.

---

[2] These responding parents are the ones who also tend to serve in real life too as the gatekeepers and axes for three-generation contacts where parents are apart. There are significantly more female linking parents than male; and this is consistent with the relative probabilities of separated parents co-residing with children.

4

DEMOGRAPHY

Becoming a grandparent

In order to understand how patterns of contemporary grandparenting operate within families, it is helpful to examine the demographic structure of British society and changes that are taking place in it.[1] The BSA 1998 survey asked respondents which categories of *relatives* they had alive, and this has enabled us to develop a profile of responding grandparents' family relationships. During the second half of the twentieth century, there was a steady fall in family size as a result of decreasing fertility rates.[2] This has reduced the *number* of grandchildren that grandparents may have, and thus the total volume of expectations on them at any moment. But at the same time, more people have become grandparents, because of the low proportion of childless women who were born in the late 1930s and early 1940s. Thus the proportion of grandparents in the population today is *higher* than during the 1960s and 1970s. Grandparents today have fewer grandchildren than in previous generations of grandparents, but are more likely to have *some*. They do not have many competing grandchildren and this may be an important factor influencing current styles of grandparenting. Figure 4.1 shows both the proportion of grandparents in the population and the distribution of the number of grandchildren among these grandparents.

Using this data, we can see that right up to the age of 90 more than half of the grandparents had only four grandchildren or less. This represents a considerable drop over the last couple of generations. Almost one in five (17%) of the grandparents interviewed in Peter Townsend's study of the family life of old people in the 1950s had ten or more grandchildren (Townsend, 1957). In the BSA 1998 survey, this had fallen to one in twenty, even though life

---

[1] For a useful discussion of trends in the demography of grandparenting see Szinovacz, 1998.a
[2] Women born in the late 1930s had the largest families: see ONS, 1999.

expectancy has risen and people are now grandparents for *longer*. The age now at which more than half of the population are grandparents is 54 ; and the mean number of grandchildren among grandparents is 4.4. This mean rises from 1.3 for those under 40, to 2.2 for those between 45 and 49. For all ages above 50, the mean is always more than 3, reaching a peak of approximately 5 after the age of sixty.

Figure 4.1 Proportions of grandparents by age with numbers of grandchildren

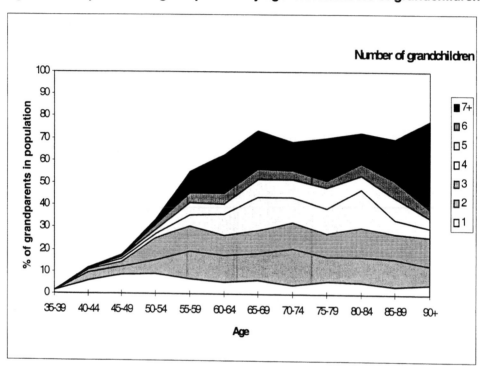

Although the majority of older people in Britain throughout the twentieth century have been grandparents, there are signs that the rates will fall. Women today are more likely to become mothers at a later age than women twenty years ago, and are also opting in greater numbers not to have children at all - both within and outside of marriage. The proportion of women in England and Wales who were still childless at age 45 was 13% in 1994 and is likely to continue to rise (Armitage & Babb, 1996; McAllister & Clarke, 1998).[3] The Office of National Statistics projects that 'the proportion of childless women will increase so that about 23% of women born in 1973 will be childless when they reach the age of 45' (ONS, 2001). Unless childbirth delayed until after that

---

[3] This trend is found also in the BSA 1998 data, where 17% of women aged 45 or more are childless.

age becomes a significant trend in the future, which seems unlikely, then a pattern of increasing childlessness must eventually also result in a decline in the proportion of grandparents. Between 1981 and 1990 marriage rates for women fell by 26% (OPCS, 1993). The proportion of women under 60 years who live in one person households has risen substantially over the past twenty years and was estimated to comprise just under 6% of total households by 2000 (Haskey, 1996). Young men are also increasingly remaining single and living alone, at an even greater pace than young women. In 2001 one in ten of all households was a man under 65 years living alone (CSO, 1995).[4]

Against this, though, there was a remarkable increase in longevity in the twentieth century, which seems likely to continue. This trend raises the proportion of life span most people spend as a grandparent, increases the number of living grandparents each grandchild has, and substantially increases the proportion of great-grandparents in the population.

Figure 4.2 Proportions of grandparents with at least one parent alive by age

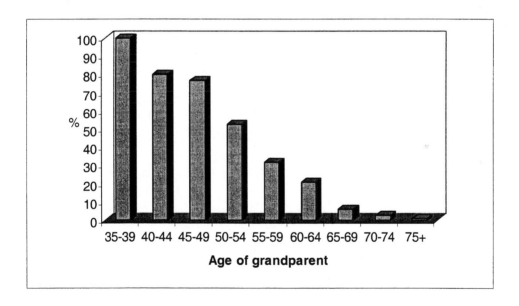

Figure 4.2 shows that virtually all of the youngest grandparents in the survey had one or more parents alive; only after the age of 53 does the proportion fall to below 50 per cent. Another way of looking at this, and using a multi-generational perspective, is shown in figure 4.3.

---

[4] By 2016, it is estimated that the proportion of male adult one person households aged under 65 years (13%) will be greater than women aged 65 years and above (12%): CSO, 1997.

Figure 4.3 Proportions of population with lineal kin by age

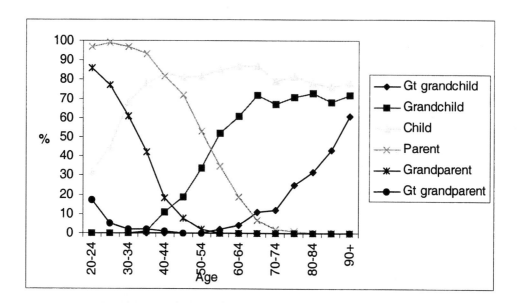

Figure 4.3 shows the proportion of each age cohort with different types of kin members alive. It indicates that almost all adults up to the age of 40 had at least one parent still alive, and over one third had at least one grandparent alive too.

The age at which grandparenthood is achieved is a function of the age of parents in successive generations. For most of this century, the average age at which women have their first child has fallen, reaching its lowest peak (23.8 years) from 1968 to 1970 (ONS, 1999). Since then the mean has steadily risen again, as more women have chosen to delay childbirth until they are in their 30s, reaching 28.4 years in 1994. The temporary lowering of the age of childbearing in the sixties and seventies means that there are a number of very young grandparents around at the moment. Thus an average woman having a daughter in 1970, at the age of 24, could expect to become a grandmother at 52 in 1998 when her daughter has her first child at 28. This is not very different from trends in the middle of the century, nor from the actual figure found in the BSA survey.[5] However, the number of young grandparents will decline as the generation span widens again.

---

[5]Peter Townsend (1957) calculated the mean age of becoming a grandfather as 55 and a grandmother as 53 years.

The BSA survey shows a wide range in the age of grandparents, the lowest age being thirty-seven. There are some social class differences as can be seen in figure 4.4.

Figure 4.4 Social class differences in age of grandparenthood
(% of age group who *are* grandparents)

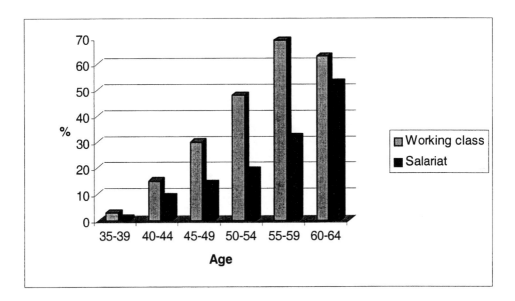

This figure shows that if we take five-year age groups up to age 64, the proportion of working-class population who are grandparents is much higher than that in the salariat. Moreover, greater age spans between the generations are found among higher social class groups. These differences reflect greater longevity among higher social classes, and greater fertility rates coupled with an earlier age of becoming a parent among lower social classes (Ni Bhrolchain, 1993). Thus the family structures of adults in the salariat are more likely to be ascending or 'sandwiched' (having at least one parent and child) than in the working class and, conversely, the working class are more likely to have descending or four-generational families. (See chapter 10 below for further discussion of this.)

On top of social class variations, the age at which men and women become grandparents also differs. Figure 4.5 uses BSA data to estimate the proportion of men and women in the population who are parents and grandparents by certain ages. It shows that the difference is *most* accentuated in the age-group 40–49 – in which most grandparents are grand*mothers*. The gap is still wide for the 50-54 year-olds, where 40% of women had grandchildren, compared with only 23% of men: but it is less for the 50-59 cohort overall, in which 47% of women have grandchildren compared with 36% of men.

By the age of 70, though, the differential has disappeared, with two in three of both men and women now grandparents. For the very oldest cohorts of men, the proportion of grandparents is in fact higher than that for women. This is because women born between 1910 and 1928 had higher rates of childlessness than later cohorts of women (a peak of 16% for women born in 1923, who were 75 at the time of the BSA survey), and because men typically marry women who are younger than themselves. Given differences in life expectancy, grandmothers today are likely to occupy this role for approximately 30 years or about a third of their life span (compared to approximately 20 years for grandfathers – about one-quarter of their life span).

Figure 4.5 Family generations by age

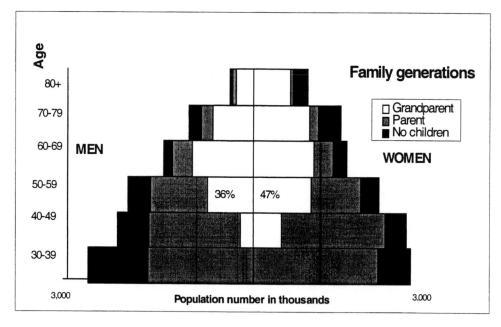

The fact that women have a greater life expectancy than men has an important effect on the relative experience of the grandparent role, and even more profound perhaps on the experience of being a grandchild. This is illustrated in figure 4.6. When grandchildren are newly born, they are highly likely to have at least one grandfather alive. But as they grow older they tend to lose their grandfathers first, and thereafter increasingly have only grand*mothers*. And those grandfathers who are around longer are rather more likely to be maternal than paternal. The same trend, continued and intensified, is evident for grandparents of adult grandchild, aged from 18 to 47 (mean age 27). By the age of 40, virtually no grandchildren have a PGF alive, and only one in ten of their grandparents are maternal grandfathers.

Figure 4.6 Proportions of grandparents per lineal category by age of grandchild

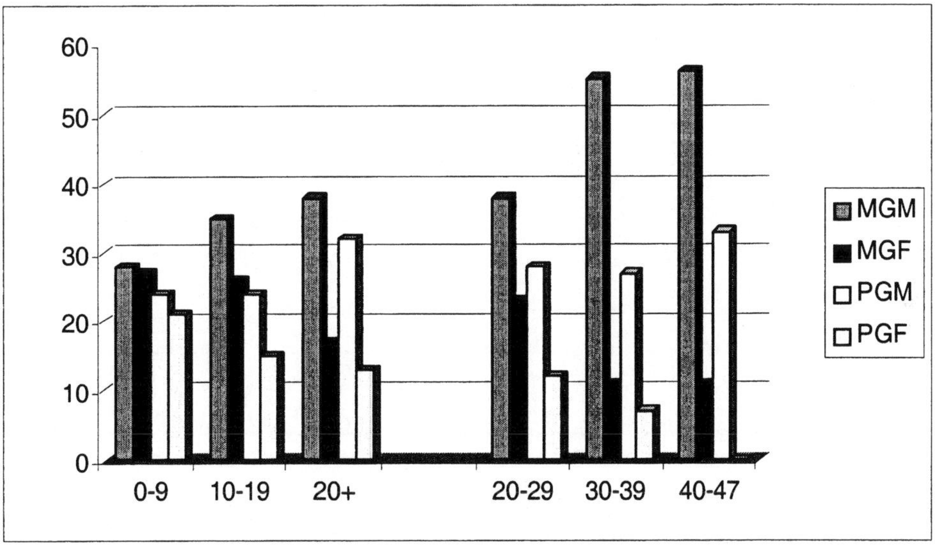

Note: (MGM=Maternal grandmother; MGF Maternal grandfather; PGM Paternal grandmother; PGF Paternal grandfather)
Left-hand columns based on Sample A data: i.e. age of selected grandchild of responding grandparent is tabulated by lineage link.
Right-hand columns based on Sample B data: i.e. age of adult grandchild respondent tabulated by lineage tie with selected grandparent.

Grandparents in the extended family

An important implication of these demographic shifts is that extended families have been changing their form. They now involve more family generations than in the past. The majority of grandparents today, 62% in BSA data, are no longer the senior generation in the family - which often contains four, five or even six generations.

The pattern revealed in the BSA survey is illustrated in figure 4.7 which illustrates the numbers of generations in general survey respondents' families according to their age group.

Figure 4.7 Number of family generations by respondent age

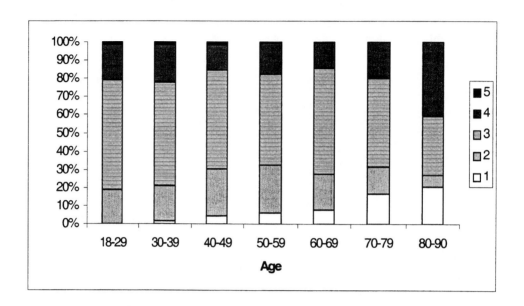

In early adult life, over 80% of the population live within three or more generational families. From middle age the proportion of one- and two-generation families increases, as grandparents die and - for childless people - are not replaced by children and grandchildren. But the majority of the adult population people still live in lineages three or more generations deep. In the later stages of the life-course childlessness increases the proportion of single-generation families, with almost one in five respondents aged 80 or above having no ascending *or* descending-generation relatives. Against this, 36% of the respondents above 80 are actually in four generation families, combining the roles of grandparent and great-grandparent.[6]

The net effect of reduced fertility and increased longevity has given rise to what some commentators refer to as a 'beanpole' type of structure of family generations (Bengston and Achenbaum, 1993). Each family has fewer members in one generation, but can expect to have members in more generations at the same time. So the focus becomes more lineal, and grandparents' support becomes more important than it might have been in the past when there was more 'lateral' support, in the form of aunts and uncles, not to mention siblings and cousins, available to play a part. In these circumstances it has been argued

---

[6] Children under 18 are not represented in the BSA survey, and no respondents were asked if they had great-great-grandchildren or -grandparents alive. If this information had been collected, it would have revealed the existence of more five, and even some *six* generation families.

that grandparents may be playing a more active role, certainly when their grandchildren are young. The time-span during which the grandparenting role is occupied can today account for half or even more of a lifetime. And in many families, young parents have their own grandparents alive, so that grandparents and, to a certain extent, great-grandparents may all be involved in helping with young children.

There are class and cultural variations here. The earlier fertility of women in the working class means that there is a greater likelihood for them of being in multi-generational families. Grandparents are younger, and generations closer together, as figure 4.8 shows.

Figure 4.8 Family generations and social class

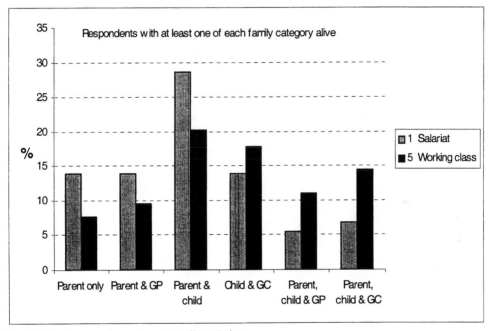

Note: Each family generation category mutually exclusive.

Differences can also be detected among ethnic minorities. Only a few grandparents from minority groups were sampled in the BSA survey - twelve Black and Asian, plus twenty-five respondents of mixed race or who refused to specify their origin. The smallness of this tally is partly a consequence of the age-structure of the immigrant population, but does also indicate some under-representation of minorities.[7] These numbers give us just about enough

---

[7] See Appendix C for a discussion of this.

information to see that because of shorter lives (and larger families) there is likely to be a lesser tendency towards bean-poling among minorities. Although no grandparent is found among them under the age of 40, the mean age of grandparents in this ethnic sub-sample is, presumably because of the absence of very old community members, around five years lower than in the white population. As we will show shortly, these differences in generation structure are accompanied by different patterns of family co-residence.

The gradual narrowing of extended families into beanpoles, organised around lineal relations, is made even more significant by the weakening of marriage ties in British society over the same period. Growth in numbers of single-parent families, plus the greater fragility of parenting relationships, means that affinity is no longer so valuable as a source of additional kin ties, and confirms the narrowing of extended family networks within a generation. In the following section of the report (chapter 5) we will outline the effect which the absence or breakdown of marriage and parental cohabitation seems to be having on grandparenting.

The increasing flexibility in conjugal relationships is, at the same time, having an effect which to some extent works against the beanpole tendency. This is to do with the increasing number of families now which involve step relationships. These can be seen in some ways as a new form of affinity, loosely and informally pulling together beanpole lineages into compound networks where many people can find a number of kin in their own generation.

The factor of step-relations has complicated grandparenting quite a bit. Before the 1960s almost all grandparents could trace a direct family line of descent to their grandchildren. The increase in divorce and separation rates since then, together with a rise in the number of births outside marriage, has changed many lines of affiliation. It is the cohort of grandparents aged between 50 and 74 which is experiencing this most, with the combined effect of separation in their own and their children's generations producing the largest proportion of step-grandchildren. The cohort of grandparents before them had a very different experience. The cohort after them - that is the parents of young parents with very young children - may prove to have a similar or even more unstable family experience. But because divorce and separation typically occur after several years of marriage many of those who will be affected have not yet encountered it. Step-families are discussed in more detail in chapter eleven.

A further effect of marriage trends on grandparenting arises out of the increase in births outside marriage. These currently account for one in four births, meaning that many 'new' grandparents have a different type of relationship with their grandchild - in which some (generally the maternal grandparents) can expect to be called on to give *greater* support, unaided by a second set of grandparents. Others, almost always on the paternal side, may find that they are largely excluded from an active role.

This is part of a trend towards matrilineal relationships which is explored in chapter six. At this point we can just note that among all parents in the BSA survey who had at least one parent alive, 6% were single parents - neither married nor living together as married. These were predominantly women (69% against only 31% men), suggesting that a large number of fathers not resident with their children may not have *reported* themselves as having children, and underlining the fact that the bulk of grandparenting carried out in relation to children of single parents is bound to be taking place in the maternal line.[8] Most single mothers were in the 20-24 age-range, however, indicating perhaps that many of them can themselves expect to be in a couple relationship after a few years, and that being a single mother is, perhaps increasingly, a common but not long-sustained stage in the developmental cycle.

---

[8] Note that this is not necessarily for parents co-resident with their children – where we would expect there to be many more mothers than fathers – but simply for men and women reporting themselves as parents but *not* living with a partner. The implication is that many men either do not know that they are fathers, or are not reporting it.

5

CHANGES IN DOMESTIC LIFE

Household composition

In this chapter we look at how current changes in the organisation of family life influence the part played by grandparents. This is mainly to do with the effects of increasing breakdown of parenting, resulting in parents of grandchildren not living together. But there are also some more general changes, which we will look at first here, in the ways in which kinship relates to co-residence.

The emerging (beanpole) form of extended families is largely invisible in existing social statistics, where the emphasis is almost entirely on co-residential household groups, and often ignores whether or not, or in what ways, these groups are made up of kin. Extended families, in which young parents may live with their own parents, and alongside siblings and even siblings' children, do still show up in those household surveys which ask questions about ties between members. But such forms are rare now. Trends in social statistics during the latter part of the twentieth century chart the virtual disappearance of this type of residential pattern. Domestic units have become smaller, and more concentrated around two-generation groups. This fact has fed a widespread assumption that extended families have simply disappeared. There has been little recognition of the continuing vitality of kinship ties outside of and between households, and very little interest has been shown in developing measures for shared activities within families that cut across residential divisions - though lately there are signs that this may be beginning to pick up.

In the meantime, provided that we do not forget the importance of ties with relatives elsewhere, there is still quite a lot that we can find out about family life from looking at household composition. The following table shows the broad pattern of household composition among BSA respondents, and some details of differences between social class groups.

Table 5.1 Household composition by social class
(column %)

| | Social Class | | |
Household composition	Salariat	Intermediate	Working class
Childless	24	13	13
Couple with child	30	30	25
Single parent and child	2	5	6
"Empty nest"	35	42	45
Other	9	9	11
Base	*986*	*1144*	*907*

Note: $p=<.001$, derived variables.

The data in table 5.1 sum up very cogently a number of class differences in the composition of households. Thus childless individuals form a relatively small proportion of respondents from intermediate and working-class groups, compared with nearly a quarter of the salariat. It is among women in higher social class groups that childbearing is more often and perhaps increasingly postponed - commonly for career reasons - or even avoided altogether (Ni Bhrolchain, 1993).

Broadly similar proportions of respondents in all three class categories are recorded as parents living with children. However there is a higher proportion of single parents in the intermediate and working-class categories, predominantly single mothers, reflecting perhaps the tendency for women to start having their children earlier where their economic opportunities (including via potential partners) are not good (Kiernan, 1999).

The 'empty nest' category also embraces considerable class variability relating to later stages in the life course. This group consists of parents whose children have all grown up and left home, and includes widows and widowers living alone. It is equally divided (for all class groups) between those who are and are not (yet) grandparents. There is a steady increase in the size of this category towards the working-class end of the spectrum, and also of its widowed component.

The final, residual category of 'other' exhibits fewer class differences, and all its component groups are quite small. The group consists of more complex households containing grandparents co-residing with their children and grandchildren, single parents living in the grandparental home, plus a miscellany of other combinations including with *non*-relatives.

These differences are detailed further in the next table, which focuses specifically on grandparents' households.

Table 5.2 Type of grandparent household
(column %)

	Social Class		
	Salariat	**Intermediate**	**Working class**
Who grandparent lives with:			
Living alone	21	20	28
Spouse/partner only	60	60	42
Dependent child	6	2	6
Adult child	10	16	19
Grandchild	1	2	4
Other type household	2	0	1
Base	*226*	*353*	*317*

Note: *p*=<.001, derived variables.

Table 5.2 exemplifies the greater *diversity* of grandparenting among working-class respondents, who become grandparents younger and so combine the status with a greater range of other life stages and family commitments. There are also higher proportions living with adult children and as part of three generation households. Rates for the latter are lower than for some European countries (and for ethnic minorities within Britain) where more traditional extended families still operate, and also than for the US where new types of extended families are developing in response to the breakdown of parenting (Casper and Bryson, 1998).

In Britain, in spite of growing instability of parenting relationships, there are few three-generation households containing grandparents and grandchildren. However the breakdown of parenting does have a strong influence on the lives of grandparents, as the remainder of this section will outline. Table 5.3 indicates the proportions of each of the BSA survey sub-samples where parenting relationships have broken down. As noted earlier, parental breakdowns in the adult grandchildren represent what is probably the most completed rate, as the age of the parents in question is greatest, while that of the linking parents are the least complete, as the families are still young. In all three sub-samples higher rates of parenting breakdown exist among the working class. What is also very interesting about the linking parents is that this association is stronger, with more than twice the proportion of split parents in the working class as in the salariat. The nexus involving young parenthood, instability of parenting and rapidly diversifying roles of grandparents has itself a definite social class dimension.

Table 5.3 Whether parents together or apart by social class

	Social Class			
% where GC's parents apart	**Salariat**	**Intermediate**	**Working class**	*Base*
GP is respondent	20	22	24	*192*
Adult GC is respondent	21	27	28	*152*
Linking parent is respondent	8	16	20	*139*

Note: Group A, NS, [264]; Group B, NS, [327]; Group C, *p*<.001[406].

Implications of parenting breakdown

One area where grandparenting is almost certainly in the throes of rapid change is in relation to grandchildren whose parents are not living together. The BSA survey reveals very important divergences in grandparenting style, following parenting breakdown, with some grandparents much more active than average and others a lot less active. Insofar as parenting relationships are becoming *increasingly* fragile in Britain, it seems safe to assume that this polarisation is currently intensifying.

The next few tables are designed to give a picture of what happens to grandparents' attitudes and behaviour after parental breakdown. Respondents have been grouped according to whether grandchildren's parents are still together or not.[1] Those where they are not have then been divided further into those where grandparents reported seeing more of their grandchildren during the separation, those who saw *less*, and those who saw them almost the same amount. The level of contact with grandparents at the time of separation seems in many cases to have set the pattern for subsequent relations. At the time of the BSA survey, contacts were generally most close and active for those grandparents who had been more involved at the time of a split (partly to do with the fact that the split often resulted in the parents with care of the grandchildren returning to their own parents' home), and least for those where separation had involved less contact. Relationships where parents were still together at the time of the survey, along with those where there had been a split with little change in grandparental involvement, fell somewhere between these two poles.

We have presented these types in the following tabulations in order of their general activity, that is with the category normally most active - 'more contact

---

[1] 'Separation' here *includes* births to single mothers who have never been co-resident with the fathers of their child, but *excludes* parents who are widows or widowers.

at separation' - on the left, and the least active - 'less contact at separation' - on the right. This arrangement helps draw attention to consistencies in the pattern of responses across a wide range of measures.[2] This grouping into four response-categories unfortunately produces rather small numbers of cases in some columns for certain questions. We have tried however to keep as many figures as possible in the tables, in order to better illustrate the wider pattern. Although some numbers *are* small, the pattern of responses they help to generate tends to recur across the different sub-samples – and this suggests that they may be more reliable than their base-sizes would indicate by themselves.[3] The first table in the set, table 5.4, looks at the relationship between parental separation and grandparents' feelings about their role.

Table 5.4 Grandparents' feelings about role by whether parents together

% of GPs who:-	Parents apart *More* contact at separation	Parents together	Parents apart *Same* contact at separation	Parents apart *Less* contact at separation
Agree strongly that grandchildren are rewarding	65	66	59	36
Agree would like a life free from family duties	36	35	39	59
Agree strongly have had to put self out to help look after grandchildren	50	30	37	19
Agree have had to cut down/give up work to help look after GCs	17	6	17	13
Base	*46*	*533*	*60*	*42*

Note: Group A, *p*<0.05, [198-201.264.269-72].

---

[2] This division of respondents where there is breakdown of parental relationships into three categories represents a more closely focused analysis of responses than was attempted in the BSA98 Report chapter on grandparents – where a distinction was made only between 'more contact' and 'same or less contact' respondents. In this fuller categorisation we have also allowed for the fact that a number of respondents suggest in their answers to one question (e.g., for grandparents, q. 269) that they had *more* contact at the time of breakup, while in others (270-272) indicating that they had *less*. In the BSA98 chapter we included these cases with the 'more contact' group, as this was the first question answered on the issue. Here we have however, after further consideration, put them into the 'less contact' category. This is because they clearly experienced difficulties at the time of breakdown – which is the key analytic issue here – and presumably had at best an ambivalent relationship during that period with their offspring. See Appendix F for syntax of categorisation of responses.

[3] Instead of leaving out all figures based on low base numbers we have placed asterisks in the base line to indicate where a total goes <u>below twenty</u> – to show that the relevant figures in the table need to be treated with caution. In the event that a base falls to <u>twelve cases or less</u> then a dash is placed in the body of the table instead of a percentage figure, as this clearly goes below a usable threshold.

Table 5.4 suggests some possible links between parental breakdown for selected relationships and grandparents' general feelings about their role. Where parents are separated and grandparents had *less* contact at separation then lower proportions of grandparents see their role as rewarding, or have put themselves out for grandchildren, and more want a free life. Where there was *more* contact at separation the opposite of this applies. Also there is a slight general tendency for *all* groups of grandparents where parents are separated to indicate that they have had to give up or reduce work commitments in order to help out.

It should be borne in mind here, if these links are not very strong, that none of the questions generating the measures tabled in 5.4 were asked in relation to *specific* grandchildren. This does not mean that there is no relationship worth looking for. Parenting breakdown in the case of one grandchild may well produce some general effect on grandparents' overall feeling about the role, and may possibly even colour their feelings about particular ties with other grandchildren. There are not enough cases in the BSA survey to allow thorough analysis of just those respondents with one grandchild (or grandparent) only. (But see table 6.7, and the discussion on pages 65-67, for some further elaboration of this issue – in the context there of unscrambling the influence of lineage on general feelings about the grandparent role.)

Responses of adult grandchildren to similar questions are set out in the next table.

Table 5.5 Grandchildren's feelings about role by whether parents together

% of GCs who:-	Parents apart *More* contact at separation	Parents together	Parents apart *Same* contact at separation	Parents apart *Less* contact at separation
Agree strongly that grandparents are an important part of their life	57	36	29	40
Disagree strongly that they would not see their grandparents as often as they do if they did not have to	29	32	25	38
Agree strongly that their grandparents are not interested in their life	5	6	8	13
Agree strongly that they do not see as much of their GPs as GPs like	19	17	21	0
Base	*44*	*301*	*64*	*24*

Note: Group B, NS, [276-79.327.332-5].

Grandchildren's responses set out in table 5.5 show perhaps even less link with the state of parental relationships. This is consistent with the points made earlier that for *adult* grandchildren parental splits will either have taken place recently, at a time when their own ties with grandparents were already established, or long enough ago for them to have had opportunities to re-establish them. But it is still evident from the data that more contact at the time of separation does appear to result in a more active bond later. However, on the evidence given here, many grandchildren do value the relationship even where they had less contact at the time of their parents' break-up.[4] A larger proportion of this category than any other asserted that they see their grandparents because *they* themselves want to, perhaps here reflecting that the contact of this group with grandparents may take place without parental encouragement to do so. As would be expected, though, this category does record the highest proportion of negative sentiments as well, with more suggesting that their grandparents are not interested in them and also fewer reporting that their grandparents would like to see more of them than they actually do.

When we come to look at specified relationships the picture is simpler and clearer. Figures for all the three main sub-samples on frequency of contact and feelings about closeness are collected together in table 5.6, where they can be seen to be highly consistent. Rates for being currently in touch (contact within two years) are as high for relationships involving separation with more contact at time of split as for those where the parents are together, and the lowest are where there was separation involving less contact. (This again, along with the high reporting in table 5.4 by this category of grandparents of finding their role rewarding, perhaps shows that grandparents feel most comfortable where families are not split.) The same general ordering applies, with even steeper gradients, for frequency of current contact and feelings of closeness. It is intriguing to see that the feelings of adult grandchildren, and the feelings of children assessed by linking parents, closely match those of the grandparents. All of these questions on contact and closeness, moreover, were dealt with in the interviews *before* those asking about the state of parental relationships and the effect of any separation on contacts at that time. So no obvious triggering or prompting of responses can have taken place.

Strikingly, the same ordering turns up also in relation to current geographical propinquity. The only exception to this is with adult grandchildren, where there is an association between frequency of contact and *integrity* of the parental relationship. Again, this may be a pointer to a counter-tendency whereby grandparents (and perhaps grandchildren too) feel more comfortable with

---

[4] It seems to be in the nature of family life that people remain interested in their relations even if splits have taken place, and may be drawn to re-establish contacts with them. See Thompson, 1999.

relationships within families that have stayed unbroken. However, the adult grandchild sample in this data set is the one which refers to the separations going back furthest in time. So there are inevitably a number of possible explanations available here, ranging from the effects of changing social attitudes to a variety of processes of personal and family development.

Table 5.6 Contact and closeness by whether parents together

% of GPs who:-	Parents apart *More* contact at separation	Parents together	Parents apart *Same* contact at separation	Parents apart *Less* contact at separation
Have seen GC in last 2 years*	**97**	**98**	**93**	**73**
See GC several times a week*	44	31	34	12
Live within 15 mins from GC**	48	35	32	18
Feel very close to GC**	**79**	**70**	**63**	**42**
*Base**	*46*	*533*	*60*	*42*
*Base***	*45*	*519*	*55*	*30*
% where GC:-				
Has seen GP in last 2 years*	100	92	83	63
Sees GP several times a week*	13	10	7	0
Lives within 15 mins from GP**	27	31	23	10
Feels very close to GP**	36	34	21	30
*Base**	*44*	*301*	*64*	*24*
*Base***	*43*	*271*	*52*	***
% where linking parent reports:-				
GP has seen GC in last 2 years*	100	96	87	64
GP sees GC several times a week *	50	21	20	7
GP lives within 15 mins from GC**	56	38	26	22
GP and GC feel very close**	70	44	43	11
*Base**	*24*	*355*	*55*	*24*
*Base***	*24*	*340*	*48*	***

Note: Group A, bold figures *p*<0.05, [232.234.238.239.264.269-72]; Group B, NS, [301.303.305.306.327.332-5]; Group C, NS, [374.376.380. 381.406.410-3].

It should be noted that for response rates other than for the items of being in touch (within 2 years) and frequency of contact the base numbers refer only to respondents who *are* in touch. The proportions of respondents in touch in the different columns vary quite a bit, with fewer than three in four of grandparents who were less in contact with grandchildren at the time of a split still actually in touch with them (compared with 97% who were more in touch). It is this smaller total which is then used as the base for all other measures in the table except those which specifically refer to behaviour within the last two years.

There are also some special response effects to be aware of in the linking parent data. As noted in chapter three, non-resident parents – mainly fathers - are excluded in this sample. Where parents are separated, relatively more respondents are mothers. As we will show later, the differences in behaviour between More contact and Less contact situations are closely related to line of descent, rather than to the sex of respondents. But the smaller proportion of male respondents does seem to have quite an influence on the *recording* of this behaviour.

In the following table, 5.7, we turn to the effect of parenting breakdown on grandparents' participation in childcare. As would be expected, rates of current activity are very closely related to what happened at a time of separation, in which of course the business of childcare would itself have been a major consideration. But the simple fact of breakdown has an effect itself. By its nature it creates a powerful demand for childcare supports, and raises levels of support for most grandchildren of separated parents above that for where parents are together. Only where grandparents were seen *less* at the time of a split is there a definite tendency for rates on indicators of routine support going to separated parents – such as help with daycare and with babysitting in the evening, plus the related matter of having a say in how grandchildren are brought up – to dip below or approximate to that for parents still together.

Table 5.7 Childcare role of grandparents by whether parents together

% of GPs who:-	Parents apart *More* contact at separation	**Parents together**	Parents apart *Same* contact at separation	Parents apart *Less* Contact at separation
Helped with daytime care weekly or more*	48	20	25	19
Helped with evening care at least monthly*	56	22	42	6
Taken or collected grandchild from school at least monthly*	16	10	8	0
Looked after grandchild when ill in last year*	28	16	20	13

Have or had at least some say in important decisions**	40	22	29	15
Have agreed with parents on almost everything on how GC is brought up**	32	39	27	17
Have not really discussed GC's upbringing**	16	16	27	26
*Base**	*30*	*333*	*34*	***
*Base***	*46*	*519*	*55*	*42*
% of adult GC whose:-				
Parents and GPs have agreed on almost everything on how children are brought up	17	24	18	0
Have not really discussed GC's upbringing	4	9	12	0
Base	*43*	*271*	*52*	***
% of linking parents who :				
Agree with child's GP on almost everything on how GC is brought up	22	31	20	33
Have not really discussed child's upbringing	11	17	23	33
Base	*24*	*340*	*48*	***

Note: Group A, NS, [250-3.264.269-72.273-5]; Group B, NS, [227.332-5.336]; Group C, NS, [406.410-3.414-16]. Base * - GC under 12.

Still more significantly, perhaps, as it takes us beyond behavioural matters into evaluative, even though grandparents are more *active* when parenting has broken down there appears to be a general tendency in all samples for the closest agreement on upbringing between parents and grandparents to occur where parents are *together*. This raises some questions about the nature of shared childcare, and the different types of grandparental involvement in it, which are looked at more closely in chapters eight and nine. But it is at the same time a further indication that grandparenting appears to be more part of a team effort where grandchildren's parents do stay together.

Finally we look briefly at the implications of parental separation for other types of mutual support between grandparents and grandchildren. Table 5.8 on the next page shows grandparents' accounts of advice and money given to grandchildren, and jobs done by adult grandchildren for grandparents.

The most active relationship overall in this batch of tabulations is that where a parental split was accompanied by more contact. But intriguingly, here, when it comes to the transfer of money, grandparents where parental separation had entailed *less* contact for them were *not* giving that much less to parents at the time of the survey. This suggests that reduced contact by no means represents the loss of a relationship altogether. Separation often means that one set of grandparents becomes more openly and actively involved. But in spite of this the other set are still able to play some part, at a distance, through provision of resources. Separation and divorce often put severe financial strain on parents. In such circumstances discreet assistance by those grandparents less involved in face-to-face supports may complement very usefully the greater *practical* supports given by the grandparents with more frequent access.[5] Where the less involved grandparents are (as normally the case) on the father's side, their help may take the form of assisting *him* to keep up maintenance payments to the grandchildren, and represent an underwriting of his *paternal* role as much as an independent *grand*parental role in its own right – if such a distinction is possible in this type of family circumstance.

Table 5.8 Advice and help in last year by whether parents together

% of GPs who in past year:-	Parents apart *More* contact at separation	Parents together	Parents apart *Same* contact at separation	Parents apart *Less* Contact at separation
Helped parent with money for GC*	33	25	27	30
Helped GC direct with money*	33	29	22	22
Given GC advice**	70	32	32	22
*Base**	*46*	*533*	*60*	*42*
*Base***	*38*	*384*	*41*	*24*
% of GCs who in past year:-				
Helped GP with shopping	50	25	15	6
Helped with house or garden work	41	29	24	13
Helped getting GP where he/she needed to go	41	25	10	6
Looked after GP when sick	14	10	5	6
Base	*44*	*301*	*64*	***

Note: Group A, NS; [258-62.264.269-72]; Group B, NS, [316-19.327.332-5].

The figures for adult grandchildren's help *to* grandparents show that their current

---

[5] If we take the responses for 'ever' having helped parents with money for grandchildren, then the highest rate is registered by grandparents who were in *less* contact at the time of separation. It perhaps becomes their role to be called on in periodic situations of greatest need. Loss of (frequent) contact is not the same as loss of all involvement.

rates of activity do reflect very neatly and consistently the broad circumstances of parental breakdown. This suggests that, unlike simple contact, where lost relationships perhaps *can* be recovered on an individual basis, the giving of intimate practical help perhaps continues to be organised more within the framework of wider family networks. This might make it more difficult for grandchildren to become closely involved with such grandparents where their tie is not mediated by, or at least consistent with, an appropriate shared bond with members of the parental generation. This is not the sort of matter which can be sorted out on the basis of survey materials alone.

6

EMERGENCE OF LINEAGE

Growing instability of parenting relationships may be contributing to a change in the type of lineages, or use of descent principles, around which extended families are effectively organised. For most legal purposes such as succession and inheritance rules, and even the transmission of family names, the male line of descent has long been privileged in British culture. But against that, and perhaps balancing it overall (or being balanced *by* it) there has been a popular attachment in British society to relationships traced in the female line. With the weakening of marriage and affinal ties in recent decades, this matrilineal principle has become more overt, and there are signs in our survey data that it is now coming to play a more significant role in structuring extended family activities.[1]

Our survey findings show clearly that where parents are not together, grandparents on the mother's side become even more likely to play a close part in helping with children, not just during the process of domestic reorganisation but in the longer term. Paternal grandparents on the other hand may have very little or no contact with their son's children after a domestic split. Where parents were never really together in the first place, as in the case of some young single mothers, these grandparents may not even know of their existence.[2] Paternal grandparents show consistently higher rates of being out of touch with grandchildren, and their substantially smaller numbers give a strong hint that there may also be under-reporting of grandchildren by them - in most such cases surely due to ignorance of them.[3] This limits the number of cases of

---

[1] We have looked at this briefly elsewhere, Dench and Ogg, 2000, and hope to do so in greater detail in subsequent publications. See also Johnson, 1998 and Hagestad, 1985, for analysis of this effect outside of the UK.

[2] A recent study suggests that one fifth of teenage mothers may have lost touch with the fathers of their children by the time that their children have their first birthdays. See Allen & Dowling, 1999.

[3] To some extent the lower proportion of grandchildren through the paternal line follows from the tendency of men to become parents at a later age than women. But the disparity in the survey figures seems greater than we could expect to account for this way.

parental breakdown that we can explore along the paternal line, and probably even means that our estimates of *average* paternal grandparents' behaviour may be too high.

Overall, parental separation has an effect of intensifying differences between behaviour along maternal and paternal lines. A range of findings are collected together in the following table to summarise this effect. When splits do occur, the general effect is to bring maternal lineages closer together and pull the paternal further apart.

Table 6.1 Grandparenting behaviour and attitudes by lineage and whether parents together

% of GPs who:-	Link To GC Through Daughter		Link To GC Through Son	
	Parents together	Parents apart	Parents together	Parents apart
Strongly agree that their GCs are rewarding*	67	62	68	31
Agree that they want a life free of family duties*	39	34	27	46
Live within 15 mins from GC**	**32**	**45**	37	27
Strongly agree have had to put themselves out*	26	45	18	15
Visit relatives and friends at least monthly***	**13**	**28**	13	5
Feel very close to GC**	73	79	**66**	**35**
Have agreed on almost all aspects of GC's upbringing**	42	34	**33**	**12**
Have had some say in decisions concerning GC under 16****	**34**	**66**	**23**	**0**
Base Grandparents with 1 GC only*	*58*	*28*	*32*	***
*Base***	*298*	*85*	*244*	*45*
*Base****:*	*306*	*92*	*253*	*56*
*Base*****	*202*	*63*	*176*	*33*

Note: Group A, bold figures *p*<0.05, [198-200.229.234.239.247.273-5].

The polarisation revealed in this table is striking. On matters of contact and shared activities, the effect of single parenting or family breakdown is to raise the frequencies in the female descent column, while lowering them in the male. Thus on the female side, the proportion of grandparents who have some say in decisions relating to a grandchild's upbringing increases from one third to two thirds where parents are apart. But on the male side, it falls from an already low quarter to no-one at all in our sample. The effect is striking.

What is more difficult to assess is how far paternal line relationships are lost or overlooked completely in the survey, and yet this is quite an important preliminary question to consider as it raises a number of issues about our sampling and selection procedures, and the drawing of inferences from the data collected.

To help illustrate and pursue this we have put together responses on what happened at the time of parental breakdowns, divided according to respondents' descent lines, and whether they were in the random or most-contact selection streams. We would expect that lineage differences in the most contact cases would mainly reflect contact choices since separation, while differences between random cases, while also reflecting differential consequences of breakdown, might also provide some hints about possible sampling and selection bias.

Thus, to take table 6.2 first, we can compare the overall proportions of broken parenting relationships in each grouping. Looking first at data from adult grandchildren respondents, whose parents are nearest to their completed breakdown levels, we can see that in three columns the rate of breakdown is around 23%, while for the randomly selected maternal grandparents it is slightly higher at 29%. As the most-contact groups in both lines of descent record the same level, we could possibly infer that by adulthood grandchildren choose to see their few remaining paternal grandparents at equal rates as their maternal, regardless of whether parental splits have taken place. It may nevertheless be the case though that they have forgotten some of their paternal grandparents. For the slight maternal bias among the randomly selected relationships needs explanation. While this is partly demographic, linked with relative age at becoming a parent, it could also reflect a greater tendency for paternal grandparents to be 'lost' after a family split. Forgotten grandparents would not be listed, and therefore *under*-represented in the random group.

Table 6.2 Parental separation rates by lineage

	Matrilineal		Patrilineal	
	Random	**Most Contact**	**Random**	**Most Contact**
% where GCs parents not together				
Respondent: - Adult Grandchild	29	23	23	22
Grandparent	23	**33**	18	**16**
Linking Parent	**22**	**21**	**5**	**4**
Base –GC	*302*	*240*	*187*	*148*
GP	*398*	*221*	*309*	*127*
LP	*292*	*183*	*166*	*117*

Note: Group A, [229.264.]; Group B, [298.327]; Group C, [371.406]; bold figures *p*<0.05.

The grandparents' data are slightly different in that there is significant variation between maternal and paternal lines for the most-contact groups, reflecting the much greater involvement of matrilineal than patrilineal grandparents where parents are not together. But there is also a modest matrilineal weighting among the random stream, which again could point to a greater likelihood where parents are not together for maternal kin to be listed and selected.

The corresponding data for linking parents are different again, with similarity between random and most-contact rates for both of the groups but significantly lower proportions of patrilineal. Given that this parent sample contains many more single mother respondents than separated fathers with resident children, we would *expect* higher matrilineal most-contact ratings. But the strong lineage disparity for random cases as well suggests a high level of non-listing of paternal grandparents by single mother respondents.

Moving to table 6.3 we now look within those cases where parents are not together, to see where separations produced more grandparental contact at the time and where they produced *less*.

Table 6.3 Contact at time of separation by lineage

	Matrilineal		Patrilineal	
	Random	Most Contact	Random	Most Contact
% where GP had *more* GC contact				
Respondent: - Adult Grandchild	36	35	30	40
Grandparent	49	57	38	41
Linking Parent	19	27	29	-
% where GP had *less* GC contact				
Respondent: - Adult Grandchild	**6**	11	**26**	15
Grandparent	4	5	25	22
Linking Parent	23	11	14	-
Base –GC	83	59	42	32
GP	110	82	72	30
LP	90	56	*	*

Note: Group A, NS, [229.269-72]; Group B, bold figures *p*<0.05, [298.332-5]; Group C, NS, [371.410-3].

The figures in this table suggest that there is a fairly consistent bias over time towards more contact with matrilineal kin during the process of separation. The adult grandchild (and longest separated) group perhaps shows slightly less matrilineal bias than the grandparent respondents. This could be a cohort effect, indicating that a generation or so ago paternal grandparents were relatively more involved during a marriage breakdown than is now the case. In addition it could be another, indirect indication of the disappearance of paternal grandparents following separations. Grandchildren seem quite likely to stay in touch with paternal grandparents who have been active, and to forget (and not even list) those who were not. For the younger parental relationships reported by grandparents there is a higher rating for matrilineal kin in the 'more contact' rows, and lower rating for them in the 'less contact' rows, which is just what the figures in table 6.1 would lead us to expect. The figures for linking parents are hard to interpret here, both because they represent the least completed generation of family life and also as the component of patrilineal respondents will be biased towards single mothers who *have* kept in touch with partners' parents. Insofar as their responses show anything at all it is that matrilineal bias in contact is probably more evident in recent separations than in earlier.

The final table in this batch, 6.4, looks at things the other way around, by listing proportions of respondents where parents are separated who reported that contacts were more difficult at the time of parental breakdown.

Table 6.4 Difficulty of contact at separation by lineage

	Matrilineal		Patrilineal	
	Random	**Most Contact**	**Random**	**Most Contact**
% where GP had difficulty keeping contact with GC				
Respondent: - Adult Grandchild	**4**	3	**19**	14
Grandparent	**9**	2	**48**	44
Linking Parent	14	13	14	-
% where GP not allowed to see GC				
Respondent: - Adult Grandchild	4	0	15	5
Grandparent	6	3	18	18
Linking Parent	2	3	0	-
Base-GC	*89*	*59*	*42*	*32*
GP	*110*	*82*	*72*	*30*
LP	*90*	*56*	***	***

Note: Group A [229.271-2] Group B [298.334-5] Group C [371.412-3]; bold figures $p<0.05$. No figure given where bases <13. (see footnote 3 on page 47)

As we would expect, it is the patrilineal ties which rate highly here, especially for grandparent respondents who are currently bearing the brunt of such difficulties – and least for parent respondents (who are both *un*typical, and also liable to deny limiting the access of grandparents to their children). There is also a possible trend over time suggested by this data, in that difficulties of contact with matrilineal kin are higher in the more recent cohorts. (We should not allow the low proportion of parents recording that grandparents have not been allowed to see grandchildren to inhibit this conclusion, as these mothers are surely the least likely group to admit that access has been hindered.)

Unscrambling sex and lineage

The breakdown of a parental relationship produces a very different effect on ties traced through the mother, to matrilineal grandparents, than on those in the paternal line, with patrilineal kin. But in order to sort out the effects properly we need to look also at the sex of grandparents themselves, as there are important differences between them too. Lineage – or sex of parent – and grandparent sex seem to interact in a variety of ways. On some of our measures these two factors operate in the same direction to produce a cumulative effect. In such cases the result is a steady gradient of response values running from mothers' mothers at one end of the spectrum to fathers' fathers at the opposite end, with mothers' fathers and fathers' mothers together in the middle. But on some other measures an interaction takes place rather than a simple cumulation. This seems to occur mainly because a paternal grandmother is not just a grandmother who happens to be on the father's side. Crucially she is not a *mother* to the grandchild's mother, but a *mother-in-law*. And this may mean that she is or may be seen as a competitor with the maternal grandmother, rather than an equivalent or ally, and may be excluded from equal access and participation. In these situations lineage (that is the sex of the lineal parent) operates *against* grandparent sex, and as it is the more powerful influence it may override the effect of the latter.

The differences between paternal and maternal grandmothers come out very graphically in the case materials collected in the parallel, qualitative study following up the BSA98 sample.[4] To help sort out these effects in the survey data we have divided grandparents into four main types, by combining the sex variables in both parental and grandparental generations to produce a single variable which we generally refer to here as lineage. Since it is the sex of the parent which seems more often to exercise the greater influence of the two components, this shorthand is not misleading. Our resulting categories are the maternal grandmother (MGM), the maternal grandfather (MGF), the paternal grandmother (PGM) and paternal grandfather (PGF). Step-relationships are excluded from this main typology, and are dealt with later on in this report, in chapter 11.

---

[4] Reported in Arthur et al., 2002.

The set of tables which follows here introduces some of the salient influences that lineage has on grandparenting behaviour and attitudes. In most of them we have also distinguished between ties where parents are together, and those where they are apart. Figures for these two sectors are put in separate rows in the tables. Inevitably, as in the foregoing table, the column totals for paternal grandfathers where parents are apart – and in a few places for paternal grandmothers as well – tend to be very small. As the figures are part of a wider pattern, which they help to illustrate, they have not been excluded altogether unless the base numbers are very low.[5]

The lineage pattern

The following tables take a range of data to compare the four main lineage types of grandparent. The first of these, 6.5a, deals with some basic contact rates – with a separate section for each of the main sub-samples, starting with the grandparent respondents.

6.5a Contacts by lineage: grandparent sample

% grandparents who report:-	Parents' relation	Link by daughter		Link by son	
		MGM	MGF	PGM	PGF
No contact with GC in last two years	Tog	0	4	**0**	3
	Apt	4	11	**10**	35
Sees GC several times a week	Tog	30	31	34	24
	Apt	54	32	14	12
Speaks on phone with GC several times a week	Tog	**27**	18	24	12
	Apt	**35**	18	10	6
Base	*Tog*	*174*	*115*	*147*	*93*
Base	*Apt*	*49*	*36*	*31*	***

Note Group A, bold figures *p*<0.05, [229.232.238.240].

The figures here for grandparents show a very distinctive pattern, which runs through a lot of the survey data that we have analysed. It is that where parents are together, so that both lines of descent are actively involved, the main response differences tend to lie between grandmothers and grandfathers. Where

---

[5] See footnote 3 on page 47 for explanation of procedure.

parents are apart, though, differences emerge between lines of descent, leading to a lineage 'gradient' in which maternal grandmothers – women linked to their offspring via women - are the most active and in touch while paternal grandfathers – men linked to grandchildren via men – are the least.

Thus although base numbers are rather small here we can see that a good third of PGFs where parents are apart are *not* in current contact. This is echoed in data for other sub-samples, and cannot be completely ignored. It is a pointer to under-representation (by non-listing) of paternal ties, which would make *real* non-contact rates even higher. The findings here on contacts mirror those on non-contact, with the rate of weekly contact for MGMs where parents are split running at several times that for PGFs.

A similar picture is given by the responses of parents, whose account is like that from grandparents though with slightly lower levels of contact for unbroken relationships. However, the lineage gradient is even stronger, largely eclipsing grandparent sex, and affects all the figures to some extent, not just where parents are apart. This may well give a clue that it is among parents, rather than grandparents themselves, that the processes which generate lineage effects are mainly operating. The linking parents are the gatekeepers regulating grandparental access to grandchildren. So it is quite understandable that their perspectives on grandparenting will exert an influence on the behaviour of everyone participating in this aspect of extended family life.

6.5b Contacts by lineage: linking parent sample

% parents who report:-	Parents' relation	Link by mother		Link by father	
		MGM	MGF	PGM	PGF
No GC contact with GP in last two years	Tog	3	11	**3**	5
	Apt	13	10	**17**	-
GC sees GP several times a week	Tog	27	23	15	18
	Apt	38	27	9	-
GC speaks on phone with GP several times a week	Tog	**16**	11	5	3
	Apt	**38**	18	8	-
Base	*Tog*	*130*	*76*	*85*	*50*
Base	*Apt*	*36*	***	*24*	***

Note: Group C, bold figures *p*<0.05, [371.374.380.382].

This point is largely but not wholly confirmed by the teenage grandchild responses. The figures in 6.5c show that where parenting relationships have broken down, there is a very strong lineage effect, with paternal line contacts virtually eliminated.[6] Numbers are very small in these breakdown groups, for reasons already discussed. But since they are low precisely because so many children are not co-resident with their fathers, it all adds up to the same thing in the end.

These grandchildren's responses go even further than (single) mothers (in the linking parent sample) in showing the thinness of paternal line contacts after separation. Even though relevant numbers are small in both samples they do reinforce each other. What also comes strongly out of the table is that from grandchildren's point of view, when parents are together the sex of grandparents is important, with PGMs quite heavily involved.

6.5c Contacts by lineage: teenage grandchild sample

% teenagers who report :-	Parents' relation	Link by mother		Link by father	
		MGM	MGF	PGM	PGF
No contact with GP in last two years	Tog	3	3	2	6
	Apt	0	12	4	6
Sees GP several times a week	Tog	22	17	16	9
	Apt	37	28	4	11
Speaks on phone with GP several times a week	Tog	**17**	5	12	3
	Apt	**33**	12	2	0
Base	*Tog*	*98*	*58*	*68*	*36*
Base	*Apt*	*51*	*25*	*45*	***

Note: Group D, bold figures *p*<0.05, [55b.57b.60a.60b].

This is rather different from the *adult* grandchild perspective, as shown in 6.5d. Here there is a similar lineage profile. But contact rates are much lower – *especially* where parents are not together - presumably because grandparents with grandchildren of this age no longer have any role in helping to look after them.

---

[6] Though interestingly there is a low figure for PGFs not seen in 2 years. Presumably some of these grandchildren may be completely unaware of the existence of their paternal grandparents, and so not have listed them even.

6.5d Contacts by lineage: adult grandchild sample

% grandchildren who :-	Parents' relation	Link by mother		Link by father	
		MGM	MGF	PGM	PGF
No contact with GP in last two years	Tog	9	8	11	13
	Apt	6	22	20	-
Sees GP several times a week	Tog	12	15	7	0
	Apt	13	6	7	-
Speaks on phone with GP several times a week	Tog	8	8	3	0
	Apt	3	0	0	-
Base	*Tog*	*158*	*57*	*102*	*32*
Base	*Apt*	*51*	*26*	*25*	***

Note: Group B, NS, [298.301.305.307].

Part 'd' of table 6.5 has rather shallow lineage gradients. There are several possible interpretations. Firstly it could be that once grandchildren are living as autonomous adults they become more detached from the influence of their parents, and with it the source of much lineage structuring of behaviour and feelings. The grandchild/grandparent relationship may become much more a matter of individual choice and taste. Since there is, if anything, a bias towards grandfathers in this table, it may be that adult grandchildren discover more interest in or affinity with grandfathers as they get older.

Or it could be a cohort effect. That is, it may only be in recent decades that growing parental separations have been feeding a maternal/matrilineal shift in family life so strongly. Older grandchildren may still operate in kin networks spread more evenly between different lines of descent. On the basis of our own data we cannot say that any of these arguments has more merit than others; it may be worth bearing all of them in mind.

Lineage and shared activities

The next table analyses some responses of grandparents relating to activities shared with grandchildren. It is organised in the same way as the preceding set on contact. What 6.6 shows, again, is that where parents are together there is not a great difference between grandparents (though there *is* more when we move to the highest frequency levels). But as soon as we look at separated parents a strong lineage effect emerges. This is also a feature of the childcare activities which are analysed in detail in chapter 9 below.

6.6 Shared activity by lineage (grandparent respondents)

% grandparents who:-	Parents' Relation	Link by daughter		Link by son	
		MGM	MGF	PGM	PGF
Often have GC stay without parents	Tog	**15**	17	15	11
	Apt	**32**	36	22	18
Visit friends/relatives with GC at least monthly	Tog	**14**	11	16	11
	Apt	**43**	14	10	0
Give/receive present with GC at least monthly	Tog	46	42	43	38
	Apt	61	37	20	12
Go on holiday with GC with parents every year	Tog	16	24	21	8
	Apt	25	21	0	6
Base	*Tog*	*174*	*115*	*147*	*93*
	Apt	*49*	*36*	*31*	***

Note: Group A, figures in bold *p*<0.05, [229.242.243.247.249].

Lineage and attitudes to role

The influence of lineage on other aspects of grandparents' behaviour is followed up later on in this report. To end here we are quickly looking at its apparent effect on some basic attitudes – specifically the four general attitudes to the role. As already explained, a problem in analysing these attitudes in detail is that they do not refer to selected relationships. So we cannot draw any confident inferences unless the analysis is restricted to cases where there is only one grandchild anyway. This cuts down the numbers heavily, which means that it is impossible to focus on one-tie-only cases *and* distinguish according to whether parents are together or not. Table 6.7 includes both sets of figures – that is, for one-grandchild only and for all respondents – to show that the pattern for the selected cases is broadly the same as in the undivided data.

These figures indicate that lineage is probably a strong enough influence to show up among the one-grandchild cases, even though there are few of them, and also to have some influence on the wider set of data too. Having both sets together helps to interpret each. Thus the relatively high ratings of PGMs in the general set of figures almost certainly reflect the fact that many of them are bound to be MGMs too, through relationships other than the ones selected for detailed analysis.

Table 6.7 Grandparents' attitude to role by lineage

% of GPs who:-		Link To GC Through Daughter		Link To GC Through Son	
		MGM	MGF	PGM	PGF
Agree strongly that GC	All	70	60	65	51
are rewarding	1-GC	68	67	61	-
Agree would like a life	All	34	41	38	36
free from family duties	1-GC	35	45	30	-
Agree strongly have put self	All	40	23	37	23
out to help look after GC	1-GC	33	3	21	-
Agree that have had to cut down or	All	12	2	6	7
give up work to help look after GC	1-GC	11	0	0	-
Base	*All*	*224*	*153*	*178*	*113*
	1-GC	*43*	*39*	*32*	***

Note: Group A, NS, [198-202.229].

On most measures, MGMs are confirmed in the one-tie-only rows as the most committed grandparents. They are the top raters in regarding their role as rewarding. They put themselves out most. And they appear to be the only category of grandparents who unambiguously (that is, in the one-grandchild situation where it is clear that they are responding *as* MGMs)[7] have given up work in order to help out.

The only measure on which they do not generally stand out in this table as the most involved is, suitably, the most ambiguous one to interpret – of wanting a free life. Their relatively high rating on this, especially in the one-grandchild row, does not fit in well with the general pattern. But it may be an indication of the discontent that can arise for grandmothers at a particular age. The drawback of basing an analysis on grandparents with one-grandchild is that these will obviously be the youngest, with MGMs (given that women tend to become parents and grandparents younger than men do etc) the youngest group of all. As the following chapter will detail, the very youngest grandparents do constitute a slightly special case, in that they are more likely to find themselves occupying the role before they are ready for it. Many such cases arise, moreover, in relation to single mothers. So there are probably a number of currents influencing the data in 6.7 which go beyond lineage in a narrow sense.

---

[7] PGFs also score zero in this row: but the base is too small for figures to be included here.

The figures in this table also help to reveal some differences between grandmothers and grandfathers which are not visible until lineage is brought into the analysis. There is for example an interesting gap between MGFs and PGFs on wanting a free life, which disappears when they are aggregated together just as grandfathers. MGFs have emerged in earlier tables in this chapter as more active than PGFs, and here record a higher level of satisfaction and seem happy to put themselves out for grandchildren. But they do also appear to harbour a greater desire for freedom. This may indicate that while they certainly find the role rewarding, it is possible to have too much of a good thing. This is in obvious contrast to paternal grandfathers, who find the role less rewarding but also are clearly less oppressed by it. The caution already applied to the data in this table referring to grandmothers is also relevant to grandfathers, though. That is, the one-grandchild respondents are all *young* grandparents, and this in itself will have an effect on their responses.

The final table here presents the responses of adult grandchildren on the equivalent set of attitude questions. In the case of grandchildren however there is no need to go beyond the figures for grandchildren with only one grand*parent*. These constitute a much larger proportion than is the case for grandparents with only one grandchild. As grandparents age they accumulate more grandchildren. As grandchildren age they lose grandparents, so that by adulthood very many of them have only one. For paternal grandfathers the numbers are small. But there are not all that many more PGFs in the set of data referring to all respondents. So the advantage of including them is not great enough to merit putting the full set in here as well.

Table 6.8 Grandchildrens' attitude to role by lineage

% of GCs who :-	Link To GC Through Mother		Link To GC Through Father	
	MGM	MGF	PGM	PGF
Agree strongly GPs are an important part of their life	**38**	**20**	**22**	**13**
Agree they would not see their GPs as often as they do if they did not have to	11	18	17	13
Agree their GPs are not interested in their life	**18**	**29**	**26**	**67**
Agree strongly they do not see as much of their GPs as their GPs would like	**22**	**3**	**15**	**0**
Base	*144*	*34*	*89*	***

Note: Group B (one grandparent only), bold figures *p*<0.05, [276-80.298].

These figures again suggest that from the perspective of adult grandchildren lineage is less important than for grandparents. Sex may be *more* so, and may play a generally important part in determining the relationship when adulthood is reached (see next chapter). Grandmothers are seen by grandchildren as occupying a more important place in their life, *and* as wanting to see more of them than they do themselves. Not grandfathers though. The 'overload' impression given by maternal grandfathers is reflected back here in the way that MGFs are seen by over one in four grandchildren as not really being interested in their lives. Paternal grandfathers on the other hand, who are *seen* less by their grandchildren, are regarded by them as even less *concerned* – with 2 out of 3 recorded as not interested. So unlike for MGFs, who may have more contact than they want, the level of involvement of paternal grandfathers may fit their actual level of interest quite well. Thus the responses of grandchildren appear to endorse those of grandparents very tellingly here.

7

THE FAMILY DEVELOPMENT CYCLE

The preceding sections have examined the influence on grandparenting behaviour and attitudes of some broad underlying changes occurring in British family life. In the light of these, we will now try to unravel the data to reveal the general pattern of grandparenting roles across the family development cycle. We do this by dividing up the data according to the age-group of selected grandchildren, starting with those less than five years old. The general finding in this chapter is that there is a tendency for grandparental interest and activity to decline as grandchildren move through these age groupings. The most involved period is immediately after grandchildren are born, and especially for first grandchildren. The participation of grandparents is perhaps most valuable here, as this is a critical stage in their *parenting* role – that is in helping their children to become successful parents themselves. As grandchildren grow up, grandparents are gradually less involved, and happier to watch from a distance – partly because they are getting older themselves. As each succeeding grandchild is born, they are less likely to be involved with it.

Pre-school grandchildren

When we focus in detail on a particular age-group of grandchildren the value of having data from complementary sets of respondents in this survey becomes particularly evident, as some differences of perspective and reporting stand out very clearly. This is evident when we collect together the responses on contact and activities with pre-school children given by grandparents and parents.

Thus it is revealing to see that not only do parents give generally lower estimates than grandparents for rates of activity, but that they give particularly lower estimates for *grandfathers*. This effect is not very marked for overall contact rates, but stands out particularly strongly for grandfathers talking with infant grandchildren on the phone and going on holiday with them. A possible explanation here is that grandfathers may be inclined to answer or speak on behalf of themselves *and* their wives, or to overstate what they do personally, while responding *parents* give more discriminating testimony.

Table 7.1 Contact and shared activities with pre-school grandchild

	Respondent is Grandparent		Respondent is Linking Parent	
% of GPs who:-	**GM**	**GF**	**GM**	**GF**
Have seen GC in last 2 years	100	94	94	88
See GC several times a week	43	44	27	21
Speak on phone with GC sev/times/wk	29	17	13	9
Have yearly holiday with parents	23	20	21	0
Go on visits w/o parents at least monthly	21	10	13	21
Play games or watch TV weekly or more	19	15	10	24
Go shopping at least monthly	13	14	10	9
Have yearly holiday without parents	8	3	8	3
Go to park weekly or more	11	15	n/a	n/a
Have high activity rate	49	44	n/a	n/a
Base	*111*	*93*	*59*	*35*

Note: Group A, NS, [229.232.238.240.244-9]; Group C, NS, [374.380.382.386-90]; grandchild aged 0-4 ; N/A=figures not available; for derivation of 'activity' rate, see Appendix F on Derived Variables.

Support for this interpretation comes from the fact that parents do give a high rate to grandfathers playing games and watching TV with grandchildren. These are things that they would believably spend their time actually doing. In the case of watching TV with a grandchild, simply being there at the same time may be all that is needed in order to qualify. Going on visits is also likely to involve grandfathers, who are often the family chauffeur. Table 7.2 provides similar data in relation to childcare.

Table 7.2 Childcare role with pre-school grandchild

	Respondent is Grandparent		Respondent is Linking Parent	
% of GPs who:-	**GM**	**GF**	**GM**	**GF**
Help with daytime care weekly or more	28	15	16	0
Help with evening care weekly or more	15	12	9	0
Take/collect GC from school monthly +	5	5	6	0
Looked after GC when ill in last year	15	17	10	6
Base	*111*	*93*	*59*	*35*

Note: Group A, NS, [250-3]; Group C, NS, [395-8]; grandchild aged 0-4.

In order to be able to help with childcare, grandparents need to live fairly close by. It is instructive in this respect to look at the association between proximity of residence and levels of grandparental involvement. Table 7.3a covers grandchildren of all ages, in order to examine the relation between age and proximity. Table 7.3b then shows the link between proximity and rates of grandparental involvement for infants.

Table 7.3 Proximity of grandchild

a. Grandchild age by proximity

| | Respondent is Grandparent | | | Respondent is Linking Parent | | |
| | *Travelling time between GP and GC* | | | *Travelling time between GP and GC* | | |
	15 min	**15-1 hr**	**1 hr +**	**15 min**	**15-1 hr**	**1 hr +**
GC age						
0-4	45	32	23	30	36	34
5-8	37	35	28	41	30	29
9-12	36	25	39	33	34	33
13-19	31	37	33	40	34	26
20+	19	36	45	49	26	26
Base	*216*	*238*	*218*	*166*	*145*	*127*

Note: Group A, $p<0.001$, [230.239]; Group C, NS, [381] **row** percentages.

b. Contact and childcare by proximity

| | Respondent is Grandparent | | | Respondent is Linking Parent | | |
| | *Travelling time between GP and GC* | | | *Travelling time between GP and GC* | | |
	15 min	**15-1 hr**	**1 hr +**	**15 min**	**15-1 hr**	**1 hr +**
Contact between GP/GC made several times a week	74	37	0	**50**	**22**	**8**
Day childcare done weekly or more	33	16	11	22	7	4
Evening childcare done weekly or more	21	13	2	8	4	4
Base	*82*	*69*	*44*	*28*	*30*	*29*

Note: Group A, $p<0.05$, [238.239.250-1]; Group C, bold figures $p<0.05$, [380.381.395-6]; grandchild aged 0-4; **column** percentages.

There are a number of interesting features in these tables. The second one shows that there is an obvious connection between nearness, on one hand, and frequency of contact and childcare support on the other. Both by their own reckoning and that of parents, and for self-evident reasons, only very small proportions of grandparents living more than an hour away are involved in regular childcare.

The relationship between proximity and grandchild age, in the first part of the table, is less clear. From grandparents' accounts, there is a strong link between closeness and grandchildren's youth. The youngest have higher proportions of grandparents living nearby, and this tails off as they get older. But this shift is not reflected in parents' responses, where there is no association between a grandchild's age and how near the grandparent lives.[1]

It may be therefore that the proximity recorded by grandparents is in part an artefact of sentiment. As will be shown later in this chapter, grandparents with young grandchildren, especially first grandchildren, feel very moved by their existence and often get emotionally caught up with them. The measures of travelling time are subjective assessments, and it may be that for GPs the emotional involvement with a young grandchild leads them to give more optimistic assessments of how near they are living. This may be an especially strong factor in the case of grandfathers. If we divide grandparents of children under five according to sex, 50% of grandfathers estimate that their grandchild lives within 15 minutes travel, compared with 39% of grandmothers. This might be because grandfathers drive faster, get around quicker, and feel the world to be a smaller place. However, if this were so it should apply to grandfathers with older grandchildren as well - but it does not. On top of this, grandfathers with very young grandchildren have a definite tendency (discussed a little later on here) to feel particularly close to very young grandchildren, and to find the role more rewarding. This enthusiasm of grandfathers for youngest grandchildren does not seem to be strongly linked to their own age – or not at least in any simple way. So it may well represent a renewed burst of interest in family life which the arrival of grandchildren promotes in them: or perhaps it is more an attachment to the idea of it, as it seems to die down again quite quickly.

Junior school grandchildren

When grandchildren start school the relationship with grandparents enters its most intensive and perhaps most significant phase. They are starting to become a little less dependent on their parents, and to have lives of their own.

---

[1] The effect of distance on childcare is explored more fully in a multivariate analysis in Appendix E.

Grandparents are there for them, as an outer shell of their immediate family, to assist them in developing some autonomy and finding out about the outside world. It is during this period that grandparents are most active in taking them around and doing things with them outside of the home. It may not involve more frequent contact than when they were toddlers, but there is a greater range of activities pursued.

Table 7.4 Contact and shared activities with junior school grandchild

	Respondent is Grandparent		Respondent is Linking Parent	
% of GPs who:-	GM	GF	GM	GF
Have seen GC in last 2 years	96	95	96	98
See GC several times a week	**43**	**22**	22	25
Speaks on phone with GC several times/week	**32**	**12**	13	10
Live within 15 mins from GC	39	33	34	40
Have yearly holiday with parents	19	20	28	18
Go on visits without parents at least monthly	27	16	17	6
Play games/watch TV weekly or more	26	13	9	12
Go shopping at least monthly	12	5	12	8
Have yearly holiday without parents	13	10	11	4
Go to park weekly or more	6	5	n/a	n/a
Have high activity rate	58	54	n/a	n/a
Base	*137*	*95*	*107*	*66*

Note: Group A, bold figures $p<0.05$, [232.238-40.244-9]; Group C, NS, [374.380-2. 386-90]; grandchild aged 5-12.

Several things are apparent from the data in tables 7.4 and 7.5. Rates of activities are higher for the older children: grandfathers in particular are more involved - perhaps reflecting the more active and out-going character of what is done. Significantly, the ratings of grandfathers' involvement by linking parents are not greatly out of line with those of the grandfathers themselves.

When it comes to childcare, too, these grandfathers are acknowledged to take a reasonable share of the load. This is most of all the case with escorting children to and from school, which is key support for this age group and also something which grandfathers are usually happy to do. Again, the credibility of this interpretation of the data is strengthened by the fact that grandparents' estimates for taking grandchildren to and from school are backed up by the parents. This is an activity which is not subject to many different meanings or definitions, and also is the sort of task that grandfathers could be expected to undertake.

Looking after sick children, on the other hand, is also important in this stage of family life but is not something which grandfathers are seen as doing as frequently as they might imagine.

Table 7.5 Childcare role with junior school grandchild

% of GPs who:-	Respondent is Grandparent		Respondent is Linking Parent	
	GM	GF	GM	GF
Help with daytime care weekly or more	26	15	9	10
Help with evening care monthly or more	30	19	9	4
Take or collected GC from school monthly+	17	9	11	14
Looked after GC when ill in last year	**22**	**9**	22	6
Have or had at least some say in important decisions	**71**	**53**	52	47
Have agreed with parents on almost everything on how GC is brought up	36	31	34	28
Have not really discussed upbringing	15	14	6	23
Helped parent with money for GC in past yr	33	32	25	20
Base	*137*	*95*	*107*	*66*

Note: Group A, bold figures $p<0.05$, [250-3.258.273-5]; Group C, NS, [375-8.403.414-6]; grandchild aged 5-12.

Grandchildren of junior school age are more likely than infants to share their grandparents with other grandchildren. This effect may partly mask the true extent of overall activity for grandparents at this key stage in the family life cycle. Our survey data only concerns activities with one selected grandchild, and so do not tell us whether grandparents look after or spend time with more than one grandchild at a time.[2] Where siblings who are close in age are concerned this seems probable. But where grandchildren belong to different sets, and are only cousins, then it is less likely.

If we look at the effect which the number of a respondents' grandchildren has on various measures then it is obvious that relations with particular children will be strongly influenced by the total volume of grandchildren around. On all measures, as shown in table 7.6., the intensity and frequency of activities is reduced where grandparents have more than one grandchild. Even the closeness of the relationship is diluted when it is spread among several grandchildren, though some of the effects here may be hard to separate out from the consequences of grandparents' ageing. There is a steady tailing off for

[2] The limitation of our survey in this respect is being addressed in the study now being carried out by Lynda Clarke & Emily Grundy.

all of the measures here, apart from proximity which is highest for one grandchild and then stays lower. This may be because it is the birth of a first grandchild which is most likely to trigger a move. But it could also, as mentioned earlier, be an indication that what is measured by this variable is psychological as much as geographical closeness, so that what is showing up here is the special feeling that a first grandchild seems to elicit.

Table 7.6 Grandparenting style by numbers of grandchildren

% of GPs who:-	Number of grandchildren		
	One	**Two to four**	**Five or more**
See selected GC several times a week	46	27	20
Live within 15 mins of GC	45	29	29
Feel very close to GC	79	67	59
Play games, watch TV weekly or more	21	12	9
Go shopping at least monthly	14	7	5
Go to park weekly or more	10	5	2
Base	*132*	*362*	*222*

Note: Group A, $p<0.001$, [202.234.238.239.244-6].

Teenage grandchildren

As grandchildren move into the teenage years, the frequency of interaction with grandparents drops off considerably. Children have now started to develop more autonomous identities in the world outside of families, and their peers are taking over the role once held by their grandparents of giving them support against parents. It is pay-back time. The new pattern is shown in tables 7.7 and 7.8 on the next page. The first brings together data from *three* sets of respondents, that is grandparents, linking parents and teenagers themselves.[3] The second reports the shared activity responses of parents and grandparents.

Compared to the previous tables, these figures show that virtually all measures of activity go down for teenage grandchildren, along with emotional attachment. One exception may be family holidays (especially with parents) which may be marginally up. By this age, several activities previously shared by younger grandchildren with grandparents have virtually ceased to exist. What is noticeable, again, in this distribution is the way in which the responses of grandfathers are brought into question. Grandfathers present themselves as

---

[3] The three sets are very comparable in terms of teenager age. See Appendix C for mean ages and standard deviations.

Table 7.7 Contact and closeness with teenage grandchild

	Respondent is Grandparent		Respondent is Linking Parent		Respondent is Young Person	
% where GP/GC:-	**GM**	**GF**	**GM**	**GF**	**GM**	**GF**
Has seen GC(P) in last 2 years	100	92	98	87	97	93
Sees GC(P) sev/times/week	23	27	26	15	21	14
Speaks on phone with GC(P) several times a week	25	22	16	7	**16**	**4**
Lives within 15 mins of GC(P)	28	35	37	30	n/a	n/a
Feels very close to GC(P)	63	62	46	21	33	30
Base	*74*	*49*	*92*	*64*	*273*	*162*

Note: Group A, NS, [232.234.238-40]; Group C, NS, [374.376.380-2]; Group D, bold figures *p*<0.05, [60a 60b 58]; grandchild aged 13-19.

Table 7.8 Shared activities with teenage grandchild

	Respondent is Grandparent		Respondent is Linking Parent	
% where GP:-	**GM**	**GF**	**GM**	**GF**
Has yearly holiday with parents	23	19	23	11
Has visits without parents at least monthly	13	3	6	0
Plays games, watches TV weekly or more	6	5	6	4
Goes shopping at least monthly	6	5	3	4
Has yearly holiday without parents	4	8	16	6
Goes to park weekly or more	0	0	n/a	n/a
Base	*74*	*49*	*84*	*51*

Note: Group A, NS, [244-9]; Group C, NS, [386-90]; grandchild aged 13-19.

being in frequent phone and face-to-face contact with grandchildren, and so on. But this just does not tally with the responses of parents and teenage grandchildren themselves. This is perhaps evidence for what may be called the phantom grandfather phenomenon. They claim to be doing a lot. But other people do not seem to be noticing them. On top of this it is worth drawing attention to the high rate of *non*-contact (during the last two years) with selected grandfathers by linking parents. This takes us back to the point that there may be a sizeable pool of grandfathers not mentioned at all, so that some of the data given here may even *over*-estimate their general level of activity.

During the teenage years, grandparental supports are becoming increasingly direct. Table 7.9 shows that whereas money to parents goes down slightly in this period, giving it direct to grandchildren, plus giving them advice, reach a peak.

Table 7.9 Changes in grandparental support with grandchild age

| | Age of Grandchild | | | | | |
| | GC 0-4 | | GC 5-12 | | GC 13-19 | |
	GM	GF	GM	GF	GM	GF
% where GP has in past year:-						
Helped GC direct with money	15	14	39	38	54	32
Helped GC parents with money	36	31	33	32	21	11
Given GC advice	n/a	n/a	40	32	54	27
Base	*111*	*93*	*137*	*95*	*74*	*49*

Note: Group A, *p*<0.05 (associations within sex for age), [230.258.260.262].

The growing detachment of teenagers from their parents is also marked by a shift in the type of involvement that grandparents appear to have in their upbringing. Table 7.10 compares the say claimed by and for grandparents at different stages in grandchild development, and the level of their agreement with parents.

Table 7.10 Grandparental involvement in upbringing

| | Respondent is Grandparent | | Respondent is Linking Parent | |
	GM	GF	GM	GF
% where GP has some say in decision :-				
Infants*	63	59	43	46
Juniors*	69	53	54	43
Teenagers (15+, *had* some say)**	68	46	56	39
% have mainly agreed with parents on upbringing				
Infants	39	43	38	37
Juniors	36	31	33	30
Teenagers	42	21	23	32

Note: Group A, NS, [230.273-5]; Group C; NS, [414-6]; see previous tables for bases.

What this suggests is that grandmothers and grandfathers follow rather different careers. As grandchildren progress from being toddlers to teenagers, and perhaps confront more complex behavioural and moral questions, grandfathers see themselves (and are seen by parents) as exercising a lesser influence on their upbringing. Grandmothers however see themselves (and are seen) as playing a slightly stronger role. For grandfathers, the loss of say coincides with a sharp decline in their level of agreement with how parents are bringing grandchildren up. Grandmothers on the other hand do not report a loss of agreement, although *parents* do report a steep decline in agreement with *them*. What may be happening here is that as parents perceive or allow an increase in say by grandmothers, they also become more aware of those disagreements that are there.

The adult grandchild

As grandchildren move into adult status, and pursue independent lives, the direction of family support gradually moves away from them. Overall frequency of contact with grandparents goes down. But the rate at which grandchildren are doing things *for* grandparents is rising. Family reciprocity is now beginning to define them as the ones to provide help. This is illustrated in table 7.11 which examines how the types of support given by grandchildren evolve as they become adults.

Table 7.11 Help from grandchild to grandparent

	Respondent is Linking Parent GC 13-19		Respondent is GC GC 20+	
	GM	GF	GM	GF
% where GC helped GP in year:-				
With shopping	44	13	29	26
With house or garden work	54	24	25	19
Getting where needs to go	9	0	24	20
By looking after when sick	16	4	9	11
Base	*92*	*64*	*335*	*115*

Note: Group C, $p<0.05$, [391-94]; Group B, $p<0.05$ [316-19].

Levels of general interaction fall to low levels after grandchildren have reached adulthood. Table 7.12 collects together some items which do not disappear completely. Thus a very small proportion of grandchildren over 20 are in frequent contact with grandparents – with phone calls to grandmothers holding up better than direct contact. Now that grandchildren are independent, and grandparents almost invariably pensioners, there is much less flow of money, and even advice sees a sharp decline.

Table 7.12 Contact and shared activities with adult grandchild

% where respondent:-	Respondent is Grandparent		Respondent is Grandchild	
	GM	GF	GM	GF
Has seen GC or GP in last 2 years	94	86	89	88
Sees GC or GP several times a week	9	0	10	7
Speaks on phone with GC or GP several times a week	9	4	19	2
Lives within 15 mins from GC or GP	18	20	27	25
Feels very close to GC or GP	64	42	38	18
Helped GC direct with money in past year	13	18	15	10
Given/received advice in past year	27	14	30	32
Base	*108*	*41*	*273*	*85*

Note: Group A, NS, [232.234.238-40.260.262]; Group B, NS, [301.303.305-7.323.325]; grandchild aged 20+.

Grandparents' feelings about their role

The evolution of relationships with grandchildren goes through a variety of behavioural stages, which are determined largely by the age of the grandchild. This developmental sequence is reflected in grandparents' feelings about their role, as expressed in our two key measures of feeling close to specified grandchildren and finding the role rewarding. It is difficult to relate the latter directly to the age of specific grandchildren, because if we selected one-grandchild only cases then we would be picking very *unusual* grandparents among those with older grandchildren. But as table 7.13 illustrates, the link with grandchild age for both variables is in fact quite similar, and it is perhaps the difference between grandmothers and grandfathers that is more noticeable.

While grandfathers with very young grandchildren do express closeness to them, they do not seem to find the role rewarding until the children are old enough to be taken out and *do* things. (Though it may also be that by this stage there are *more* grandchildren around.) The interest of grandfathers also tails off much more steeply than that of grandmothers, so that by the time grandchildren are adult their grandfathers feel neither very close nor rewarded. Perhaps, unlike with grandmothers, the more grandparenting that they actually do the less satisfaction they derive from it. Novelty is the key.

Table 7.13 Shifts in grandparents' attitudes by grandchild age

		Age of Grandchild			
		0-4	5-12	13-19	20+
% where GPs:-					
Agree strongly find role	GM	75	68	65	62
rewarding	GF	55	61	57	46
Feel very close	GM	73	78	63	64
	GF	75	65	62	42
Base	*GM*	*111*	*137*	*74*	*108*
	GF	*93*	*95*	*49*	*41*

Note: Group A, NS, (associations within sex for age) [198.230.234].

The age of grandparents themselves is obviously a factor in all this. Grandparenting is a stage in life where most people are withdrawing from very active involvement in childrearing. They remain concerned about the well-being of their descendants - but mainly pursue this through helping their children to become successful parents themselves. In modern British society they have little direct responsibility for their grandchildren. A common ideal seems to be one of meeting children and grandchildren quite often, watching them develop, and being able to help out a bit - especially in times of need or pressure – while staying free from more arduous and demanding responsibilities (Cherlin and Furstenberg, 1988). We have seen that most people do find grandparenting very rewarding, but perhaps this depends on not being too closely involved. Part of the reward for a parenting job well done may lie in being able to stand back at last and see family life carrying on smoothly without having to organise it oneself.

In looking here at how the age of grandparents affects role satisfaction, we have chosen to focus on the responses of the most-contact grandparents, because the differences are more accentuated than among the random group. It should also be borne in mind that contact with this category of grandchild may either be actively sought by the grandparent or be much less solicited, as for example when 'surprise' visits to the grandparental home are made by the parents of the grandchild.[4] Table 7.14 looks at the same measures of

---

[4] See Appendix B for more discussion of how responses of the most-contact group may differ from those of the random group.

satisfaction as in table 7.13, plus putting self out, but according to the age of grandparents in the most-contact group.

Table 7.14 Shifts in grandparents' attitudes and circumstances by grandparent age

	Age of Grandparent		
	<50	**50-65**	**66+**
% where GPs:-			
Agree strongly find role rewarding	**61**	**73**	**56**
Feel very close	**75**	**91**	**74**
Put self out (agree strongly)	32	35	35
Parents of GC not together	**47**	**29**	**18**
Are separated or divorced	**23**	**6**	**3**
Have a dependent child at home	**55**	**23**	**12**
Are providing long-term care for someone	7	**19**	9
Base	*48*	*128*	*172*

Note: Group A, 'most contact', bold figures *p*<0.05, [198.201.234].

The shifts with age are very clear. Both young and old grandparents feel more distanced from their grandchildren than do middle-age. At the same time young grandparents, of course, differ substantially on key socio-demographic variables from older grandparents. They belong to different generations, are still likely to be working, and have much younger grandchildren. Above all, it seems that young grandparents still have too much other family work to be able to stand back properly. Most of them still have at least one dependent child of their own at home, presumably needing time and attention themselves. Perhaps more tellingly, rates of separation and divorce of both grandparent and the parents of grandchildren are significantly higher among young grandparents. This does not necessarily mean that becoming a grandparent at a young age results from family breakdown, since separation and divorce are more associated with younger than older cohorts. But the link between the two, and the lower rates of grandparental satisfaction associated with young grandparents, do raise questions from the grandparents' perspective about the timing of grandparenthood and types of family structures that may provide the most rewarding experience. In the U.S., this being a grandparent at too young an age is sometimes called 'time-disordered'.

Finally, we examined the commitment of grandparents to time-consuming support of other family parents – mostly ageing parents. Looking after a parent on a regular basis mainly affects the middle age grandparents, with one in ten (random) grandparents in this age group providing long-term care to someone -

which may take up a lot of their time. Balancing obligations towards ageing, often disabled parents with the help given to the parents of young grandchildren is no doubt a delicate task, particularly given that many of the grandparents in this sandwich generation position within the family are also still in paid employment.

The BSA survey does not contain enough data for us to be able to examine in detail the supports given to ageing parents and other relatives, but this is clearly an aspect of grandparenting which will become more prominent in the future. We did however find that nearly four times as many grandparents involved in looking after an ageing parent, compared with their counterparts who are able to focus their time and energy on descending generations only, would like a life free of family duties. At the same time it is interesting to note that role satisfaction with grandparenting does *not* seem to diminish if a grandparent is also looking after an ageing parent. Taken alongside what is known already about carer stress, it therefore seems almost certain that dissatisfaction with family duties is related to the heavy involvement of these grandparents with their own parents rather than with their grandchildren.[5]

---

[5] See also Arthur et al., 2002, which finds that looking after *offspring* (as opposed to members of ascending generations) does appear to carry some intrinsic satisfactions.

8

CARING AND PAID EMPLOYMENT

Having sketched out the broad pattern of grandparental activity over the family development cycle, we can now look more closely at key aspects of the role – starting with a part which lies right at the heart of intergenerational family life, that is the help given to parents through participation in the care of young children. This is a matter of great public interest at the moment. And this salience itself may make it that much harder to sort out exactly what is going on and in particular how grandparental roles may be changing. For whenever behaviour is subjected to close public scrutiny, it becomes difficult to distinguish what may be new in it from what is simply made more visible.

Thus there is a common perception, reflected and reinforced by heavy media coverage over the last few years, that because of both the shortfall in supply and perceived problems with care outside of the family, childcare by grandparents holds a key to fuller entry of young mothers to the British labour market.[1] As a result many are being drawn into providing ever more of it, whether they want to or not.[2] Such thinking presumably informed the high level of approval found in our own survey for the view that working mothers need help from grandparents. The performance of such family supports could even be seen as representing a public duty of older citizens, which some policy commentators might regard as part of an implicit intergenerational contract underlying the legitimacy of state pensions and provision of healthcare for the elderly.

We have already published some of the findings of our survey that have a bearing on this debate (Dench, Ogg & Thomson 1999). However, the more detailed analysis that we have undertaken since then has changed the picture a little. The conclusions we reached originally remain broadly valid. But there are some new configurations emerging which point in different directions and which are relevant to several concerns about social change that feed contemporary issues of public policy.

---

[1] See for example Young, 1997; Hansard, 1998 and Home Office, 2000.
[2] E.g. Orr, 2000.

The BSA98 survey did not explicitly address social change. Our own primary concern was to establish what is happening at present, not least so that *future* developments could be charted more easily. So while it did look at current attitudes towards the general role of grandparents, it did *not* consider whether they were doing more childcare, or were needed to do more of it, than in the past. Nor have there been comparable studies in the past exploring these issues, producing findings that could be directly compared with our own. So we do not have any unambiguous evidence against which assumptions about growing activity or demand could be tested. There is in any case a limit to what can be found out in a single survey.

But having made these qualifications, there is perhaps some light which the survey can shed indirectly on how the volume of childcare carried out now by grandparents compares with the past. Insofar as our data does have a bearing on this question, it does moreover point to a rather different situation than is commonly assumed. It would support the view that while some grandparents may now be very heavily involved, the overall levels are perhaps reducing. The current childcare gap and debate may not be prompted by growing demand for help from mothers so much as by declining supply from grandparents.

The study does not contain sufficient material to allow confident adjudication between alternative accounts. What it can help to do though is identify some key questions that now need to be considered, and to clarify the terms in which these questions are phrased.[3]

Interpreting the data

The first things that we need to look at here are the measures of childcare used in the survey and the sort of findings they generated. One of the problems with the public debate on child care is the rather loose and interchangeable usage in it of terms like 'child care' and 'looking after children'. There is clearly a world of difference between having the responsibility for a pre-school child for up to twelve hours a day, five or more days a week on one hand, and looking after a ten-year-old for a couple of hours a week on the other. Yet it is not uncommon to find these two situations considered together under the same rubric of 'child care', and this can encourage false assumptions and unrealistic policy objectives. When the government states that '47% (of grandparents) help look after their grandchildren'(Home Office 2000, p.18), it is not clear which part or parts of the spectrum they have in mind. Without detailed information on the amount and regularity of time spent, on whether grandparental care substitutes or

---

[3] We are intending to publish *fuller* analyses of BSA98 data relevant to these questions in the near future, bringing in more factors relating to the work situation of mothers and grandmothers. There is not room within this present volume for this further material.

complements other sources of care, and how arrangements are negotiated and maintained, the place of grandparents in the child care system remains open to misinterpretation.[4]

The BSA survey does not itself meet these exacting criteria, but it has tried to clarify the position a bit, in order to help dispose of some of the grosser misconceptions concerning levels of grandparents' support. It did this firstly by defining a number of types of childcare. Four main types were considered. These were childcare during normal working hours; childcare or babysitting during the evening - covering for parental leisure or unsocial working hours; taking children to and from nursery or school - which frequently embraces a period of care before or after school; and finally looking after a sick child - which represents an unscheduled form of care which may or may not be related to parents' work commitments. Responding grandparents were asked how frequently they had performed each of these forms of care over the preceding year. Response categories ranged from at least once a week to not at all. The rates of activity recorded for each of these are detailed in the following table.

Table 8.1 Frequency of childcare by type, and by age of grandchild

Type of care	**Frequency**						
	Once a week+ often	Several times/ month	Every month or so	Every six months	Once in past year	Never in past yr	No contact in 2yr
Grandchild age 0-4							
Look after in day	22	14	18	7	8	29	4
Look after in evening	13	9	16	16	8	35	4
Escort to/from school/nursery	3	3	3	3	3	83	4
Nurse sick child	0	1	3	1	11	81	4
Grandchild age 5-12							
Look after in day	21	8	21	11	5	31	4
Look after in evening	16	9	17	16	7	32	4
Escort to/from school/nursery	10	4	12	8	6	57	4
Nurse sick child	0	1	2	6	9	80	4

Note: Group A, [230.250-3]; *bases*: GC 0-4 (*155*), GC 5-12 (*187*); **row** percentages.

All of these measures relate to situations in which grandparents help out parents

---

[4] Ideally we should also take into account the duration of caring over the longer term, and level of responsibility, as done by Hirshorn, 1998.

by taking responsibility for children. But as we have noted, helping out for short periods, even on a regular basis, is not directly comparable to what is done by childminders or nannies, or in nurseries and crèches, and for school age children by teachers. For this reason we selected out grandparents in the survey who are extensively involved in child-care. We defined these as grandparents whose specified grandchild lives in their household, or those respondents who help with baby-sitting/childcare during the day weekly *and* spend time during the day with the grandchild without his/her parents often *and* have that grandchild to stay overnight without his/her parents often. About *one in eight* grandparents emerged as involved in all of these activities on a regular basis with grandchildren aged under 13.[5]

This proportion then has to be considered in the context of the broader pattern of caring. So we next looked at data about general contacts, and about lower-key, *less direct* forms of support.[6] For general contact with selected grandchildren, including with parents present, the frequency range in the survey was from 'daily' to 'not at all in the past year'. The overall distributions of responses for these questions are as follows.

Table 8.2 Frequency of contact by age of grandchild

Type of contact	Frequency							
	Daily	Several times/wk	At least once a week	At least once a frtnght	At least once a month	Several times a year	Less often	Never
Grandchild age 0-5								
How often see	15	27	22	9	7	12	3	5
How often speak on phone	9	17	18	7	4	3	3	39
Grandchild age 6-12								
How often see	8	22	16	13	9	22	6	4
How often speak on phone	5	16	26	11	11	13	5	13

Note: Group A [230.238.240], *bases*: GC 0-5 (236), GC 6-12 (191), excludes grandchildren living in the same household as grandparent.

Similarly, for a selection of activities without a parent present (but which could form part of a visit that involved parents) the range was from several times a week to not in the last year.[7] The frequency distribution arising is as follows.

---

[5] See Appendix E for more detailed analysis on 'extensive' childcare.

[6] It is of course not easy in a family situation to distinguish between formal and informal care. For a useful recent discussion see Land, 2002.

[7] For details of frequency ranges used in BSA questions see Appendix F.

Table 8.3 Shared activities by type, and by age of grandchild

Type of activity	Frequency						
	Once a week+ often	Several times month	Every month or so	Every six months	Once in past year	Never in past yr	No contact in 2yr
Grandchild aged 0-5							
Go park/playground	12	8	14	11	6	45	4
Go shopping/cinema/event	9	5	12	9	5	57	4
Play indoor games/watch TV	2	13	13	6	3	42	4
Visit friends or relatives	6	3	7	7	9	64	4
Go away weekends/holidays without parent	0	0	1	1	5	90	4
Grandchild aged 6-12							
Go park/playground	6	6	24	15	7	38	4
Go shopping/cinema/event	4	4	20	14	7	48	4
Play indoor games/watch TV	19	15	24	16	5	18	4
Visit friends or relatives	2	7	13	9	10	55	4
Go away weekends/holidays without parent	0	0	4	3	5	85	4

Notes: Group A, [230.244-8], *bases*: GC 0-5 (236), GC 6-12 (191), excludes grandchildren living in the same household as grandparent.

These figures for general contact and for shared activities show higher rates than for direct childcare. Between a third and one half of grandparents saw children under six several times a week, and nearly a third shared *some* activity with them without their parents at least several times a month.

This all adds up to a broad pattern in which between one quarter and one third of respondents with grandchildren under 13 have a fairly regular childcare role, about one quarter appear to have no role at all, and just under a half fall between these two positions. Thus there is a considerable amount of activity taking place which may contain elements of care without being primarily oriented to it. It is perhaps these more general types of inputs that inform responses of grandparents to those surveys which conclude that high levels of childcare are normal.

The problem of grandfathers

There is, however, a further complication in all of this, which relates to grandparents' sex. The survey findings tend to show that more childcare is done by grandmothers than grandfathers. But the magnitude of this differential varies greatly according to the status of the respondent. Grandfathers seem to regard and report themselves as really quite active childcarers. But when we look at parents' responses on this, their claims are *not* endorsed. This discrepancy may be largely to do with the wording of our survey questions, which refer to 'helping parents by doing childcare'. This formulation does not distinguish between having full responsibility for care and giving assistance. Consequently grandmothers with primary responsibility and grandfathers who take part by helping *them,* or even just being there when it happened, could both end up recording the same levels of caring activity, on the basis of very different degrees of involvement in it.[8] Presumably *parent* respondents would regard grandmothers as doing more, and be less likely to see grandfathers as really involved.

Wording of the questions on childcare may therefore be producing a 'halo effect' in grandfathers' responses, whereby they appear - by virtue of co-residence with a genuinely involved grandmother – to be doing more than they really are. The limited nature of much grandpaternal activity is revealed however not only by *parents'* assessments of support but also in that (as we shall see in the final chapter) the self-reported rates of activity by those grandfathers living alone are markedly lower than of those living with a partner.

So it seems very likely overall that the actual role of grandfathers is mainly one of assisting grandmothers. Even where support is given by grandfathers as frequently as by grandmothers, it is almost certainly less intensive. For these reasons, the remaining analysis of childcare which follows in this chapter will concentrate principally on that carried out by grandmothers.[9]

Support for working mothers

Having made these points about the nature and meaning of the measures of care given to grandchildren, we can begin to examine the factors which determine the amounts provided. Given the political value attached to help for working mothers, we rather assumed at the outset of the analysis that the dominant factors would be on the demand-side - that is linked to the working status and commitments of mothers - with factors of supply such as grandparental availability playing a secondary or limiting role.

In fact the pattern was more complicated than this, and has needed more patient analysis than expected. Our first wave of analysis, published in the BSA report, failed to find any clear relationships involving *grand*parental work, and even the link with *mothers'* work status - the demand factor - was not straightforward. Some of the data figuring in the original BSA analysis is reproduced in the following table.

---

[8] This ambiguity is clearly something that the wording of questions should try to avoid in future research.

[9] This is not a distinction made in our original analysis in the 16th BSA report. As will become clearer over the next few pages our failure to do this is in part responsible for the limitations of that earlier analysis.

Table 8.4 Care of grandchild by mother's work status – original analysis

| | Employment status of grandchild's mother | | |
	Full-time	Part-time	Not in paid employment
% of grandparents who:-			
Agree strongly being a grandparent is very rewarding	66	65	70
Want a life free from family duties	35	34	40
Have agreed on almost all aspects of grandchild's upbringing	**29**	**49**	**27**
Have had holiday at least once in year with grandchild (without parents)	9	13	7
Look after grandchild when ill at least once a year	17	19	14
Look after grandchild during the day weekly or more	**20**	**32**	**15**
Take grandchild to school or collect at least monthly	13	12	7
Look after grandchild in the evening at least monthly	21	27	25
Base	*81*	*154*	*180*

Note: Group A, bold figures $p<0.05$, [198-9.230.235.249-53.273]; children aged under 13.

Findings here show that the least childcare by grandparents overall was done where mothers were not working, and where need for help was therefore less. However, the most was done where mothers were working only part-time. In part, this probably reflects that mothers working full-time are the most likely to be able to use nursery places and childminders, rather than having to rely just on family ties.

But those grandparents who were involved in looking after the children of full-time working mothers also appeared to find it a rather less satisfactory experience. This suggested that grandparents may be more likely to get involved helping part-time working mothers, and to say yes if asked, because the load is not too great and can be fitted in smoothly with the rest of their lives. Thus supply-side factors do have some relevance here, in that family negotiations around childcare may be a factor steering mothers into part-time working. The flexible nature of part-time work meshes better with family life, and a whole tranche of measures – from grandparents being most thoroughly involved, and feeling closest to children and grandchildren, to being happiest in their role – were clearly linked with it. Where mothers are working part-time, grandparents clearly feel needed and useful, and have regular contact with grandchildren –

including some time alone with them – but without becoming overwhelmed by it.

The compatibility of care within families and *part*-time work by mothers can be underlined by adding in some further measures to those used in the original report. This is shown in the figures below dealing with frequency of contact, feeling close and having a say in a grandchild's upbringing. The measure for giving money to parents indicates that grandparents may also be concerned to help out parents financially where family income is low, and provide a supplement for non-working mothers which reflects levels of the latters' workforce commitment.

Table 8.5 Care of grandchild by mother's work status – further data

	Employment status of grandchild's mother		
	Full-time	Part-time	Not in paid employment
% of grandparents who:-			
Feel very close to GC	64	76	76
See GC several times/week	**30**	**49**	**36**
Help parent with money (in year)	23	35	39
Have big/some say in upbringing	24	38	29
Base	*81*	*154*	*180*

Note: Group A, bold figures *p*<0.05, [234.235.238.258.274], grandchild aged under 13.

But the further work done since the first report has also exposed a limitation in our original analysis, which obscured the effects of grandparental behaviour on the supply of childcare. As suggested earlier in this chapter, the mistake was not to allow properly for differences between grandfathers and grandmothers. For distinguishing the work status of grandfathers and grandmothers, and analysing them separately, reveals entirely different patterns.

Full-time working grandfathers have *more* contact with grandchildren than do non-working, and claim to do more childcare too. What this probably means in practice though is that working grandfathers may be more likely to have *partners* who do not need to work, or at any rate full-time, and who are therefore free to take on more childcare. Grandfathers with such partners would live in households where there is more coming and going of grandchildren, and where they would by virtue of this regular involvement acquire an 'active' halo themselves - even if their own activity was only indirect and marginal. It would certainly be more frequent than most full-time working grannies could manage. For their part, full-time working grandmothers recorded *less* childcare than others. When grandmothers and grandfathers are left together in an undifferentiated category these differences become cancelled out, and the true significance of the work status of either is obscured.

The working granny

So we carried out a new analysis which excluded grandfathers from the supply-side altogether. The results have proved extremely revealing.[10] In the first place, we soon found that in mother-grandmother pairs containing a grandmother of working age and where the grandchild was young there were more grandmothers than mothers who were actually working. This gave an early sign that the working status of grandmothers would be at least as important a consideration as that of mothers. We then ran a series of computations to explore the effect of grandmothers' work status on their levels of child care. This is summarised in the table 8.6. Unfortunately by the time that grandfathers have been cut out of the reckoning the number of cases becomes reduced considerably. Some columns in the resulting tables have rather small totals, and we have consequently left out altogether here a small column for the few grandmothers working after the retirement age of 60.

Table 8.6 Grandmothers' work status by involvement with grandchild

	GM under 60			GM 60+
% grandmothers who:-	**Working Full-time**	**Working Part-time**	**Not working**	**Not working**
Agree strongly role rewarding	68	87	65	70
Feel very close	74	83	75	70
See GC several times week	**49**	**60**	**50**	**32**
Spend time wGC w/oP often	**37**	**60**	**33**	**41**
Have GC stay w/o P often	18	35	20	21
Have big/some say in upbringing	**37**	**50**	**30**	**25**
Mostly agree upbringing	37	30	23	36
Give money to parents	**49**	**50**	**25**	**26**
Day childcare at least monthly	31	50	43	33
School escort at least monthly	2	15	13	15
Evening baby sit weekly or more	16	23	20	12
Nurse sick GC in past year	14	20	30	19
Base	*37*	*32*	*40*	*76*

Note: Group A, bold figures p<0.05, [198.234.235.238.241.242.250-3.258.273.274]; grandchildren under 13.

What the first table in this series perhaps shows is the compatibility of caring with part-time employment of grandmothers themselves. Grannies working part-time are clearly the most involved group overall. They do most day and evening

---

[10] See Appendix E for multivariate analysis.

care, pretty well as much escorting to and from school and nursing of sick children as non-working grannies, and (reflecting their involvement) have significantly more say in upbringing. Their levels of 'social' contact are well above those of other groups and they also record both the highest level of closeness with their grandchildren as well as by far the highest rate for general role satisfaction.

Following this we looked at the *combined* working status of both mothers and grandmothers, to see how these factors operate together.

Table 8.7 Involvement with grandchild by work status of grandmother *and* mother

| | Who works:- | | | |
	GM only	Both	Mother only	Neither
% grandmothers who:-				
Agree strongly role rewarding	89	69	64	77
Feel very close	89	71	76	71
See GC several times a week	**61**	**51**	**45**	**25**
Spend time wGC w/oP often	**57**	**38**	**46**	**27**
Have GC to stay w/o P often	29	17	28	15
Have say in upbringing	**36**	**48**	**31**	**33**
Mostly agree upbringing	36	40	43	27
Ever give money to parents	43	48	25	33
Day childcare at least monthly	36	43	41	33
School escort at least monthly	11	8	23	4
Evening baby sit weekly or more	14	20	20	15
Nurse sick child in past year	14	15	29	15
Base	*39*	*61*	*80*	*60*

Note: Group A, bold figures $p<0.05$, [198.234.235.238.241.242.250-3.258.273.274]; grandchildren under 13.

This second table underlines the relative importance of grandmothers' working status. There are several aspects to this which interest us. Firstly, it is noteworthy that the highest rates of social contacts, not involving direct childcare as such, occur where only the grandmother is working, while higher rates of childcare involvement are found where both mother and grandmother or only the former are working. This rather suggests that for many grannies, where they have a choice their own priority may be to help out in ways other than simply through providing childcare themselves.

Again there is some sense here of intergenerational partnership (rather than exchange) in that both the biggest grandparental say in childcare as well as (marginally) the highest overall rates of childcare are found where both are working. There is a large overlapping of roles here, with both mother and grandmother in paid work and sharing childcare. However, the groupings used for table 8.7 may obscure some important parts of the pattern because they pool together full- and part-time working mothers. We have tried re-sorting the cases a bit, into columns with bases as small as we dare go in the circumstances. In this next tabulation all grandmothers over normal working age (i.e. 60+) are removed in order to simplify comparisons, and mothers are split into part-time and full-time groups. The outcome is very revealing. Organised this way, the data shows not only the higher satisfaction of grandmothers where mothers are not working but also very considerable differences according to the *amount* that mothers work.

Table 8.8 Grandmothers' involvement by combined work status

	Who works:-			
	GM works [mother does not]	**Mother works FT** [GM may or may not work]	**Mother works PT** [GM may or may not work]	**Neither works**
% grandmothers who:-				
AS role rewarding	88	58	74	75
Feel very close	88	68	79	71
See GC several times week	**62**	**35**	**67**	**35**
Spend time wGC w/oP often	**54**	**47**	**43**	**15**
Have GC stay w/o P often	31	21	29	5
Have say in upbringing	**36**	**25**	**55**	**40**
Mostly agree upbringing	**32**	**11**	**49**	**15**
Ever give money to parents	46	35	49	35
Day childcare weekly or more	39	47	50	37
Takes to school weekly or more	8	11	12	0
Evening baby sit weekly or more	15	20	31	21
Nurse sick child in past year	15	26	24	25
Base	*35*	*27*	*46*	*20*

Note: Group A, bold figures *p*<0.05, [198.234.235.238.241.242.250-3.258.273.274]; grandchildren under 13: grandmothers under 60.

The figures in 8.8 provide a summary of the family childcare marketplace. Thus at one end of the spectrum - where grandmothers are working but the mothers are not - we find a situation of low demand for childcare combining with low supply of grandparental time. Such grandmothers appeared to be in a relatively strong position to play the role on their own terms and derive maximum pleasure from it. They saw their grandchildren very often, recorded by far the highest levels of satisfaction with the role and general closeness to grandchildren, and in addition felt that they had a reasonable say in their upbringing. However, they did little formal childcare. They were also at least as likely as other grandmothers to have given money in the past year to their children and grandchildren.

The simple fact of working outside of the home clearly has an empowering effect on grandmothers. For when we look at the cases in which *neither* grandmother nor mother is working – that is where there is low demand but high supply – there are signs of a reduction in satisfaction, presumably because it is harder to say 'no' to what *is* taken on. Thus a little more childcare is done overall, but casual contacts are fewer, and agreement with grandchildrens' upbringing, closeness to grandchildren plus general satisfaction with the role are all down.

Then there are cases where mothers are working and grandmothers may be. These have been sub-divided further according to whether the mother is full-time or part-time. Only the mother's detailed working status is used here because there are not enough cases to allow fuller division, and very few grandmothers work full-time if the mother is working at all. In those cases where grandmothers are working full-time, most mothers are not; this may itself say something about the importance of the supply side factors.

The split between full- and part-time working mothers revealed some crucial differences. Where mothers are full-time we have a situation in which demand for grandparental childcare is potentially very high - though it can be less so if the mother uses a nursery or childminder. The result is that grandmothers are more active in childcare than where mothers are not working at all. But it is only a little more. And against that they are much less in agreement with upbringing, perhaps partly because of the use of childminders and nurseries. They also have less say in it all, do not feel so close to their grandchildren and above all have a markedly lower level of satisfaction with the grandparent role. So there are definite indications of stress in this group.

Where mothers are working only part-time, though, there appears to be greater involvement of grandmothers, even though they are more often than not working too. Levels of childcare are the highest, informal contact is also frequent, say and agreement in upbringing are the highest, and closeness to grandchildren is high. Role satisfaction and social contacts are not quite so high as where *only* the grandmothers are working. But where mothers are working part-time, grannies do seem to achieve a reasonable balance of involvement and satisfaction, while managing to carry out a large portion of the direct childcare which is actually done by grandparents. So this pattern may well be valuable from the point of view of a family as a whole.

Working and caring

What is most striking in these tables though is that the grandmother's role does seem to be most enjoyed where mothers are not working at all - and so cannot make demands - and above all where the grandmother herself is working. This is extremely pertinent, as it may be a pointer to a new type of division of labour within an extended family, in which grandparents are closely involved with their grandchildren but much of the daily care is left to mothers themselves. As we have seen, the working but non-caring granny is able, and likely, to give money to her offspring. So it may be that as the effects of new career-patterns among women work their way through the family cycle, the support given by grandparents may increasingly take *either* financial or practical forms. Work and care are to some extent interchangeable, as they are for parents.

This does not mean of course that some grannies will do one, while others do the other. Many may not do much of either while others, the Supergrans, will do both. Our sample is too small to contain many supergrans who are active across the board. But we have arranged the working grannies as best we can in the next table to show how many of them are also active carers for their grandchildren, and how these differ from the rest. The first column (A) contains the supergrans - working grannies who do day and evening childcare at least several times a month. The second (B) has those who do this only infrequently - once every month or so or once every six months. The third (C) has working grannies who very rarely look after their grandchildren or not at all. The final column gives figures, for comparison, of non-working grannies of working age.

Table 8.9 Profile of the supergran

	Work/care category			
	Supergran (working and caring)	**Medium gran** (working and some caring)	**Uninvolved gran** (working and no caring)	**Non-working gran under 60**
% grandmothers where:-	A	B	C	D
Ag. strongly role rewarding	73	82	59	74
Feel very close	90	77	58	73
Trace tie via daughter	**74**	**53**	**27**	**47**
Child's parents split	37	19	23	29
GC *mother*'s work status:				
FT	26	16	11	19
PT	53	42	45	30
Not working	21	44	44	51
Grandmother social class				
Salariat	11	30	25	24
Intermediate	60	46	45	40
Working class	31	24	30	35
Base	*44*	*24*	*49*	*29*

Note: Group A, bold figures *p*<0.05, [198.229.234.235.264]; grandmothers under 60.

Although numbers are rather small, this table can help to delineate a number of styles of grandmothers' involvement. Social class has an influence here. Choice between types of support obviously depends on a grandmother's income, and the balance between financial and practical help will vary between class groups. Thus relatively few grannies with professional jobs are also involved in active childcare, and this would tie in with this class group giving greater financial support - as confirmed by data given later in this report (chapter 10). The typical supergran (col. A) is an intermediate worker - that is in a non-manual job but without the income or responsibility level that would enable her to avoid doing childcare. It is worth noting too that there is a much higher proportion of working mothers in the supergran column, especially mothers working full-time. This is an indication of the pressure on supergrans to provide across-the-board help.

There are also a markedly higher proportion of *separated* parents in supergrans' families, adding further to the pressure on them and in addition helping to produce a higher matrilineal percentage. Looked at another way, when a mother's need is great, heavy demands become concentrated on maternal grandmothers, whose own role is then likely to become many-stranded and to combine material and caring elements. The daughter is both freed to work herself and can also expect to receive financial assistance from her mother.

These different styles of grandparenting support seem to have an outcome in terms of quality of relationships, with a clear gradient of felt closeness to grandchildren running down from supergrans through the lesser degrees of involvement. This is in line with the general link found between direct participation in childcare and closeness. But very significantly, and as we might now expect, this does not coincide entirely with role satisfaction. It is (again) those working grannies who do only a little childcare who come out top here. The life of the supergran is too hectic to allow the top rating.

A new division of family labour?

These various types of working granny may together be a sign of the splintering of the mould of British grandparenting. From the mists of time until very recently it has been assumed that insofar as grandmothers continue to make a contribution to family life this is through looking after children and generally joining in *domestic* activities. Public policy still seems to assume this. When families were larger, and domestic work less mechanised, this probably *was* the most valuable contribution. Raising a family was extremely demanding, and few women continued to work outside the home into middle age. Those who were still employed by the time that they became grandmothers would retire, and incorporate childcare into their domestic routines so that their daughters or daughters-in-law could work, rather than soldiering on themselves.

Some would have been, or would become, co-resident with their children anyway. We noted earlier that well into the 1960s researchers were estimating a fifth of households to be three-generational. (Rosser and Harris, 1965) Since then co-residence in UK has dwindled.[11] But many grannies still went on looking after grandchildren for working mothers, so that the Women and Employment survey carried out in 1980 found them even then to be (at 44% of the total) by far the most important source of full-time care for pre-school children. (Martin & Roberts, 1984 p.39)

There has been rapid change since then, with smaller families, greater availability of independent housing, more women spending longer in the labour force, greater geographical dispersal and so on. But perhaps the most significant *current* change in terms of extended family life may well be that fewer older women are choosing to give up work when grandchildren are born. They are giving priority to their economic role and contribution instead. The main trend in women's employment since the seventies has been the expansion of careers as opposed to mere jobs - which can be readily dropped and picked up again - and the corresponding virtual disappearance of housewives. Grandmothers of present-day young grandchildren are much more likely than in the past to have interesting work, which in some cases may also be better paid than that which their daughters have or could get. For it is in the nature of a career that remuneration increases with age. This is not the case for the less skilled jobs to which most women, by virtue of the shortness of their working lives, were on the whole previously confined.

Even women who are not in career jobs are increasingly being encouraged to remain in the labour force well into their 50s and beyond (Council of the European Commission, 2002). Ageing populations mean that decent pensions can only be achieved by working longer over the life course, and grandmothers in their 50s are now much more aware of the importance of financial security for an extended period of old age.

On top of this, many of them have spent all of their adult lives at work, and have never been engaged in extensive childcare anyway. So the traditional division of labour between generations may be facing a new challenge. The public perception that grannies are in demand, plus their own claims to be under great pressure, may actually reflect a growing tendency for grannies themselves to say no. The present market imbalance in family childcare may be less a matter of escalating demand than of declining supply. Given that most women have fewer children, later in life, or none at all, net demand may itself even be falling - though with supply falling faster at the moment.

We cannot test this argument from the BSA survey as we do not have

---

[11] Not least because older people living with children found that their entitlement to benefits was lost. See Wenger, 1984; Lewis & Meredith, 1988 and Wall, 1992.

equivalent data for the past. We know from ethnographic studies, and from anecdotal sources like our own recent collection of personal testimonies, that grandmothers in the past were often rather taken for granted by working mothers as sources of childcare (Dench, 2000). Many mothers have always preferred to use a grandmother than to put children in a nursery, and some would not go to work at all otherwise (Thomson, 1995). But in the past they have mostly just assumed that their mothers would help out. Indeed, many of the women who led the movement towards giving work greater salience in women's lives were only able to do so because their own mothers were free to help them. Now that they are grannies themselves they are finding that this expectation is in conflict with their own careers, and many are feeling the 'guilt of the working granny' (Neate, 2000). Part-time work arrangements do however allow balance to be achieved between mothers' and daughters' work aspirations (Nelson, 2000; Winterson, 2002).

To return to the original question, what is arguably new therefore is not so much the pressure on grannies to do childcare as their *resistance* to it. The revolutionary generation of women who challenged and adapted convention as they passed through earlier life-stages are perhaps in revolt against the traditional expectation of daughters - which they exercised themselves as daughters - for family childcare support. And this would help to explain our findings that, at a time when grandparents publicly claim to be providing more help than previous generations, many do not seem to be doing much at all. There may be many families in which wholly new types of negotiations and battles are emerging, with ripples from these private revolutions producing the impetus for public debate.

If this *is* what is happening, then we would expect to find a definite class dimension in changing generational divisions of labour – as shown above in relation specifically to supergrans. For women with middle class occupations would have greater opportunity than others to substitute economic support for hands-on childcare help. Later on (in chapter 10) we will scan for any such tendencies by looking at the influence of class on childcare activities. But before considering class variations we need first to develop a little further the conceptual model for understanding grandparental roles. Having found that material support of young mothers and the provision of direct childcare seem to be alternatives for some grandmothers, we will go on now to see what the survey data can tell us about different styles of grandparental involvement in bringing up grandchildren, and the main pattern of their distribution.

9

Patterns of Involvement in Upbringing

Having concentrated in the previous chapter on some links between employment patterns and the family care of grandchildren, we can go on now to develop a broader model of contrasting styles of grandparental involvement in bringing up children. This will be presented mainly in terms of lineage, as it is the lines of family articulation which appear to have the strongest general influence on these styles. But before looking at the lineage pattern itself we will briefly consider the meaning of the key variables in the survey which are crucial in identifying styles of involvement.

There are two key measures in the BSA survey that are relevant here. The first deals with the amount of say that grandparents have, or feel they have, in decisions about how grandchildren are brought up. The second is to do with the level of agreement that parents and grandparents feel over childrearing issues. We assumed from the outset of the study that the extent of say and agreement would have a close link with the degree of commitment to childcare which grandparents would be able to sustain, and with their satisfaction in the role.

It is important to be very clear about what these variables actually measure, and may mean. The first of them, say, is essentially a behavioural measure, whereas the second, agreement, is almost wholly concerned with attitudes and evaluations. But there is some overlap between them and also – we suspect – a common factor in that both are touching on sensitive issues and not likely to be answered simply and bluntly. There are some indications in the distribution of responses that both questions elicited diplomatic answers, and require very careful interpretation. The following table shows the responses to these two questions by grandparents and linking parents.[1] Only 5% of grandparents - and even fewer parents - felt that grandparents did actually have very much say (either now or in the past) in decisions relating to grandchildren. The figures in

---

[1] Note that there are two separate questions in the survey relating to 'say', one relating to selected grandchildren currently under 16, the other (retrospective) for those 16 or over. The profile of responses on these two questions turned out to be fairly similar, so for most purposes they have been pooled.

this table may however under-state the actual part played by grandparents. Both groups of respondents may have been influenced by the idea that grandparents *should* not really have much say, and that where they do - or certainly where it is publicised - this risks breaking the golden rule of non-interference. 'Say' implies that there is disagreement with parents, and that grandparents' views are allowed some influence. But rather different considerations may apply for the question of agreement about the basis on which upbringing is carried out. Where there is agreement, the issue of interference need not arise. Accordingly there is a more positive picture in these findings, with the majority of respondents indicating agreement all or most of the time. This presumably reflects the exercise of diplomacy in a contrary direction. Being in agreement is more of an attitude of mind, and does not require manifest expression. So it is possible for grandparents to appear to agree (or say they do) when what they are really doing is more a matter of trying not to interfere. The responses on agreement may therefore be an *over*-statement of involvement, and conceal a certain amount of tongue-biting. Responses on say, on the other hand, seem likely to understate the influence that grandparents actually have.

Table 9.1 Grandparental say and agreement in upbringing

	Respondent is:-	
	Grandparent	*Linking parent*
% reporting that grandparents have (1):-		
a big say	5	3
some say	26	16
not a very big say	30	27
no say at all	38	54
Base	*478*	*323*
% reporting that grandparents had (2):-		
a big say	5	1
some say	23	14
not a very big say	27	30
no say at all	45	55
Base	*204*	*115*
% reporting that grandparents and parents:-		
agreed about almost everything	35	29
agreed more often than not	37	42
disagreed more often than not	7	9
disagreed about almost everything	1	1
upbringing has not really been discussed	18	18
Base	*681*	*438*

Note: Group A [273-5]; Group C [414-6]; (1) Grandchild aged under 16; (2) grandchild aged 16+.

In this table the figures given are for the actual response categories used in the survey. For subsequent analysis though say is reduced by incorporating 'big say' into 'some say' - giving us three working categories of 'some say', 'little say' and 'no say'. To simplify references to the agreement variable, we differentiate between agreement all or most of the time (abbreviated in places as harmony), agreement at least some of the time (which we call stable), disagreement – which combines two original categories but still contains rather few cases - and not discussed. This last response-value seems to be rather different to the other three, and perhaps does not form the end of a simple continuum of attitudes. In practice it overlaps with behaviour, and seems to indicate a certain *distance* in the relationship between parents and grandparents, whereby they are not able to talk about the upbringing of children at all, or simply have no occasion to do so. It helps to clarify the nature of both variables if we look at their association. This is done in table 9.2

Table 9.2 Relation between say and agreement in upbringing

	Level of Agreement			
	Harmony	**Stable**	**Disagree**	**Not discussed**
Respondent is grandparent				
Some say	42	33	22	4
Little say	21	42	37	15
No say	37	25	41	81
Base (100%)	*230*	*258*	*52*	*141*
Respondent is parent				
Some say	22	22	20	0
Little say	26	39	17	13
No say	52	40	63	87
Base (100%)	*128*	*182*	*50*	*78*

Note: Group A, $p<0.001$, [273-5]; Group C , $p<0.001$, [414-6].

The figures generated here show that there is a strong association between the two variables and that the distributions of the harmony and stable values are very similar when cross-tabulated with say. Of those grandparents claiming some say, roughly equal proportions fall into the harmony and stable categories for agreement. This possibly suggests that the higher level of agreement – that is occurring most of the time - does not necessarily indicate a *closer* relationship. For some grandparents, declaring almost complete agreement may reflect awareness of their inability to actually influence decisions. It seems possible therefore that the harmony respondents will include not just those grandparents who do agree wholeheartedly but also some who prefer to stand back from active participation and leave decisions to parents. For parents on the other hand, claiming high levels of agreement may help to conceal lack of readiness to allow grandparents any actual say. For where there is complete agreement the issue of say does not arise. Intimacy is not the same as agreement, and may encompass the right to disagree. It may be important to appreciate these matters if the distributions found in the data are to make sense. The tabulation suggests that although these variables do measure different things, there is a good deal of correspondence between them.

Lineage and childrearing

In the preceding chapter, on work, we argued that when looking at childcare activities it was particularly important to distinguish between grandmothers and grandfathers. But as shown in other chapters before that, there are also very significant differences between grandparents according to their lineage connections. It is only when we divide grandparents into the four main types according to sex and lineage that we start to get a clear picture of the main styles of grandparenting.

During the rest of this present chapter we will examine variations of input to raising children between these four sex-lineage categories. We will also distinguish between relationships where children's parents are together, and those where they are apart. Chapters five and six have indicated that parental separation is not just a very influential factor on family relationships in its own right, but is also a major determinant of the differences between maternal and paternal line relationships. But as the data presented in this present chapter should help to confirm, parental breakdown is not the only source of lineage differences. It is helpful to look at both factors at the same time, line of tie and whether parents are together, in order to understand the roots of the divergent grandparenting styles which emerge here.

We begin this analysis by looking at participation in those activities which count very explicitly as childcare. These are looking after children during the day, most commonly while a mother is at work, babysitting in the evening, taking children to and from nursery and school and nursing a sick child. Lineage rates for these forms of childcare are summarised in table 9.3a, with separate rows containing rates for where parents of the child in question are together, and where they are apart.

The first important point to notice is that *where parents are together* there is little difference in reported childcare between grandparents according to lineage, though there is by sex. This is just as found in the analysis of simple intergenerational contact rates, and sharing of social activities, reported in chapter six. Take for example the data on daycare. The table shows the rates for two frequency levels – daycare provided more than once a month, and daycare done at least once every six months. Thus 38% of maternal grandmothers looked after their selected grandchild (under 13) several times a month where parents were together, and 72% of them did so at least every six months. Reading along these two rows, it becomes clear that there is no significant difference between grandparents by lineage, but that grandmothers mostly report more care than grandfathers.

When we move however to the row below, dealing with the care of children whose parents are not together, strong differences do emerge. Unfortunately the numbers of cases here are rather low, particularly for paternal grandparents where there are fewer than twenty in each column. However, even if the actual figures have to be regarded as rough estimates, the differences between maternal and paternal lines are so strong and so consistent with the pattern of general contact rates for lineage, as shown in table 6.4a in chapter six in which the total numbers are greater, that they seem highly likely to have some validity. What the figures indicate is that rates of childcare increase considerably for maternal grandparents, especially grannies, while declining heavily for paternal.

Very similar distributions occur for the other measures of childcare. Grandfathers are more likely to report evening babysitting than daycare, so that sex differences as well as lineage are minimal in the first line for this variable – where parents are together. But the centrality of maternal grandparents, and above all maternal grandmothers, is very evident where parents are not together. Escorting children to school has a slightly different pattern, though given small numbers and low frequencies not too much can be made of it.[2] This activity is one that typically entails a lot of co-ordination between parental and grandparental households and their regimes. Parents drop off and pick up children at very *social* points in the day – often around mealtimes – and may themselves stay for a while when doing so, especially when collecting. So it is probably not surprising that paternal grandparents take no part when parents are split, and relationships are tenuous. At the same time, it is an activity which extends outside of the home, and is something that grandfathers (the chauffeurs of extended family life) may be quite heavily involved in, resulting in less marked sex differentials than for other forms of care. Nursing sick children is even less frequent, with once or more in the year the only value used in this table; but at higher rates it does become more sex-related.

---

[2] Because it is also less common than the first two types of care listed here, lower frequency measures (at least once per month, and once per year) are used for it.

Table 9.3a Childcare by lineage: grandparent responses

% GPs who do:-	Parental relation	Type of relationship			
		MGM	**MGF**	**PGM**	**PGF**
Day care several times a month	Tog	**38**	**27**	39	24
	Apt	**70**	**44**	17	-
Day care at least every 6 months	Tog	72	59	61	60
	Apt	87	72	36	-
Evening care several times a month	Tog	**22**	**21**	29	18
	Apt	**61**	**44**	9	-
Evening care at least every 6 months	Tog	67	57	48	56
	Apt	87	72	36	-
Take to school at least every month	Tog	21	48	21	13
	Apt	22	28	0	-
Take to school within year	Tog	33	26	29	22
	Apt	32	44	8	-
Nurse sick grandchild in year	Tog	21	16	17	11
	Apt	35	22	9	-
Base	*Tog*	*97*	*73*	*84*	*64*
	Apt	*29*	*23*	*	*

Note: Group A, bold figures *p*<0.05, [229.250-3.264].

Data collected from the other BSA sub-samples broadly supports this picture. The sample of parents is rather smaller than that of grandparents, so that once the analysis is narrowed down to grandchildren under 13 there are not enough cases of split parenting to allow comparison with families where parents are together. The figures in table 9.3b are *only* for where parents are together, and these indicate not only much lower overall frequency of childcare than estimated by grandparents but, in particular, a rather lower estimation of PGM than MGM activity. Contrary to what one might suppose this is not a direct consequence of lower assessments of PGMs by daughters-in-law than of mothers by daughters. For if parents are divided by sex, daughters-in-law give rather higher ratings of PGMs performance than do sons, whereas sons-*in-law* give MGMs a similar rating to that of daughters! Against this though sons tend to give (on this as on a number of questions) a higher rating to paternal grandfathers than do daughters-in-law, suggesting either less knowledge of what goes on in the family or perhaps a tendency to (over)report things that they, the sons, have been concerned with personally and therefore know about.

Table 9.3b Childcare by lineage: other respondents

	MGM	MGF	PGM	PGF
% Linking parents who report:-				
Day care several times a month	20	20	16	17
Day care at least every 6 months	62	52	54	29
Evening care several times a month	13	17	8	4
Evening care at least every 6 months	49	47	42	33
Take to school at least monthly	13	23	14	13
Take to school within year	20	47	24	17
Nurse sick grandchild in year	23	7	14	13
Base	*70*	*35*	*47*	*28*
% Young people who report:-				
GP ever looked after (parents together)	55	35	40	26
GP ever looked after (parents apart)	49	36	29	17
Base	*149*	*83*	*113*	*54*

Note: Group C, NS, [371.395-9], parents together only; Group D, NS, [62.a]; [*Lineage* designation of teenagers derived from their parents' responses].

A second source of data in this table comes from the responses of adolescent grandchildren in the Young People sample. Although no longer children, they do still receive some care from grandparents, and were asked a question about whether they were ever looked after by their selected grandparent. Their replies point to *more* of a maternal bias in those families where parents are together, and *less* maternal bias where they are not, than revealed in the grandparental and parental data. This might be because we are dealing here with children of an age where they are able to organise their own lives for themselves. However, it could simply be that answers to the (broader) question used for this sample encompass activities before *and* after parental breakdown, and do not show the effects of separation so clearly.[3]

---

[3] It is important to remember that tables comparing the activities of different categories of grandparents do not take into account that there are not equal proportions of each category alive. There are always more maternal grandparents alive, in particular grandmothers, than paternal. And the imbalance increases, the older that grandchildren become. Thus, by adolescence and even more so young adulthood, most people's actual experience of grandparents is predominantly of maternal grandmothers. Where there are paternal grandparents still alive, and especially paternal grandfathers, these are likely to be several years older. So in practice the effective differences, on the ground as it were, will be even greater than shown in the tables.

The quality of involvement

Materials relating to the frequency of childcare do seem to show that, even if there is relatively greater involvement by maternal grandparents, the differences are not great from the grandparents' perspective, and are mainly a consequence of their heavier involvement where parents are not together.

But does this mean that *without* parental breakdown there would be equal lineage involvement? The answer is probably no. Several aspects of the survey data point to important differences in the quality and style of maternal and paternal contributions to childrearing. It is no accident that where parenting relationships do break down, that it is the maternal line which then becomes much more active. There are differences in *closeness* which are not eradicated by similar frequency of contact – though they may remain fairly unobtrusive so long as parents do remain together.

The key evidence for this comes from answers to the questions on agreement and say – even though their inherent sensitivity may make it rather hard to interpret findings with certainty. Table 9.4 sets out the responses of grandparents to these questions. As in some previous cross-tabulations, cases where parents are not together are shown separately, although such PGF cases are too few to offer reliable indicators. With these new variables, we do begin to get a more rounded impression of the different styles of grandparental involvement.

As we would expect, MGMs record the highest overall levels of agreement with the way that parents are bringing up children – including the highest level of strong agreement and the lowest levels of not discussing upbringing. They also have the greatest sense of a significant say in how things are done. Given that their rates of contact and childcare and so on are no higher than paternal grandmothers', these findings must surely indicate a difference in the depth and quality and closeness of their relationships. This would obviously reflect their place as the mothers of the main childrearers – and as such both more likely to share basic ideas about family life with the parenting household in the first place *and* to be in a better position to talk about it if they do *not* share them. Interestingly, their levels of agreement go down, while disagreement and non-discussion both go up, where parents are split. However, related to their greater hands-on involvement where parents are split, their say goes up. Thus where parents are apart, the greater closeness of MGMs may put them in a situation of some stress, through being more involved but less in sympathy. The conflict or contradictions which can arise are revealed in some of our findings discussed elsewhere.

The next highest overall volume of agreement is recorded by MGFs, although they also admit to a higher proportion of non-discussion. As fathers of the main childrearer, and partners of the generally on-tune MGMs, MGFs can be expected to share many of the family ideas about how things should be done, even though they may not (as men) be very active personally in applying or debating them. Where parents are apart, MGFs do not greatly reduce their agreement, though they do scale down their emotional commitment by increasing their levels of non-discussion.

Paternal grandmothers occupy the position in three-generational family life which is most routinely delicate, and they show rather divergent responses as a consequence. PGMs are mothers themselves, who are likely to hold definite opinions on childrearing which may or may not coincide with those of their daughter-in-law. Where they do coincide the PGMs are, presumably, glad to be in agreement. But where they do not it may be safer not to discuss issues than risk conflict through open disagreement. So there is a tendency towards polarisation between expressing strong agreement on the one hand and avoiding disagreement through non-discussion, all of which adds up to a modest level of say claimed in upbringing – though even this may be overstated for reasons of diplomacy. When parents are not together, PGMs' levels of declared agreement drop substantially, and their say virtually disappears. This is linked with the very heavy reduction which takes place in paternal line contacts.

Table 9.4a Involvement by lineage: grandparent responses

		MGM	MGF	PGM	PGF
	Parental relationship				
% GPs who:-					
Agreement:					
Almost always	Tog	43	41	39	26
	Apt	31	40	17	0
Mostly	Tog	39	39	27	48
	Apt	40	36	28	36
Disagree	Tog	8	7	6	11
	Apt	17	4	17	27
Not discussed	Tog	11	14	28	15
	Apt	11	20	39	36
Say:					
Big or some	Tog	**40**	24	**26**	19
	Apt	**64**	48	**0**	8
Base	*Tog*	*174*	*110*	*146*	*90*
	Apt	*46*	*33*	*27*	***

Note: Group A, bold figures *p*<0.05, *=base<20, [229.264.273-5].

Paternal grandfathers illustrate the least involved pattern. They are not women, with a close interest in childrearing issues, nor are they parents of the children's main carer. So they neither expect to agree very intimately with the way in which the grandchildren are being brought up nor, we can imagine, mind very much whether or not they have a say. The commonest response of PGFs is to agree mostly with how things are being done. And in their case this may not entail very rigorous or critical assessments. They are accordingly the most detached grandparents, perhaps watching what is going on more than seeking to influence it. When parents are not together, though, and contacts are seriously diminished, this mode of fairly passive approval switches off and appears to be replaced not only by much higher levels of non-discussion but by more outright disagreement too.

Other views of involvement

These four styles are perceived, or at least presented, in a slightly different manner by family members in other positions. The next table (9.4b) lists responses by parents and adult grandchildren to the same questions, though in the case of the grandchildren the reference is retrospective - often over a considerable period. For both of these further sub-samples, the numbers of cases where parents are not together are too small to allow reliable estimation, and in addition to this in the case of grandchildren may frequently involve separations that have taken place *since* the respondents have grown up. For these reasons, only the figures for families where parents are together have been included in this table.

Table 9.4b Involvement by lineage: other respondents

	MGM	MGF	PGM	PGF
% Linking parents:-				
Agreement:				
Almost always	30	37	23	32
Mostly	53	31	44	44
Disagree	5	14	15	10
Not discussed	13	19	18	15
Say:				
Big or some	56	44	38	41
Base	*126*	*69*	*83*	*48*

% Adult grandchildren:-
Reporting agreement:

Almost always	25	22	20	27
Mostly	53	50	46	46
Disagree	13	20	23	9
Not discussed	8	8	9	18
Base	*145*	*50*	*90*	*26*

Note: Group C, NS, [406.414-6]; Group B, NS, [327.336]. Figures for where parents *together* only.

There are several overall differences apparent between these responses and those of grandparents, which refer to more than one type of grandparent. As we have already seen earlier on, parents generally tend to report less agreement and say than grandparents do. But against that, both parents and grandchildren report more disagreement than acknowledged by grandparents themselves and, in particular grandchildren, mention less non-discussion. So what grandparents see or present as non-discussion may either be interpreted as disagreement (more by parents) or even as broad agreement (especially by grandchildren). Altogether, both of these groups of respondents seem to make less tangible distinctions between the four categories of grandparents than the grandparents do themselves.

In spite of this it is still possible to recognise the varying styles through these accounts. Parents do appear to regard grand*fathers* as more often being in full agreement with them than grandmothers, and presumably interpret grandfathers' relative indifference or holding back as positive approval. However the largest overall agreement, together with lowest levels of disagreement and non-discussion, are attributed to MGMs, and this corroborates or reciprocates their own sentiments. When it comes to having a say, though, parents do not seem to echo the greater sense of having an influence on upbringing that MGMs themselves articulate. This effect may however partly be a consequence of pooling the 'have say' and 'had say' responses. For among parents where grandparents are currently involved with *young* grandchildren (the 'have say' sector) there is a gradient of responses, from MGM down to PGF, similar to that found in grandparents' answers.

There does not seem to be much in the experience of parents to distinguish between the other types of grandparent. Again, though, this may be a technical effect, arising in this table from putting the focus solely on lineage categories of grandparents, and neglecting the characteristics of respondents themselves and their exact relationship to the grandparent. Grandparents may present divergent faces to different categories of relatives. Thus, when we divide responses concerning paternal grandparents according to the sex of the *respondent*, we find that rather more (20%) of daughters-in-law see the PGM (their mother-*in*-

law) as being in disagreement over childrearing, than as not discussing upbringing (14%). Equally, and balancing this out in the pooled figures for PGMs, many more sons (20%) see them (their *mothers*) as not discussing the issues than as disagreeing (10%). Exactly the same effect applies to daughters' and sons-in-laws' assessments of maternal grandfathers - 18% of daughters see their fathers as disagreeing with them over childrearing, compared with 8% of sons-in-law. But 38% of sons-in-law see MGFs as not discussing upbringing (diplomatically perhaps) compared with only 9% of daughters. In both situations it is interesting that the male parents see the grandparents as merely not discussing matters of childrearing, while the female parents – who are the more directly and closely involved in childrearing practice – regard them as actively disagreeing. Different interests are bound to generate divergent ways of conceptualising each people's behaviour. And in a sense these are all components of the larger pattern. But unfortunately there are simply not enough cases in the sample to allow a detailed unravelling of the different perspectives which go to make it up. This is one of the areas where we badly need much more qualitative research, to get greater purchase on contemporary family behaviour.

Other aspects of support

We can differentiate further between the main lineage styles of grandparenting by looking at some other ways in which grandparents help their offspring. For example, we asked respondents about advice given to grandchildren. This is not something that is restricted to young grandchildren in the way that childcare is. But it is still very closely bound up with issues of upbringing, and the ways that things get handled within particular families. So it can reasonably be expected to be influenced by the same sort of sex and lineage factors as childcare itself.

This is indeed what the available data, summarised in table 9.5, do suggest. Parents were not asked this question, on the assumption that they would not be reliable informants regarding events in which they might well not take a direct part. Also, the data for adult grandchildren whose parents are not together has been excluded, as numbers of cases are not large enough to make proper allowance for relative recency of domestic splits. So the table contains only three categories – grandparents where parents are together, those where parents of grandchildren are not together, and adult grandchildren whose parents are together. Percentages are given for grandparents who have *often* in the last year given advice, and for those who have *ever* given advice.

The responses given by grandparents fall into a pattern remarkably like that for childcare. Where parents are together, grand*mothers* report more giving of advice than grandfathers, but there is really no difference between lineages in this. Where parents are not together, rates go up for maternal grandparents and down for paternal. Sex and lineage factors then combine to produce the familiar gradient, which appears repeatedly in lineage distributions, whereby frequencies run downwards from MGMs at the top to PGFs at the bottom.

Table 9.5 Advice by lineage

GP respondents	Parental Relation	MGM	MGF	PGM	PGF
Advice given often	Tog	**10**	3	11	2
	Apt	**25**	18	6	-
Advice given ever	Tog	**37**	**25**	38	22
	Apt	**66**	**63**	19	-
Base	*Tog*	*137*	*74*	*112*	*63*
	Apt	*36*	*23*	*23*	***
GC respondents					
Advice received often		6	16	7	5
Advice received ever		51	49	35	43
Base		*145*	*50*	*90*	*26*

Note: Group A, bold figures $p<0.05$, [229.260-1.264]; Group B, NS [298.324-5.327], 'Parents together' only.

The responses of grandchildren do not form such a neat profile. This does not necessarily contradict grandparents' responses. What sounds like advice to the recipient may not be intended as such. Grandmothers perhaps tend to have stronger views than grandfathers on how one needs to behave, and so would be more conscious of offering advice. For their part, grandchildren may experience the comments of grandfathers as containing instructive content when none was in fact meant. Or, since this question was decidedly retrospective for many of the adult grandchildren, it may be that they recall advice from grandfathers more readily because they had fewer contacts with them, and the events were more noteworthy. Either way, perceptions of advice obviously differ according to standpoint.

When it comes to the next form of support, though, such ambiguities are less in evidence as the nature of the behaviour is more objective: giving *money*. All respondents (except for the Young People) were asked about direct transfers of money from grandparents to grandchildren, and (except here for grandchildren) about indirect payment, via parents but 'for' grandchildren. Findings are set out in table 9.6. Figures where parents are apart are included for grandparent respondents, even though the paternal columns contain rather small numbers. But they are *not* included for the parent or grandchild samples, as too many of the relevant tables would be too small to offer even an approximate idea of the effect.

Table 9.6 Financial help by lineage

% GP respondents who:-	Parental Relation	MGM	MGF	PGM	PGF
Give money to parent often	Tog	10	3	5	6
	Apt	11	12	0	27
Ever give money to parent	Tog	24	23	25	27
	Apt	35	39	10	27
Give money to GC often	Tog	15	11	19	10
	Apt	14	12	5	27
Ever give money to GC	Tog	24	27	36	24
	Apt	31	21	29	31
Base	*Tog*	*174*	*110*	*146*	*90*
	Apt	*46*	*33*	*27*	***
% GC respondents who:-					
Receive money from GP often		2	5	0	0
Ever received money from GP		42	38	28	24
Base		*145*	*50*	*90*	*26*
% Link parents who report GPs who:-					
Give money to parent often		4	3	3	2
Ever give money to parent		20	14	21	14
Give money to GC often		**7**	**7**	**9**	**12**
Ever give money to GC		**19**	**14**	**25**	**46**
Base		*130*	*76*	*85*	*50*

Note: Group A, NS, [229.257-60.264]; Group B, NS, [298.322-3.327]; Group C, bold figures *p*<0.01, [371.402-5.407]. Groups B & C, 'Parents together' only.

To take first responses to the question about money given to parents, the data in this table support the argument that the apparent greater strength of relationships in the maternal line does *not* operate right across the board. Where parents are together, the payment of money to parents hardly seems to be influenced by lineage in any systematic way, or even by sex. In fact on the evidence of the parents themselves, there may even be slightly more transfers from paternal grandparents to grandchildren direct, with PGFs well represented.

There are several possible implications of this. It may be that caring and providing material resources are genuinely complementary ways of giving family support. We have seen earlier how grandmothers who work, and because of working do little or no childcare, are more likely to give money to their offspring. So there is a clear sense in which these different types of support are understood as alternatives. There is an obvious sex angle to this, which chimes with conventional sexual divisions of labour. Women traditionally provided more direct care within families, while men 'enabled' this by producing the necessary resources. And this principle may to some extent embrace the inputs of grandparents too, with lines of descent supporting parents by taking on some of the aspects of that parent's role.

This is perhaps manifest here in what happens when parenting relationships break down. The female parent role assumes and requires closeness – both physical and emotional. The male role on the other hand can be performed at a distance, in that personal contact is not imperative for transferring material resources. It is therefore interesting to see that paternal line money transfers to parents in the paternal line do not seem to be significantly reduced where parents are apart, in the way that paternal line *caring* is, and may even be increased. The case numbers are too small to be more than rough pointers here, but the largest increase in regular contributions where parents are not together are recorded by PGFs, with MGFs in second place. Male providers are still to be found, albeit in the grandparental generation, to replace missing male partners.

As far as PGFs are concerned, this process is presumably helped along a little by the child support agency. Many non-resident fathers may have difficulty in keeping up maintenance payments, and it should be noted that it is male parent-respondents, that is sons, rather than female, that is daughters-in-law, who seem the more likely to report paternal grandparent financial contributions for grandchildren when parents are apart. Notwithstanding this, and *not* forgetting that the number of cases on which figures for payments where parents are not together is very small, it should also be noted that according to grandparents' accounts a large increase in financial support where parents are separated comes from MGMs – perhaps in many cases grannies who are choosing to make a financial rather than hands-on caring contribution.

The position is even more complicated when we come to direct payments to grandchildren. These are presumably quite small amounts usually, and may just constitute (possibly regular) pocket-money. Thus they cut across the distinction between caring and providing. And this is reflected in their distribution, as the tabulated figures show. What is immediately striking in these figures is the prominent position of PGMs, certainly on their own evidence. A possible reason for this could be that high rates of activity here help them to resolve difficulties inherent in the PGM role. As we have seen, PGMs face obstacles in playing a fully maternal role. They have frequent contact, and do regular childcare, but many do not feel that they are allowed to really get involved in the moral deliberations and decisions on which upbringing is based.[4] To compensate for this exclusion from having a say, some PGMs may become more inclined to give money to grandchildren, as something that is 'value-free' in that it is less likely to be seen as attempting to exercise direct influence over their behaviour, and which can be done in a more detached way. It is perhaps avoiding competition with the children's mother and maternal granny, by expressing affection at a slight distance.

The ambiguous nature of money transfers direct to grandchildren is further confirmed by the absence of any clear response pattern embracing all sub-samples of respondents. Parents, although not themselves involved and so, possibly, not aware of all that may be going on, do not back up the claims of PGMs. Paternal grandfathers appear well ahead in parents' views, though again this may be a consequence of male tunnel vision, as it is high responses by sons (who also provided the main testimony to PGFs' position in giving money to parents) rather than daughters-in-law which produces this rate. Adult grandchildren, for their part, produce a classic matri-centred gradient of responses, running down from MGM to PGF. However most of the gifts they refer to are well in the past, so that it may be an artefact of memory more than a reflection of actual grandparental behaviour. Also, if we *do* look at data for grandchildren whose parents are now apart – not included here because numbers are so small - PGFs do seem to stand out again. So perhaps the safest conclusion is that there *is* no definite pattern here. This would support the general argument that a number of different influences operate in this domain, and paternal line relations are less weak than in caring activities.

Role satisfaction

The various aspects of grandparenting analysed here embrace enough of the whole spectrum to sketch out the overall outlines of different sex-lineage patterns. But these do not come fully to life until we have related the findings to how grandparents actually feel about their roles. This final section of the chapter takes key measures of role evaluation and looks at how they fit in with the preceding data. The first table here summarises grandparents' own responses on these matters.

The measure which distils the emotional heart of grandparental relations is that of closeness. Maternal grandmothers predictably come at the top of this league, even where parents are together and contacts are evenly spread across

---

[4] This again comes out in the ethnographic study which has complemented the 1998 survey (see Arthur et al., 2002) and the work of Gillian Douglas' team on post-divorce grandparenting in Wales.

descent lines. The quality of ties is obviously different, as suggested by the greater say that MGMs enjoy, plus the clear and strong tendency for contact to increase along that line at times of special need - as when parents are not together. The other two measures listed here confirm this dominant position, even though they do suffer from technical limitations which may partly obscure lineage effects.[5] Thus MGMs, in this instance alongside PGMs, come top for feeling that the grandparent role is very rewarding and also (by a notable margin, given the muffled nature of the measure used) are well at the bottom end of wanting more freedom from family ties.

Table 9.7a Role satisfaction by lineage: grandparent responses

		MGM	MGF	PGM	PGF
% GPs who:-	Parental relation				
Feel very close to GC	Tog	**77**	68	69	65
	Apt	**92**	72	44	36
Agree strongly grandparenting rewarding	Tog	70	63	69	51
	Apt	69	52	43	47
Agree want free life	Tog	32	40	36	36
	Apt	43	52	45	27
Base	*Tog*	*174*	*110*	*146*	*90*
	Apt	*46*	*33*	*27*	***

Note: Group A, bold figures *p*<0.05, [198.199.229.243.264].

These measures also provide a neat summary of the effects of parental separation. Closeness with grandchildren is increased, in line with their greater dependence on MGMs and time spent with them. However, the stresses that are entailed in taking on more burdens look as if they do make the role less rewarding. The actual drop recorded here is very small. But given the muffling effect of other factors blunting measurement, and also the confirmation which is given by the perceptible rise in the proportion even of MGMs wanting a freer life, it does seem likely to be real.

Maternal grandfathers arguably are shown by these figures to be near their limit of rewarding participation in grandparenting, even *before* parental

---

[5] As explained earlier these questions do not refer specifically to selected grandparental relationship. Consequently tabulations cannot isolate the effects of lineage from that of other factors – and this obviously reduces the strength of lineage effects in them. There are not enough cases for analysis if we restrict tables here to those cases in which there is only one grandparent where we can be more sure of the direct effect. (Confining analysis in this way might not entirely solve the problem anyway, as it would also bias findings towards youngest grandparents and grandchildren.)

separations increase the demands on them. As men they may have less desire to become heavily involved in family life. But as *maternal* grandfathers they may be liable to be pulled into it anyway, and co-opted to its regime, a little more than they would ideally like. Thus they feel less close than MGMs to grandchildren, find the role less rewarding and show high levels of wanting a freer life – and all this where parents are still together! Where parents are apart, and demands on them are greater, their role satisfaction goes down and their desire for freedom steps up even further.

Paternal grandmothers are confirmed in this table as the grandparents who lose out most through parental separation. Where parents are together, most PGMs feel reasonably close to grandchildren – though because they are excluded from equal influence and say not so many feel as close as do MGMs. They also find the role as rewarding, and experience a desire for freedom which is only slightly above average. Where parents are apart though the proportion feeling very close drops heavily, role satisfaction plummets, and there is a clear increase in the proportion who say they would welcome a reduction in family obligations. Unlike for MGMs, this is presumably not often related to the burden of practical demands on them, but almost entirely to stress generated by intensified exclusion from involvement.[6]

Paternal grandfathers by comparison appear to have a far less stressful position. As men they are probably less drawn to intensive participation in grandparenting, and so feel less excluded when not closely involved. For them any stress is more likely to be secondhand, and to arise from sharing the feelings of their partners. Their experience of closeness accordingly mirrors that of PGMs, and co-varies with the volume of grandparenting activities taking place in the household. However, only half of PGFs definitely find much satisfaction in the role. In line with this relative detachment, PGFs express a desire for freedom which is only slightly above average. Most PGFs already have as much freedom from family duties as they want; although numbers are too low for clear conclusions to be drawn here parental separation does not appear to create extra burdens or direct stress for them.

Complementary perspectives on these grandparenting models are given by the responses of parents and grandchildren to equivalent role questions, which are summarised in table 9.7b. Parents were asked to assess the closeness of relationships between selected grandparent-grandchild pairs. Grandchildren, including the teenage sample, were asked both how close they felt to their *selected* grandparent and also how they felt about their grandparents in general.

---

[6] This effect is well documented in the US, from Furstenberg & Spanier, 1984 onwards. Reading between the lines of Secker, 2001 leads us to suspect that PGM stress may also be a significant factor driving separated fathers to seek greater access to their children.

As with the questions to grandparents on how rewarding they found their role, and whether they would like more freedom from it, although these further measures were not focused specifically on the selected relationship they would clearly be influenced to some extent by it. Grandchildren's responses summarised in this table relate to the following two propositions: 'My grandparents are an important part of my life,' and 'My grandparents are not very interested in my life.' All of the figures here are for where parents are together.

Table 9.7b Role satisfaction by lineage: other respondents

	Respondent relation	MGM	MGF	PGM	PGF
Linking Parents' views					
GP/GC feel very close		**55**	**42**	**43**	**33**
Linking Parents' views *by sex & relationship*					
	Daughter	**62**	**38**		
	Son-in-law	46	46		
	Daughter-in-law			**50**	**31**
	Son			33	33
Base		*126*	*69*	*83*	*48*
Teenage GC's views					
Feel very close		37	38	29	20
Agree strongly GP important		37	38	50	31
Disagree strongly GP not interested in me		47	41	37	20
Base		*98*	*58*	*68*	*36*
Adult GC's views					
Feel very close		47	28	24	23
Agree strongly GP important		37	38	31	29
Disagree strongly GP not interested in me		48	46	26	21
Base		*145*	*50*	*90*	*26*

Note: Group B, NS, [276.278.298.303]; Group C, bold figures $p<0.05$, [371.376]; Group D, NS, [47a.47c.55b.58]. Parents together only.

Felt closeness of relationship remains the most reliable measure here – in that it is the only one which refers unambiguously to selected ties – and on this the collected responses were broadly consistent. MGMs tellingly rated the highest proportion of 'very close' in all groups (though this was shared with MGFs for teenagers), and PGFs the lowest, with MGFs and PGMs more or less on a par in between. In passing, it is worth noting that when responding parents are divided by sex (as in 9.7b) female respondents can be seen to rate grandmothers as closer than grandfathers, while male respondents rate maternal grandparents as closer than paternal and within that do not differentiate between grandmothers and grandfathers. Clearly there may be some difference here in how men and women define or perceive closeness. This indicates that the sex effect has further dimensions than those which have been analysed and examined in this report, and which themselves probably deserve fuller attention.

For teenage grandchildren, who have the widest range of grandparents alive to influence their assessments, there is a shallower gradient of closeness to grandparents than there is for adult grandchildren. We cannot say though how far this relates to the latters' current experiences or arises from memories of childhood. On the question of the importance of the relationship (which is not related to specific ties) there is understandably little difference between the lineage columns. But this then makes the existence of a strong gradient on the last item, for teenage and adult respondents alike, all the more striking. It means that if we take the lineage columns as indicating that, whatever *other* grandparents they may have, respondents in them *do* have an MGM, MGF or whatever, then *simply having* an MGM appears to make grandchildren *much* more likely to feel that grandparents are interested in them, than does having a PGF. This clearly reflects back, and very strongly confirms, grandparents' own differential evaluations of their solicitude towards grandchildren.

This then represents the overall lineage patterning of grandparenting styles, with MGMs and PGFs arguably representing the clearest 'sex-line' models. Thus MGMs could be seen as mothers who are able to retain and develop a motherly role into later life, because the tie is mediated through another mother – their daughter - while PGFs are fathers who can retain a fatherly role. MGFs would then be identifiable as fathers who become pulled by three-generation lineage ties into a maternal relationship with grandchildren, and PGMs perhaps as mothers who get drawn into a paternal relationship with theirs. On this basis, we might perhaps predict that both MGFs and PGMs would be more liable to experience contradiction and stress in their roles, even (or perhaps especially) where the parents are together and relations between households are operating normally. But more *qualitative* work will be needed to explore these differences, and to help define measures, before they can be approached confidently in survey research.[7]

---

[7] This has been started, in Arthur et al., 2002.

10

EFFECTS OF SOCIAL CLASS

We have now established what appear to be the main determinants of grandparenting style. Age and the family development cycle, employment patterns and lineage – with instability in parental relationships liable to trigger variations in all of these – seem to account between them for the bulk of variability. But there are other considerations such as social class which manifestly have some pertinence too, even if this mainly constitutes a shorthand way of referring to different settings within which the key variables may interplay in particular ways. This qualification is important. It would be a mistake to regard class as a 'hard' factor in its own right – as age and sex are for example – which has a direct and determinable effect on grandparental relations. The idea of class encapsulates a number of lifestyle alternatives which have an essentially analytic relevance here. It is an abstraction which is itself subject to a variety of competing definitions. And even when definitions and appropriate measures have been selected, there are still many difficulties in applying these to multi-generational sets of people and data. So the discussion of its relation with grandparenting which follows here is bound to be both tentative and problematic.

We have taken as our basic definition and measure of social class the Goldthorpe schema (as applied in many BSA analyses) and organised the categories into three main groupings. The top and bottom groups here are the Salariat, embracing relatively secure middle-class and professional occupations, and the Working Class, covering the least-skilled and most precarious. Between these there are a number of intermediate categories which we have grouped together for most purposes. We sometimes found in the course of the analysis though that the small-business and self-employed category within this intermediate grouping stood out as the most distinctive and most different from both salariat and working class. So there are some references in the text which are more specifically to this group.

As already emphasised, these classes should not be seen as self-conscious groupings, in some way 'for themselves' in a Marxist sense, and with distinctive family cultures, but simply as categories of people likely to share lifestyle factors relevant to extended family life. The nature of people's work and economic opportunities obviously generate a number of such factors. Thus salariat jobs involve high levels of qualification and commitment to an occupation, commensurate high rewards and structuring of life around career progression, which will clearly have implications for family life. These features of salariat work mean for example that people may have to be geographically mobile, and cannot expect to live so near their kin or, to look at the other side of it, have better excuses when they don't want to. Higher pay and greater personal security widen their choices generally, and allow them to enjoy better health and longer lives. People in such jobs may be more self-reliant and altogether less likely to be dependent on family ties.

The following tables illustrate some of these general implications of class for family life. The first tabulates the class of grandparents against the time it takes them to travel to where selected grandchildren live. It shows that salariat grandparents, and especially grandmothers, tend to live furthest away while it is, intriguingly, the intermediate group that live nearest to grandchildren. This is one among many indications in the data that members of this class have the greatest overall capacity to organise their lives around extended family life, and this could be because of the particular mix of resources available to it. People in the salariat have more financial resources than the other groups, but have little time to become involved in family activities and may not be able to confine themselves to a localised lifestyle. The working class in general may have more time, and tend to be locally-based, but have limited financial resources to expend in family activities and less opportunity to control how closely they live to relatives. People in between have reasonable amounts of both time and money, and may as a result have greater overall inclination and power to organise their lives around family ties if they want to.

Table 10.1 Proximity of kin by social class

	Salariat		Other		Working class	
%GPs who:-	GF	GM	GF	GM	GF	GM
Live within 15 minutes	26	18	48	40	39	35
Live within 15 mins-1 hour	33	34	22	33	36	40
Live more than 1 hour	41	48	30	27	25	25
Base	*87*	*90*	*80*	*173*	*91*	*133*

Note: Group A, *p*<0.05 (associations of class with sex), [239].

The next table considers demographic issues, and organises data from the BSA sample as a whole to unravel the relationship between class, sex and reproductive

Table 10.2 Family status by social class

Sex, age and family status		Salariat	Other	Working class
Male, up to 40, with-				
	Parent alive only	56	52	51
	Both parent and child	43	45	42
	Child only	1	2	2
	Neither parent or child	1	1	5
	Base	*207*	*176*	*210*
Male, 41-59, with-				
	Parent alive only	**10**	**8**	**7**
	Both parent and child	**61**	**54**	**43**
	Child only	**24**	**34**	**41**
	Neither parent or child	**6**	**4**	**9**
	Base	*165*	*139*	*131*
Male, 60-, with-				
	Parent alive only	1	0	1
	Both parent and child	10	7	4
	Child only	84	84	79
	Neither parent or child	5	9	17
	Base	*138*	*108*	*113*
	Base – all males	*510*	*423*	*454*
Female, up to 40, with-				
	Parent alive only	**55**	**32**	**23**
	Both parent and child	**43**	**64**	**71**
	Child only	**2**	**4**	**5**
	Neither parent or child	**0**	**1**	**1**
	Base	*212*	*289*	*167*
Female, 41-59, with-				
	Parent alive only	13	5	2
	Both parent and child	49	58	57
	Child only	30	33	38
	Neither parent or child	8	3	3
	Base	*182*	*232*	*134*
Female, 60-, with-				
	Parent alive only	3	1	1
	Both parent and child	7	6	9
	Child only	63	79	75
	Neither parent or child	26	14	14
	Base	*87*	*209*	*138*
	Base - all female	*481*	*730*	*439*

Note: bold figures $p<0.01$, [190-5].

status. Respondents are grouped, within age-bands, according to whether they have either or both a parent and child alive. Several relevant effects of class stand out. Firstly, although women in all groups begin to have children younger than men, this difference is far less apparent among the salariat than lower down the social scale, where people who become parents do so earlier. By middle age this class-sex divergence has intensified as a result of lower fertility among salariat women, with salariat men overtaking them in being parents, while in the working class men retain the higher rate of childlessness. Differences in longevity compound these differences in fertility, so that from the age of forty onwards salariat men and working-class women are increasingly *more* likely than working-class men and salariat women to have both a parent and a child alive. On this basis it seems arguable that the first two groups enjoy rather greater chances for involvement in extended family life than the latter two.

Social class and sex

These demographic tendencies point to a inter-linking of class and sex which requires some further consideration before the survey data can be interpreted. In particular we need to look at how measures of class are constructed and relate to position in family life. Until quite recently the social class rating of a woman tended to be based on the occupation of her husband. Whatever else may be said about this, it did at least enable class to be attributed to a household, rather than just individuals. But now that more women are working longer, and are more committed to their own jobs, they are given their *own* class, which may or may not be the same as their partners'. In reality, there is a high chance of non-correspondence within a household, as the numbers of men and women in particular classes is rather different. Because of the continuing demands of family life on them, not only do fewer women have work of salariat status, but disproportionate numbers of those who do remain childless. For men on the other hand, professional status increases the chances of reproduction. At the other end of the social scale the opposite applies. The main concentration of women's work now is in services and clerical-administrative occupations, which cluster in the intermediate class. So women are under-represented in manual, unskilled jobs, just as they are in the salariat. But whereas salariat men are more fertile than salariat women, working-class men are less fertile.

The upshot of this is that there are far from equal proportions of male and female respondents in our three class groups. The salariat is quite strongly biased towards fathers and grandfathers, the intermediate class group is biased towards mothers and grandmothers, and the working class – because of low male fertility – just about balances out. And this brings us back to the problem of households, in that many respondents are bound to have partners in a different class, which raises all manner of complexities for the analysis. For what happens in a household, and determines its lifestyle and the pattern of parenting and grandparenting, may relate much more to a partner's class than to the respondent's own.

This report is certainly not the place for a full exploration of this. But it is helpful, for interpreting the data here related to respondents' class, to have some idea of the ways in which partners' classes do combine. Table 10.3 looks firstly at the association of respondents' own and their partners' class for the BSA sample as a whole, and then for that of the *grandparents* within it.

Table 10.3 Respondent social class by partner social class

	Respondent's social class			
Spouse's social class	Salariat	Other	Working class	DK
Men – all respondents				
Salariat	**40**	22	13	-
Other	48	**50**	40	-
Working class	11	27	**44**	-
Base	*336*	*243*	*215*	*
Women – all respondents				
Salariat	**59**	32	13	30
Other	25	**36**	30	14
Working class	14	30	**55**	32
Base	*279*	*419*	*216*	*26*
Grandfathers				
Salariat	**30**	10	10	-
Other	50	**47**	37	-
Working class	18	41	**48**	-
Base	*93*	*88*	*76*	*
Grandmothers				
Salariat	**56**	30	7	-
Other	27	**41**	35	-
Working class	17	28	**54**	-
Base	*52*	*126*	*74*	*

Note: Main survey data & Group A, all associations (spouse class*respondent class) *p*<0.01, bold figures highlight correspondence, [192].

This table shows a fairly clear tendency for respondents to have partners of the same or at any rate adjacent class identities. The tendency is weakest for salariat men – whose wives are more likely to have intermediate occupations themselves or, in the case of salariat grandfathers, are almost as likely to be working class as salariat themselves. It is *strongest* for salariat women – more than half of whom have same-class partners. The small category of salariat grandmothers is thus the most endogamous group of grandparents in class terms, and this may have a bearing on the fact that, as the coming tabulations illustrate, this category stands out as the most distinctive in its family behaviour.

Class and family contact

Having made this lengthy qualification about the meaning of our survey data, we can go on to look at what the findings actually show. The first tables here are concerned with the data on contacts and shared activities.

Table 10.4 Contacts and activities by social class

% GPs who:-		Salariat	Other	Working Class
See GC Several times a week	GF	23	26	37
	GM	**15**	**39**	**38**
Speaks on phone to GC several times a week	GF	13	18	20
	GM	24	27	32
Gives/receives present at least monthly	GF	43	37	44
	GM	57	47	38
Often has GC stay without parents	GF	**14**	**30**	**14**
	GM	16	19	20
Visits friends/relatives at least monthly	GF	7	17	7
	GM	13	21	21
Visits friends/relatives at least yearly	GF	26	36	25
	GM	33	37	33
GP/GC go holiday with parents in Yr	GF	22	16	18
	GM	16	17	22
Base	*GF*	*73*	*78*	*76*
	GM	*64*	*133*	*102*

Note: Group A, bold figures $p<0.05$, [238.240.242.243.247.248].

Several of the distributions here indicate fairly strong effects of class lifestyle. With regard to simple frequency of contact, for example, salariat grandmothers report materially lower rates – lower even than salariat grandfathers, many of whom of course will have non-salariat wives setting higher activity-rates for their households. So it is almost certainly the class of grand*mothers* which is the key variable here, directly influencing their own involvement and indirectly having an effect on grandfathers. Interestingly, this class pattern is reversed with gifts, where higher-paid (but time-constrained) grannies seem to compensate for their lack of contact by giving relatively more frequent presents. The bipolar grandfather distribution concerning gifts is probably itself a further consequence on them of their partners' behaviour.

When it comes to family activities, though, it is the intermediate group respondents, for both grandmothers and grandfathers, who show the highest ratings, reinforcing the impression that it may be within this class, or perhaps in the effects of these types of women's occupations, that the most vigorous extended family networks are found.

Involvement in childcare

This impression is strengthened further by the findings on looking after grandchildren. Grandmothers in intermediate occupations are considerably more likely to undertake the routine childcare tasks of daycare, babysitting and school runs. The more unpredictable help with nursing sick children is distributed very evenly between classes, in line with its random nature. There are fewer differences for grandfathers, although working-class men do appear to take part in more daycare, perhaps because of higher rates of unemployment or early retirement.

Table 10.5 Childcare by social class

% GPs who:-		Salariat	Other	W. Class
Do daycare several times a month	GF	23	26	31
	GM	**21**	**48**	**40**
Babysit several times a month	GF	19	29	18
	GM	18	34	25
Take GC school/nursery in year	GF	30	29	29
	GM	24	34	28
Nurse sick GC in year	GF	13	15	14
	GM	20	19	21
Base	GF	*64*	*54*	*57*
	GM	*64*	*104*	*74*

Note: Group A, bold figures $p<0.01$, [250-253].

Greater childcare activity is also linked with greater say, and as shown in 10.6 intermediate grannies record the highest levels of big or some say, and the lowest levels of not discussing upbringing. But activity is *not* the only class-linked factor with a strong influence on agreement. There is also the matter of moral values. It is well documented (Evans, 2000) that the salariat is generally most progressive in its social and moral attitudes, as befits its elite position in a fast-changing society. So salariat grandparents, especially perhaps grand*mothers*, are rather more likely to be in tune with younger generations on issues of childrearing. This is probably why salariat grandmothers, in spite of their lesser hands-on participation in childcare, record very high levels of agreement with the way that grandchildren are being raised, and minimal *dis*agreement. It would equally suggest that the low levels of agreement indicated by working-class grandmothers, and surprisingly high rate of non-discussion, may be related to the more traditional moral and social values held by them. The high rates of '*mostly* agree' registered by intermediate grandmothers presumably reflect a combination of these two factors – that is their greater participation and say - in a context of moderate ideological compatibility.

Table 10.6 Involvement by social class

% GP responses:-		Salariat	Other	W. Class
Agreement:				
Almost always	GF	41	28	32
	GM	45	39	31
Mostly	GF	35	39	37
	GM	31	49	33
Disagree	GF	12	7	10
	GM	5	7	12
Not discussed	GF	13	18	20
	GM	18	15	24
Say:-				
Some or big	GF	19	27	28
	GM	34	39	30
Base	*GF*	*73*	*78*	*76*
	GM	*64*	*133*	*102*

Note: Group A, NS, [273-5].

Data from other sub-samples

This is a good place to raise the problems of using responses from the parent and grandchild samples to fill out and corroborate the class picture, because it would obviously be very convenient at this point to be able to analyse parents' views about agreement according to class. The problem though, which is self-evident as soon as it is stated, and which turns out to have some bearing on our interpretation of grandparental data too, is that we have no way of knowing from the survey how far grandparents' and parents' households share class positions and lifestyles. In the case of grandparents, we do have survey data about partners' occupation and work status that can be used, as earlier here, to cross-tabulate with respondents to see how many mixed-class households there are. But we cannot do this across generations.

This sort of problem does not arise with lineage, which is clear and objective so that it is not hard to construct complementary categories in different generations, and make precise comparisons of their accounts. We can't do this with class, and it would be a mistake to just assume that class status is commonly enough inherited between generations. Quite apart from anything else, the salariat has grown considerably over the last generation, so that many more parents in the sample belonged to it than grandparents. Similarly the working class has shrunk. Assuming continuity along lines of descent is very risky.

There are sex differences involved too. Because work is a key aspect of male identity, there are many social pressures and processes operating which can lead to class positions being transmitted in a paternal line. For mothers though, certainly for women outside of the working class, work has only quite recently played an important part throughout their adult lives. In the past, women who had careers tended not to have children, and those who had children tended not to have careers. On top of that, since middle-class women had heavy domestic responsibilities until recently, those who did have careers generally needed to have a lot of *non*-career women around them and supporting them. Therefore, very few daughters of women with a strong commitment to work will have been in a position to follow their mothers' paths. All in all, there has been and probably largely still is much less tendency for succession of class status to operate between generations of working women – or even more generally (that is, including sons) in a maternal line.

What this means for present purposes is that we probably cannot expect to find much consistency in the responses of different generations according to class; insofar as we do it is more likely to feature between the accounts of fathers and grandfathers, than between mothers and grandmothers. We should not assume the daughter of a salariat grandmother to be a salariat member herself. Even less should we expect the mother of a salariat mother to be one herself.

Money and advice

The rates of grandparental material and non-material support do not appear to vary greatly according to social class. This is particularly the situation for grandfathers, whose levels of advice to grandchildren, plus frequency of payments to parents to help with grandchildren, show little difference between class groups. When it comes to payments direct to grandchildren, there is perhaps a slight increase as you move down the social scale, in line with simple rates of contact. But the trend is not marked.

Among grandmothers there are more indications of variation. Advice increases with lower social status, reflecting greater time spent with grandchildren and perhaps also, we can surmise, their lesser direct and agreed control over grandchildren's upbringing because of disagreement over values with parents. The most salient variation occurs though with financial transfers to parents, where salariat grannies are well ahead of others – adding to the impression that better off grannies provide less direct caring but more material contributions. There is no clear pattern for payments of money direct to grandchildren. The small differences which do exist here suggest that higher rates of transfers to children form part of the hands-on, proximate and intimate style which includes advice, rather than the more distant relationships associated with higher rates of financial help to parents.

Table 10.7 Money and advice by social class

% GP respondents who:-	GP Sex	Salariat	Other	Working class
Give advice to GC often	GF	9	2	2
	GM	5	13	15
Give advice to GC ever	GF	32	38	27
	GM	32	45	42
Give money to parent often	GF	6	6	7
	GM	18	5	5
Give money to parent ever	GF	36	39	36
	GM	**55**	**32**	**31**
Give money to GC often	GF	10	11	14
	GM	15	17	16
Give money to GC ever	GF	29	35	38
	GM	32	40	42
Base	*GF*	*73*	*78*	*76*
	GM	*64*	*133*	*102*

Note: Group A, bold figures $p < 0.05$, [257-262].

Data from parents on these matters show broadly compatible effects, though not very strongly. Fathers in different classes, just like grandfathers, do not report differences in money payments to parents. The most likely reason for this would seem to be that such material providing is part of men's role in all class contexts, and is fairly constant throughout British society. Mothers however do show a different pattern to grannies. Whereas salariat grandmothers reported most payments, mothers are more likely to indicate it the *lower* their class position. This is, of course, entirely consistent with the grandparental information. For what they are reporting is giving money, which will be related to wealth. Mothers on the other hand are reporting the receipt of money, which will be associated with relative *need*. On the matter of giving money direct to grandchildren it is the fathers and mothers in the intermediate class category who report the highest levels. This does not in the same way match the grandparent data – possibly because of differing class proportions. But it *is* compatible with the parents' reports for frequency of shared activities and care contacts.

Class and role satisfaction

Although class shows a number of interesting links with variations in grandparent activity, it does not stand out in this analysis as a major determinant of grandparenting style. This may be partly because of the problems in measuring and analysing it; but is no doubt also because class factors simply do not have that much effect on lifestyle. This relative lack of importance is endorsed by the findings concerning evaluations of the role, where there are no strong differences. There is a slight tendency for grannies in intermediate occupations to give more positive responses, 74% feeling very close to grandchildren, 70% agreeing strongly that the role is rewarding, and only 32% expressing a desire for a freer life. This is in line with these grannies' slightly closer involvement. But the margins are quite thin.

Table 10.8 Role evaluation by social class

% GPs who:-		Salariat	Other	W. Class
Feel close:-				
Feel very close	GF	65	67	66
	GM	66	74	73
Find Role Rewarding:-				
Agree strongly	GF	58	59	53
	GM	67	70	68
Want free life:-				
Agree/agree strongly	GF	37	47	33
	GM	34	32	36
Base	*GF*	*73*	*78*	*76*
	GM	*64*	*133*	*102*

Note: Group A, NS, [198.199.234].

For grandfathers the comparisons are even tighter, with intermediate grandfathers only fractionally ahead on closeness and role evaluation. However, they are considerably higher on wanting a free life – the only figure in the table to register as significantly different, and also the most divergent from same-class grandmothers. This out-of-step finding may indicate that the greater involvement in family life of this class-category of grandfathers may be taking them towards the edge of their enjoyment of the role. Intriguingly here, if we focus just on the self-employed sector of this class grouping, a definite sexual division emerges which takes grandmothers' rates higher in satisfaction (in both closeness and role evaluation) and grandfathers' lower. So this particular lifestyle looks as if it may be the most consistent with more traditional sex roles (as also fits its conservative political orientation – see Evans, 2000). But the numbers in this class fraction are not large, so that perhaps not too much should be made of this result.

Overall therefore it seems possible that, although there are some variations between class lifestyles, people's satisfactions (and presumably expectations) may be largely contained within them, and the role is judged according to criteria intrinsic to family life which can be met equally within them all.

11

STEP-RELATIONSHIPS

There is one further aspect of variability in grandparenting which should be looked at here, that is step-relationships. The importance of this issue does not lie in its already being an important component of the overall pattern so much as that it is growing in volume and *could* become a significant part of the whole. Step-parenting has always been a part of family life. But in the past it was mainly related to early death, and was more of a constant. More recently it has been linked with the increasing instability of parenting relationships, often followed by (re)marriage to new partners, which is producing a new sort of step-tie that overlaps with natural ties and indeed with other step-bonds. It is this form of step-relationship which is growing, and may become a significant dimension of extended family life. [1]

Step-grandparents in the BSA survey

Step-grandparenting does not yet constitute a very large proportion of the total, and is moreover not that easy to define rigorously. Is formal marriage and then remarriage required, in order to generate it, or does simple cohabitation serve to do this. And if the latter, cohabitation for how long? There is no general consensus on these questions, so in the survey we simply asked people to include step-ties in their lists of relations, and then left it to them to decide what they meant by it, and whom to include.

The numbers of step-relationships for the various sub-samples are given in table 11.1. Step-relationships are shown in the *right-hand* column, with natural descent relationships (grouped by lineage) in the first four columns.

---

[1] There is likewise a growing literature on it, especially in US where it has been a part of most people's lives for some time, e.g. Stacey, 1991, but which is also quite extensive now in Europe. For a range of UK treatments see Elliott, 1996; Dalley, 1996; Haskey, 1996; and Batchelor et al, 1994.

Table 11.1 Numbers of step-relationships in selected ties

Nature of link	MGM	MGF	PGM	PGF	STEP
Respondents:					
Grandparents	*310*	*197*	*229*	*142*	*55*
Adult grandchildren	*256*	*92*	*153*	*53*	*30*
Linking-parents	*287*	*123*	*157*	*82*	*25*

Note: Group A, [229]; Group B, [297]; Group C [370]. (All unweighted).

Comparing natural with step-grandparenting

The numbers of step-relationships are very small in all of the BSA sub-samples, far too small to allow firm conclusions to be drawn from any of them taken by themselves. However, it is also the case that on most issues the pictures emerging from the findings in each of these essentially independent sub-samples are remarkably similar. The effect of step-relationships appears to be definite and consistent, and given this it is certainly worth treating the findings as having some indicative value.

We have therefore organised the data into a set of four-column tables which compare the position of natural grandmothers and grandfathers with *step-*grandmothers and –fathers. As we have seen throughout this report, grandmothers consistently show higher rates of contact and activity than grandfathers. With step-grandparents however this effect is mainly reversed, and it is step-grand*fathers* who mostly record higher levels. In order to make this quickly apparent in the tables, and ease the reading of the data, we have arranged the four columns to run from natural grandmothers on the left, to step-grandmothers on the right. This means that most ratings descend a gradient from high levels on the left of the table to low on the right.

At first sight the nature of this divergence between grandmothers' and step-grandmothers' behaviour may seem paradoxical. After all, they are all *women*, and surely it is the factor of sex which underlies most differences between grandmothers and grandfathers. So why should natural and step-grandmothers be so much less alike than are natural and step-grandfathers?

The answer to this seems likely to be that not only are men and women different, as individuals, but they have a different sort of link with family and community. Women are much closer to the centre of British family life, with men playing a more supporting, marginal role that depends moreover very much on their relationship with a woman or women. Men tend mainly to slot into family structures that are organised by and around women, and their participation is mediated by their relationships with their partners. For many practical purposes it does not make much difference for men whether the offspring in these family groups are their own or their *step*-children/grandchildren. Their role is much the same, and is also more mobile. Men can and do detach themselves from one family group and move on to another. And just as they may become easily incorporated into a new family, they may find it relatively easy to scale down their attachments in previous families. The genial step-father/grandfather is probably an absent or non-resident and inattentive father/grandfather elsewhere.

By contrast, women do not so readily detach and move on. When parents split, it is far more common for mothers to have greater subsequent contact with the children, and to build any new relationships around these children. So while – to consider the extreme scenarios here – fathers or grandfathers may keep moving on to new relationships, largely leaving previous ones behind, mothers who have several partners will tend to collect children from several fathers together in a single household which revolves around her but may involve some continuing ties outside with diverse fathers. At any particular moment, the mother of these children may have a co-resident male partner, who may be an active father or step-father (variously) to them. But the chances of that mother herself being an active step-mother to children of that partner, let alone to children of previous partners elsewhere, are very slender, as are those of the mothers of those other children being active step-mothers to *hers*. A step-father does not have to compete with much continuing interest from a natural father, to the extent that a step-mother will from a natural mother. Indeed, part of the disparity between men and women in the numbers of step-relationships reported may not just lie in a greater tendency for men to remarry and have multiple partners, but also in a lesser tendency for women to regard the offspring of their various partners *as* step-children of their own.

In the grandparental generation the differences are not quite so glaring. Children will have left home to live in their own households, and other partners may well be dead. Where step-grandmothers are replacing maternal grandmothers who are dead, rather than competing with ones who are still alive, then it is easier for them to develop maternal relations with their partners' offspring. Also, many grandmothers are steps not on account of their relationship with their own partners, but as a result of their children's ties with *their* partners. But even here, being a step-grandmother involves ties *through* men (whether sons or daughters' male partners) to offspring whose stronger, maternal ties lie elsewhere. It is a sort of intensified paternal grandmother status, with the added problem of not having a biological tie with the step-offspring to give it all meaning. Thus in all of these situations the essential logic of step-parenting applies – which is that step-fathers/grandfathers are tied into the natural family as adjuncts of a female member of it, and can share in her role in that family, whereas step-mothers/grandmothers are tied into their new family via a male member, and have their new relationships mediated by them. This is surely what produces the reversal of sex-related behaviour which these tables reveal.

Contact and activities

Table 11.2 deals with types of contact and shared activities, and shows that on most counts step-grandparents are by their own reporting less active than natural. On several of them step-grandfathers come top though. Those activities, such as taking grandchildren on family visits, giving and receiving presents, going on holiday together and so on, are in fact just the sort of things that a new member of the family might well spend more time doing. They are fully consistent with the notion that step-grandfathers might feel pulled into more intensive contact with partners' offspring than natural grandfathers would expect to maintain. Step-grandmothers however come at the bottom on virtually all counts, including - very notably – living near to grandchildren. This probably reflects greater mobility by step-grandfathers, who move into a new family's territory, while step-grandmothers may stay closer to their existing, natural families. Geographical proximity is both a measure of, and a reinforcing factor behind, their lesser involvement in their step-families. One measure on which step-grandmothers are above step-grandfathers in this table is frequency of contact by phone – which is both very much a *female* form of behaviour and also something that does not actually depend on nearness.

Table 11.2 Contacts and activities by step-relationships

% of GPs who:-	GM	GF	Step-GF	Step-GM
See GC several times a week	36	30	20	11
Speak on phone several times a week	38	15	5	11
Had no contact in past 2 years	2	6	10	20
Live within 15 minutes	35	38	39	18
Often have GC stay without parents	17	15	20	6
Give/receive presents at least monthly	44	37	50	23
Visit F/R with GC at least monthly	19	11	5	11
Go on hol. with GC w/parents in past year	17	15	15	9
Go shopping etc with GC at least monthly	11	6	10	6
Play games with GC at least monthly	17	12	5	0
Base	*539*	*338*	*21*	*35*

Notes: Group A, (unweighted data), NS, [228.232.238-40.242-3.245-7.249].

The responses of grandparents are broadly replicated in the information given by parents and grandchildren. However, there are definite signs in these other accounts that the reports by step-grandfathers may somewhat inflate their activity.

Not a single respondent in the parents, young people or adult grandchildren groups reported contacts with selected step-grandfathers at a rate of several times a week or more, and all three of these sub-samples gave them generally lower ratings for specific shared activities – in most cases ratings above those for step-grandmothers but well below natural grandfathers.

Childcare and involvement

A very similar picture emerges in relation to looking after young grandchildren. On the routine childcare tasks of daycare, babysitting and taking to-and-from school, step-grandparents show lower rates than natural, with step-grandmothers as the lowest. Step-grandmothers though, as confirmed in parents' responses too, are possibly a little more involved than grandfathers in giving emergency help with sick children. But this is probably more related to sex than to actual closeness. This may also be reflected in the figures given here by Young People on grandparental involvement in looking after them, although it has to be emphasised that in all these groups the number of step-grandmothers referred to in relation to childcare questions is *extremely* small.

Table 11.3 Childcare by step-relationships

% GPs who do:-	GM	GF	Step-GF	Step-GM
Daycare at least monthly	41	29	7	0
Evening care at least monthly	29	24	7	0
Take school/nursery at least monthly	22	18	21	13
Nurse sick child in past year	24	14	0	11
Base	*303*	*204*	*	*
Teenage GC responses:-				
GP looked after in past year	46	30	10	14
Base	*266*	*141*	*20*	*

Note: Group A, (unweighted data), NS, [228.250-3]; Group D (unweighted data), NS, [62.a].

When we come to the quality of involvement in upbringing, these differences stand out clearly again. Thus step-grandfathers themselves adopt a very affable stance here, and see themselves as heavily in agreement with parents, fully participant in discussions (and able to disagree) and enjoying considerable say over what goes on. But again this may give an over-positive view of their role in their newly adopted families, and it has to be said that other participants' perspectives do not produce the same picture. According to parents' responses (not detailed here) while step-grandfathers are seen as having a high level of strong agreement, they are also assigned a higher rate of non-discussion (second only to step-grandmothers, who score a massive 40% on this) and are seen as having no say at all, which is less even than step-grannies.

Insofar as figures based on such small samples are valid, this points to a serious disparity between the way in which step-grandfathers see their own contribution and the evaluations made by other participants in the family. Possibly it shows the enthusiasm for their new families of men who have left behind situations of some tension and difficulty. More realistically, and not entirely in contradiction with the previous point, it may indicate that step-grandfathers become involved in more than they bargained for in their new families, so that what they *do* do feels a lot to them. This interpretation would fit the findings on role satisfaction reported at the end of this chapter.

Table 11.4 Involvement by step-relationships

% GP responses:-	GM	GF	Step-GF	Step-GM
Agreement:-				
Almost always	35	30	53	25
Mostly	39	41	26	32
Disagree	7	8	11	0
Not discussed	19	21	5	39
Say:-				
Some or big	34	25	29	24
Base	*539*	*338*	*21*	*35*

Note: Group A, (unweighted data), NS, [228.273-5].

Money and advice

We find the same sort of pattern here, though less markedly, with natural grandparents predictably coming top on most measures, and step-grandfathers' claims inviting some sceptical attention again. Thus relatively a high proportion of step-grandfathers reported ever giving advice to grandchildren and money to parents, although fewer claimed to give money often, and came behind even step-grandmothers in that respect. Doubts about step-grandfathers' reports are supported by the fact that both the parent and grandchild samples produce *lower* ratings for money transfers from step-grandparents generally.

Table 11.5 Money & advice by step-relationships

% GPs who:-		GM	GF	Step-GF	Step-GM
Give advice:-					
	Often	13	9	0	4
	Ever	45	36	38	22
Give money to parents:-					
	Often	8	6	5	7
	Ever	22	27	30	17
Give money to GC:-					
	Often	16	11	11	11
	Ever	29	26	20	11
	Base	*539*	*338*	*21*	*35*

Note: Group A, (unweighted data), NS, [228.257-62].

Role satisfaction

Responses on role satisfaction present some difficulties of interpretation. But there are ways of pulling the data into a coherent pattern. It is set out in 11.6.

Table 11.6 Role evaluation by step-relationships

% GPs who:-	GM	GF	Step-GF	Step-GM
Feel very close	74	68	58	21
Agree strongly role rewarding	66	57	48	54
Agree /strongly want free life	36	40	57	26
Base	*539*	*338*	*21*	*35*
Linking-parents views:-				
GP/GC are very close	55	44	21	-
Base	*429*	*190*	***	***
Teenage GCs who:-				
Feel very close to GP	34	31	25	-
Agree strongly GP important	37	41	45	-
Disagree strongly that GP not interested	41	40	50	-
Disagree strongly prefer see GP less	27	23	15	-
Base	*266*	*141*	*21*	***
Adult GCs who:-				
Feel very close	34	30	-	-
Base	*285*	*54*	***	***

Note: Group A, NS, [198-9.228.234]; Group B, NS, [297.303]; Group C, NS, [370.376]; Group D, NS, [47a-c.55a].

There is no problem here with the key question on closeness, which refers to specifically selected relationships, and where there is very obvious consistency in the data from each of the sets of informants. Natural grandmothers feel and are felt to be closest, followed by natural grandfathers, then (for all sections except adult grandchildren, where the numbers of relevant cases are *extremely* small) step-grandfathers followed by step-grandmothers. This is one of the most robust findings in the whole survey.

The data becomes harder to interpret though when we move on to the general questions about the role, which do not refer only to selected relationships. Here it is impossible to separate conclusively any effects of *step*ness from the combined effects of other relationships that respondents may have, for if we confine analysis to where respondents have one relationship only there are far too few cases. But this does not make it impossible to draw any inferences at all from this data. Where a question refers generally to grandparenting roles, responses to it can be influenced by any of the grandparenting relationships that a respondent has. This probably has the effect of averaging out their responses a bit, pulling all respondents with several relationships towards the mean level, and thereby flattening response-profiles. But it is, in principle, unlikely to remove the influence of selected relationships altogether.

What in practice this means, to phrase it in a way relevant to the present table, is that we cannot simply interpret step-grandmothers' responses on the question about how rewarding the role is to their being a step-grandmother. Instead we have to phrase the analysis in terms of all that we know about the ties that they may have with grandchildren. What we do know is that, whereas some of the natural grandmothers in the first column may also be step-grandmothers, all of the grandmothers in the fourth column – whether or not they are also natural grandmothers – are definitely *step*-grandmothers. Thus in our four-column comparisons in this present table, where there are clear differences between natural and *step*-grandmothers, which cannot be better explained by reference to other factors, we are entitled to take the step/non-step difference seriously. It is also pertinent to point out here that the general questions on grandparental roles were asked *before* respondents had listed their relationships and one had been selected for detailed investigation.

On this basis, we can say that being a step-grandmother does appear to be related to a somewhat lower evaluation of the role. In spite of being objectively *higher* than step-grandfathers in the reporting of closeness, and clearly regressing towards the mean for all grandmothers, their ratings on the rewarding nature of the role are not only lower than for grandmothers as a whole but nearly as low as for step-grandfathers. Only basic sex-differences, it would seem, ensure that being a step-grandmother holds more value for women than being a step-grandfather does for men. By the same token, it seems safe to conclude that in spite of higher levels of contact, involvement, activity and closeness, step-grandfathers find the role *less* rewarding than do step-grandmothers, as well as than natural grandfathers.

This inference is reinforced by responses on the next variable, as step-grandfathers record much more desire for a life free of family obligations, suggesting perhaps that a heavy burst of involvement in a new family may be quite stressful for a man at that stage of life, particularly if it entails detachment from a previous set of commitments. The divided step-grandfather is pulled in several directions. By contrast, a remarkably low proportion of step-grandmothers express this sentiment. This may in part be because – given the tendency for older men to re-marry younger women – step-grandmothers are on average younger than all other categories of grandparents, and also in some cases may be childless. So other family pressures on them may be minimal. But it is unlikely that these factors would be sufficient to counter any general tendency to find the new or additional step-role stressful if it was. So it is more likely that, because step-grandmothers are not so much pulled into their partners' families, there are few new demands made on them and there is less need to feel over-committed or have any desire to escape. If you are largely excluded from things anyway, there is little to escape *from*.

Equivalent analysis of role satisfaction in the complementary sub-samples is not really possible. Parents were only asked to evaluate closeness of grandparents and grandchildren, and not about other issues or any feelings of their own. Grandchildren were asked to assess a number of propositions relating to three-generational ties, but because of small numbers the only group for which remotely reliable figures are available are in the Young People's survey, where it is possible to compare natural with step-grandfathers (but not step-grandmothers). Step-grandfathers emerge quite well. So either adolescent grandchildren are well-disposed towards them, or make little distinction between them and natural grandfathers. The latter seems quite plausible because young people with step-grandparents are likely to have quite a lot of grandparents altogether, and to get a reasonable amount of attention from them. And it seems to be levels of attention in their lives that grandchildren are responsive to. So they may be likely to have generally positive feelings towards family ties as a whole, where they have more grandparents. This could make family life generally more *important* for them, even though in detail we have seen that levels of closeness toward selected step-grandparents tend to be rather low. So not all perspectives on step-relationships will be informed by the same set of feelings.

Looked at more generally, the growing numbers of step-ties can also be seen as part of a wider process whereby, as sexual partnerships become increasingly unstable, men (in particular) are having a larger number of shallow and shifting family ties, and the relationships that people can trace through them become increasingly short-term. This represents a fracturing of men's social identities, and some marginalisation of their roles – though it also gives them an escape from responsibilities and commitments which they may be finding irksome. For women and their offspring the opposite may apply, as the same process may entail a deepening of *maternal* ties.

Thus the changes which appear to be taking place in grandparenting need to be assessed in relation to changes in extended family life as a whole. The final chapter will broaden the focus of this report by considering what some of the survey findings suggest about the nature and implications of the key changes which have placed grandparenting in greater salience.

GRANDPARENTS IN CHANGING FAMILY LIFE

The BSA survey of grandparenting in Britain is only a *baseline* study. There have been no similar studies in the past with which its findings could be compared. So no direct conclusions about change can be drawn from it. However, it is because grandparenting is, or is assumed to be, changing that the study was carried out at all. And we do have some ideas about the ways in which other (and documented) shifts in family and social life generally could be having an influence on it. So we felt that we should be able to say something about change – even if it was no more than rule out certain hypothetical possibilities.

In the event, though, we feel that it is feasible to suggest with some confidence ways in which grandparenting does appear to be changing, and relate these to some general trends in family life. In particular, the growing fragility of parental relationships, and consequent rising number of single-parent families, are fairly clearly linked to current patterns of external family ties and have an impact on grandparenting. In turn, the materials we have collected in this survey – as also in the related qualitative study documented elsewhere (Arthur et al., 2002) – may themselves help illuminate the state of extended families. We cannot properly understand grandparenting relationships unless we look at them in the context of wider kinship networks and family ties. They are not just bonds between individuals. Grandparental relationships exist because of, and are constantly mediated by, the ties of both parties to other kin, and in particular to the parental generation in between. Even in those very rare (in Britain) instances where parents are minimally involved and grandchildren are being brought up by grandparents, the present or past relationships with these parents set parameters for what is possible and appropriate.

One important aspect of wider family life that we consider to be significant here is the position of men. Greater fragility in parenting ties obviously leads to changes in male participation in domestic and family life. If men and women had the same predisposition to stay with or in touch with children, and similar rates of repartnering and so on, then the fragility of relationships by itself might not augment differences. But these tendencies are not equal. So fathering and mothering are perhaps becoming more different than they were a generation ago, and this has implications for maternal and paternal grandparenting.

We have already plotted a number of sets of effects on grandparenting of male mobility and detachment – as for example in the effects of parental breakdown on lineage patterns and, in the last chapter on step ties. But the materials collected in the survey also allow the isolation of other effects, relating to patterns of residence, which give additional perspectives on sex differences in parenting and grandparenting.

The first set of tables following here presents some of the effects on grandparents' behaviour and attitudes of breakdown in their own relationships – in this case according to whether or not they are *living with* a partner. BSA data does not distinguish between respondents who are still married to and living with their original partners and those who are divorced or separated and now living with new partners. So we cannot analyse the effects of grandparental breakdown in the way we could for parental. But we can look at patterns of behaviour which go with having or not having a current partner, and this proves to be extremely revealing of sex differences. The following tables divide grandparents by sex and according to whether they are currently living with a partner, widowed and living alone, or 'other alone' – that is, separated or divorced and living alone.

Table 12.1 Contacts and activities by who grandparent living with

	Grandmothers			Grandfathers	
% GPs who:-	Other alone	Widow alone	Living with partner	Widower alone	Other alone
See GC at least several times week	**30**	**20**	**36**	**29**	**15**	**27**
Had no contact in past 2 years	**0**	**5**	**2**	**7**	**5**	**9**
Talk on phone several times week	**30**	**18**	**27**	**15**	**10**	**9**
Have GC stay often w/o parents	22	8	19	17	5	9
Visit friends at least mnthly	**17**	**9**	**21**	**10**	**10**	**0**
Give-receive present at least monthly	50	25	50	42	10	18
Holiday with parent in past year	22	11	19	19	5	0
Go shopping at least mnthly	17	16	24	21	15	10
Play games at least monthly	**44**	**21**	**46**	**44**	**20**	**18**
Base	*43*	*167*	*224*	*213*	*43*	*25*

Note: Group A, bold figures *p*<0.05, [232.238.240.242-3.245-7.249].

The first of these tables, 12.1, looking at rates of contact and shared activities, reveals a clear and consistent difference between grandmothers and grandfathers. What it shows is that where grandfathers are living alone, their interaction with grandchildren goes down. For grandmothers on the other hand this is not the case. Widows are lower on all contacts than those living with partners, and this is related above all to greater age. But separated and divorced grandmothers are much on a par with those living with partners, although there is a slight tendency for lower ratings, with (perhaps predictably) a considerably lower frequency of visiting friends and relatives with grandchildren. Interestingly though, they record higher rates of going on holiday with children and grandchildren, and this may point to a common way in which family members keep in touch with grandmothers who are distanced by family breakdown from the rest of an extended family life. Shared holidays, on neutral territory, avoid the risk of awkward encounters.

The figures in this table indicate an important sex difference, and confirm grand*mothers* as the key people around whom most grandparenting activities revolve. Basically the behaviour of grandfathers appears to be more affected by whether or not they are living with a partner.[1] Where grandfathers do live with a partner this is, given their generation, highly likely to be the natural grandmother of their grandchildren, and their contacts with their grandchildren are nearly as high as those of grandmothers with partners themselves. We do need to recognise though that the quality of grandfathers' involvement is unlikely to be so intense. Some of the difference in responses between those grandfathers living alone and those with a partner may come down to the halo effect produced by contact with grandmothers. That is, where grandfathers share a household with an active granny, the heavy involvement of the latter with grandchildren rubs off on the contact levels reported by the grandfather. The existence of this (one-way) effect is itself part of the sex difference in grandparenting.

Any sex differences largely disappear though when it comes to grandparental inputs which do *not* require direct contact. Thus, and as we might expect after findings already presented, widowed grandparents living alone seem no less likely than those living with a partner to give money to parents or grandchildren, and they may even give *more* advice to grandchildren. Perhaps they feel that they have more experience to impart. Grandfathers are rather more like grandmothers here, not only in the frequency of their transfers of money and advice but also in that frequencies are not influenced by cohabitant status. All separated/divorced

---

[1] We do not entirely agree on how to interpret these findings. One of us (J.O.) feels that the best explanation lies in socialisation to sex roles and gender identity, as in Maccoby and Jacklyn 1966; Rossi 1983; Arber and Ginn, 1995. The other (G.D.) feels that the data give support to the argument that male family behaviour is *more* defined and influenced by external, social factors than is female behaviour - which may arise more directly out of internal feelings and sex-linked dispositions. See Mead 1949; Barnes 1973; Dench, 1996 and Hrdy, 1999.

grandparents have low rates of giving money direct to grandchildren too, though this could presumably arise out of the economic consequences of living alone more than from their attitudes, as they share it with widows.

Table 12.2 Grandparents and advice/money by who living with

% GPs who give:-	Grandmothers			Grandfathers	
	Other alone	Widow alone	Living with partner	Widower alone	Other alone
Advice ever*	43	31	41	29	35	-
Money to parent ever	**22**	**11**	**31**	**27**	**25**	**18**
Money to grandchild ever	17	20	33	26	30	18
Base	*43*	*167*	*224*	*213*	*43*	*25*
Base*	*25*	*154*	*150*	*133*	*37*	***

Note: Group A, bold figures *p*<0.05, [257-62].

Sex *differences* show up again when we look at the effect of co-residence on feelings about the grandparent role. For grandmothers there is no real variation in feelings of closeness according to residence. Any slight differences which do emerge here can be attributed to age. For grandfathers though there is a very different picture. Those living with a partner feel nearly as close to their grandchildren as do grandmothers. But those living alone, and especially those separated or divorced, record much lower levels of closeness, indicating that without the influence of a cohabiting partner men may be much less inclined to develop or experience strong emotional attachments to grandchildren.

Table 12.3 Grandparents' role evaluation by who living with

% GPs who:-	Grandmothers			Grandfathers	
	Other alone	Widow alone	Living with partner	Widower alone	Other alone
Feel very close to grndchild	**68**	**65**	**73**	**69**	**40**	**33**
Agree strongly role rewarding	**44**	**59**	**73**	**58**	**48**	**40**
Agree want free life	43	35	33	41	19	50
Base	*43*	*167*	*224*	*213*	*43*	*25*

Note: Group A, bold figures *p*<0.05, [198-9..234].

Distributions on the other two variables here are a little different, reflecting perhaps that they relate more to family life in general rather than to specific relationships. Grandmothers with partners, then widows, show the highest valuation of the role, together with only moderate levels of desire for a life free of kinship obligations. Next come grandfathers living with a partner, who both find their family role less rewarding than do widows and record a higher rate of desiring a free life. For their part, widowers show rather less appreciation of the value of the role, but then record very low rates of wanting a free life, suggesting that (by their age) they have become thoroughly socialised to family life and/or are not being expected to put much into it.

The responses of separated grandparents show some interesting variations on this, illustrating that they do not react to the breakdown of relationships in quite the same ways. Grandmothers living alone, but not grandfathers, express high levels of emotional closeness to selected grandchildren. However, and *like* grandfathers in this respect, they have very low levels of role satisfaction, combined with a high degree of interest in a life free from family obligations. This perhaps indicates that although separated grannies are still very active in their role this does not hold quite the same meaning for them as for grannies with a partner, who find it the most rewarding and show the least desire for freedom. There is some tension and stress suggested here for lone grannies, though not widows, which could arise from problems to do with family splits among offspring following from their own divorce or separation. The breakdown in relationships takes much of the pleasure out of being a grandparent.

It may be different for men. Lone grandfathers are *like* separated grannies in not finding the role very rewarding. But they are *un*like them in that they are not very close or active, and perhaps feel less personal need to be involved in looking after their offspring. So there is less of a contradiction for them.

Effects on Young People

A general consequence of conjugal breakdown - which shows up in our parenting breakdown tables, in the material on step-relationships, and now in the figures linked to grandparental residential status - is for men and for people related *through* men to become less firmly tied in to family networks. As one of us has argued elsewhere (Dench, 1996) this may be producing, insofar as relationships are becoming increasingly fragile, a growing de facto sexual division of labour in which, even though a few men may be doing marginally more family work than before, the domestic realm is increasingly a female domain.

There is another category of respondent who can add a further perspective to this picture, and that is the teenage grandchildren in the Young People sample. Materials organised in terms of their *parents'* relationships have already been considered as part of the parenting breakdown analysis, which draws data from all of the sub-samples. But we have also looked at Young People's responses according to their own living arrangements, to pick out the effects which may derive from *lone* mothering and fathering.[2] The tables which follow here for Young People have three columns. One is for where responding adolescents are living with two parents. One is for those living with a single mother. One is for where they are living with a single father or, in six cases, their natural father and a step-mother. A residual category of around fifteen young people who are not living with either parent is excluded from the tabulations.

Although these three categories do not exactly match those used in other sets of tables, the pattern of findings is comparable. It shows that there is very little difference in the rates of interaction with grandparents between those young people living with two parents (including some step-fathers) and those living with a single mother. This similarity holds in spite of the fact that many grandchildren living with single mothers have very little contact with their paternal grandparents. So the increase in contacts with maternal grandparents for these respondents must balance out for them any reduction in contact with paternal.

Table 12.4 Teenage grandchildren: contact and activities with grandparents by who living with

	Young person lives with:-		
% Grandchildren who:-	**Both parents**	**Single mother**	**Single father**
See GP several times a week	18	20	10
Talk on phone to GP several times a week	12	14	5
Often see GP without parents	25	23	15
Stay with GP without parents in year	33	35	20
GP ever looked after	40	33	30
Base	*332*	*104*	*23*

Note: Group D, NS, [60a-b.61a-b.62a].

There is however a substantial difference between both of these groups and those respondents who are living with a single father (including a few step-mothers), with the latter group often recording only around half the contact frequency of the other two. What these distributions suggest is that the lesser interest of fathers in

---

[2] The categorisation is complicated by the fact that there were rather few (only 17) young-person respondents living with a lone father. So we boosted that group by adding to it the handful of cases where fathers living with their children also had a partner *other than* the respondent's mother. This did not alter the profile of responses noticeably, but it did lift the category just over the threshold of 20 cases which we have taken as a threshold for treating columns seriously. There were however plenty of children living with lone mothers. So where respondents were living with mothers whose partners were *not* their fathers we included these in the 'two parents' column, leaving that for single mothers restricted to *only* that.

family life has implications for the behaviour of their co-resident children – whose interaction with grandparents is rather less than that of children living with their mother, whether or not she is alone. Thus where parents are split, children living with their mother seem to keep in better general touch with grandparents than those living with fathers. But as there are so few single fathers with co-resident children it is impossible to make a close comparison of who the contacts are *with*. Young People's data could not be linked with parents who were not living with them (and not BSA sample members) themselves. Co-resident fathers are presumably more likely than non-resident to be in touch with their children's grandparents, on whom as single parents they would be dependent for a lot of support. The low levels of grandparental contact via single fathers (compared with single mothers) suggest that *either* children living with single fathers are far less likely to be in touch with maternal grandparents than children living with single-mothers are with paternal grandparents – which seems possible but implausible – *or* that fathers are generally less solicitous than mothers in getting children (in this case teenagers) to keep in touch with any grandparents. The latter explanation seems more consistent with the wider flow of findings.

Some support for this interpretation is given by figures showing the effect of Young People's living arrangements on their evaluation of their role as grandchildren. As shown in the next table, there is a clear gradient of closeness running down from the both parents column to single fathers.

Table 12.5 Teenage grandchildren: role evaluation by who living with

	Young person lives with		
% Grandchildren who:-	**Both parents**	**Single mother**	**Single father**
Feel very/fairly close	78	70	55
Agree GP important part of life	82	81	61
Agree would *not* see GP so often if did not have to	9	13	17
Agree GP not very interested in them	8	11	9
Base	*332*	*104*	*23*

Note: Group D, NS, [47a-c.58].

It has to be remembered here that because of the way that the survey questionnaire was constructed, responses in all tables refer to selected ties with grandparents in both lines. We should not therefore expect children of single parents to be in a position to achieve closeness scores (with randomly selected grandparents) as high as those living with both parents, who would in most cases be in contact with grandparents on both sides. In view of this it is striking that children living with single mothers, whose selected grandparents would randomly include paternal as well as maternal, should achieve a rating here almost as high as that for grandchildren *living* with both parents and in touch with both lines.[3]

Note that the value tabulated here, 'very or fairly close' is not the same as used in earlier tables for grandparents' responses (which is 'very close'). The numbers of grandchildren saying they feel very close is much smaller than for grandparents. So the level of closeness we have used here is one which is the equivalent majority measure. If we do select 'very close' instead, then Young People living with single fathers actually come at the top. This is perhaps because the dependence of separated or divorced fathers with co-resident children on paternal grandparents is particularly heavy, so that where grandchildren *are* close to them in these circumstances and at this age it is likely to be *very* close.

But the more general tendency is towards detachment. As the next two variables in the table show, children of single fathers both accord their grandparents a lower level of importance in their life and also more often express a desire not to see them so frequently. This is presumably as a result of spending more time with fathers and picking up male attitudes towards kin. However, they do not seem to blame their grandparents for this, or project their own feelings onto them, as there are equally small proportions in all columns agreeing with the fourth proposition that grandparents are themselves not really interested in the respondents.

Living arrangements and attitudes towards family

The implications of men living alone can be illustrated further by looking at the links between residential status and views on family life in general. To do this we analysed the responses of all survey members to a few attitude questions included in the BSA general survey – not simply the grandparenting module in it.[4] As many respondents were neither grandparents nor parents we have categorised their living arrangements slightly differently, though still with the broad objective of exploring sex differences in family attachment. Three categories were used, generating six columns when divided by sex of respondents. The three groups of living arrangements are as follows:-

> *Traditional.* This grouping includes all married respondents who are either still living with their partner or are widowed. All age groups are represented in this category, although there is some bias towards older people. (Perhaps because widowhood does not involve a split in the

---

[3] Though of course the loss of contact with paternal grandparents would in part be made up for by greater intensity of relationships with maternal.

[4] Not all questions were given to all sample-members though, so column totals vary – adding up variously to one-third, two-thirds or all of the sample.

family, there are few differences in attitudes between widowed and married people that are not matters of age.)

Neo-Conventional. This category embraces those people 'living together as married', both with and without children, plus childless people who are living without a partner. It consists mainly of younger people, but not entirely. The rationale for this category is that it represents that sector of the population which has the most progressive attitudes towards family life, which do however constitute *conventional* views among younger age groups.

Unconventional. The third group consists of people who are parents, but are not living with a partner. Many of the female respondents in this group are single mothers living with children. More of the male respondents are non-resident fathers, living alone. There is a slight bias in this category towards younger people.

When we take these categories and look at the attitudes of people in them towards family life and values we find that there are some interesting differences between men and women, above all within the unconventional category. This does not show up much in relation to those views (to do with sexual mores and gender roles) that are usually regarded as constituting family values. Three typical examples of these are included in table 12.6, as rows three to five, and the responses of the unconventional groups, both male and female, can be seen to lie generally *between* the traditional and neo-conventional categories – certainly with no values falling *outside* of that axis. This is because these values are very much public statements about lifestyle choices, and as such are largely determined by age cohort ideology. On the first of these items here, which is focused on gender, there is a much stronger age effect for women than for men. But the overall principle is the same.

Divergence between men and women emerges when we look at feelings about actual family ties rather than abstract principles. Here unconventional men clearly show greater indifference to these ties, or even hostility, than women. Thus (on the second item in the table) unconventional women record the highest rates of asserting that they themselves try to keep in touch with members of their family – higher even than traditional women. Unconventional men on the other hand show the lowest levels of agreement with this proposition. Given that the general rates of agreement with this statement are higher for women than for men, the unconventional women represent the most female category here, while unconventional men produce the most male response. Sex differences appear to be at their greatest within the unconventional category. There is similar but less extreme divergence in other expressions of the valuation of family life, for example (as shown here in the first item) with more unconventional men than women arguing that they would rather spend time with friends than family.

Table 12.6 'Family values' by living arrangements
(For BSA survey respondents as a whole)

% who:-	Men			Women		
	Trad	Neo-Con	Unconv	Trad	Neo-Con	Unconv
i. Disagree "would rather spend time with friends than family"	**59**	**47**	**42**	62	60	62
ii. Agree "try to stay in touch with (all) my family"	49	46	36	64	61	71
iii. Agree "family life suffers when women work FT"	37	25	35	**30**	**8**	**26**
iv. Agree "good idea live together before marry"	**56**	**80**	**61**	54	74	74
v. Agree sex before marriage is "not wrong at all"	64	81	64	**57**	**84**	**73**
Base (i-ii)	*404*	*179*	*72*	*620*	*199*	*174*
Base (iii-v)	*194*	*90*	*35*	*322*	*89*	*72*

Note: main survey, bold figures $p<0.05$ (within sex).   Meaning of categories as follows: -
Traditional: Married and living with partner *or* widowed.
Neo-Conventional: Living as married (with or without children) or childless
Unconventional: Parent, but **not** living with partner. Either single parent (living with children) or parent living alone.

Here again the data seems to be showing that that fragility in parenting relationships is producing an overall decrease in men's commitment to family life. Fathers not living with partners, whether or not they have direct responsibility for children, have the least positive attitudes towards family relationships, even less than men who have not yet, or have only just, entered into adult family life.[5] Mothers without partners on the other hand (who are of course also more likely than men to have and be influenced by direct parental responsibilities to children) have the most positive attitudes to family life, even more so than mothers in conventional marriages. Thus, paradoxically in view of current stereotypes, 'independent women' may now be the staunchest champions of family values in the sense used here of recognising the importance of family ties. It is the men they are not living with (but *would* have been a generation or so ago) who are the ones actually liberated from family ties, and who show least sympathy for and understanding of them. For women it is having children which produces attachment to family, whereas for men it is living with a partner with children.

This divergence between men and women largely disappears when it comes to views about the role of grandparents. If we run the six propositions concerning grandparents into these analytic categories the results suggest that male and

---

[5] This is a finding that has also been replicated in data from other sources (see Ogg, 2001).

female unconventionals hold a similar, and fairly distinctive, point of view. This combines a more critical assessment of family processes than made by other categories with a tendency towards higher expectations of family support. It adds up to what might be called an outsider view of family life, which is quite similar in many respects to the pattern of responses on these propositions given by BSA sample members who are not part of three-generation families (see table 2.1). It is consistent with their being single parents and requiring greater help, while perhaps at the same time failing to receive all they need or not getting it on the terms that they would like. In the case of men this pattern could perhaps be seen as related to an abdication from direct family roles themselves, and leaving much more to grandparents. The similarity of women's views here suggests that in relation to grandparents some may be drawn to a similar strategy.

Table 12.7   General views on grandparenting by living arrangements
(For BSA survey respondents as a whole)

% who agree:-	Men			Women		
	Trad	**Neo-Con**	**Unconv**	**Trad**	**Neo-Con**	**Unconv**
i. Grandparents have little to teach grandchildren	10	12	11	10	7	9
ii. People don't value grandparents	**53**	**49**	**67**	49	54	52
iii. Parents don't appreciate help GPs give	**41**	**32**	**55**	41	38	52
iv. Grandparents should be involved in upbringing	19	20	29	19	19	25
v. Grandparents interfere too much	11	14	19	**9**	**9**	**15**
vi. Working mothers need the help of grandparents	**74**	**66**	**71**	**78**	**71**	**80**
Base	*624*	*297*	*106*	*925*	*296*	*272*

Note: BSA main survey, bold figures $p<0.05$ (within sex) [incl. A11.a-f].

This effect does not show up in the first variable, concerning whether grandparents have much to teach grandchildren, and where responses seem to be mainly influenced by age. Equally, the second is altogether rather ambiguous (see the commentary in chapter 2) so that it is hard to tell whether the high level of agreement by single fathers should be read as an anti-family response or as a romantic defence of the importance of grandparents. It could even be some of each.

Responses to the next three propositions however show a definite convergence between unconventional men and women. On item three, this entails a firm criticism of parents for not appreciating grandparents, which again could be seen as part of a conservative pro-family reaction to contemporary mores. In item *iv* there is a shared endorsement of grandparental involvement, which is also accompanied by lower levels (not shown here) of *dis*approval of this. Item *v* on the other hand shows stronger criticism of grandparental interference (and weaker disagreement with that proposition) than coming from conventional respondents. Overall this rather suggests that unconventional parents are more inclined to be conscious of the importance of grandparents' behaviour, while perhaps more resentful of the consequences. The sixth proposition is, again, one that is influenced mainly by age.

Impact on Young People

Whatever the exact factors and processes may be which generate this 'outsider' orientation, it is significant that it too seems to rub off onto the children growing up with parents who develop it. When we look at the responses of Young People respondents to the same propositions to do with grandparenting, we find that the children living with single fathers reflect quite closely the unconventional male, and those living with single mothers the unconventional female, points of view. This is illustrated in the next table.

Table 12.8 Teenage grandchild views on grandparenting by who living with

	Young person lives with		
% Grandchildren who agree:-	**Both parents**	**Single mother**	**Single father**
i. Grandparents have little to teach grandchildren	13	13	26
ii. People don't value grandparents	46	51	52
iii. Parents don't appreciate help grandparents give	25	30	35
iv. Grandparents should be involved in upbringing	32	30	44
v. Grandparents interfere too much	11	15	17
Base	*332*	*104*	*23*

Note: BSA Main survey questions, NS. Young people were not asked the question about working mothers.

It is impossible to say how far this pattern of attitudes is likely to be taken with them by these young people when they leave home and join the neo-conventional sector of the population. But it is difficult to imagine that those with unconventional parenting will merge completely into it and just become an indistinguishable part of their cohort.

The future

There may be a risk of indulging in speculation if we venture too far from the actual survey findings. But there does seem to be a case for arguing that the various data collected together here do indicate, even if in a tentative sort of way, that many of the people who have participated most directly in new family forms over the last decade or two do seem now to be among the strongest *supporters* of kinship ties. There is much ambivalence and uncertainty indicated here, to be sure. But what we most certainly do not find in the data is any evidence of a group of people moving eagerly and confidently into new lifestyles which leave behind kinship ties as the basis for their social life. On the contrary: there is, if anything, a holding-onto kinship values among those people who are at the centre of new families – though *not* among those (men) who have moved to their margins. Even the latter, though, albeit for possibly different reasons, do seem to appreciate grandparents and to be in favour of their active involvement. In this respect, the surge of public interest in grandparents can also be interpreted as part of a broad reaction to problems that arise from recent changes in family life generally.

It is important to understand that grandparenting cannot be looked at in isolation from the rest of family life, and in ignorance of wider connections, otherwise social policies relating to it may simply upset other things. As discussed at the outset of this report, the 'disappearance' of grandparents in Britain (during the seventies) took place at a time when kinship ties outside of the household were becoming increasingly defined by the intellectual heirs of the Fabians as infringements of personal liberty and impediments to efficient meritocracy. Mechanisms of the burgeoning welfare state, attempting to rationalise and universalise citizenship entitlements, were busily redefining families as 'benefit units' consisting of no more than one or two adults with the care of (and responsible to the state for) dependent children. Anything beyond this was not just administratively messy but also, in the view of many, hostile to democracy and social justice itself (Barrett & McIntosh, 1982). Even parents had to be treated with caution, lest they hinder their children's emergence in their late teens as capable, self-respecting and autonomous adults.

This mindset came to dominate official data-collection on family life for much of the last decades of the twentieth century, and still informs most academic analysis. It was not surprising to see, for example, that the recent book from the BHPS team in Essex, detailing the lives of modern families, labelled the stage of life after one's children have left home (and are starting – often with more than a little parental help – to establish themselves in the world) as the *Older Childless*. (Berthoud and Gershuny, 2000, p.236.) Continuing denial of extended family; or just male wishful thinking?

To a very large extent, the public commentaries on grandparents over the last few years that have marked their rehabilitation arise out of the notion that the state can no longer manage without them, whether because of declining state resources, growth in need occasioned by parenting crises, or out of realisation that some types of supports for parenting are more appropriate coming from grandparents than from the state. The spirit of these commentaries is epitomised in the call from

Lord Brentford in a House of Lords debate in 1998. "I would plead ... for the Government to say, 'Grandparents, come out of the woodwork. We need you. You are important' ". (Hansard, 1998: {col 1171}) The point is made more generally by Uhlenberg and Kirby that as modern states have started to realise their own limitations, public conceptions of grandparents have changed from interfering and obsolete villains to valued family elders. (Uhlenberg and Kirby, 1998.) Grandparents now, accordingly, are seen as a sort of reserve army of retired parents who, as suitably qualified and related individuals, can be recalled when needed to join the national effort.

But the findings of this present survey indicate that the situation is more complex. Firstly they show that the grandparent/grandchild tie is not just a relationship between individuals that can be understood adequately as a dyad. It is part of a web of overlapping kin relationships which cuts across many households to bind people into all sorts of combinations and collectivities. Secondly they suggest very powerfully that even though modern states may have chosen to overlook their existence, these extended families have been quietly working away all the time in most people's lives, out of the limelight, to provide lifelong mutual personal supports. Paradoxically, new rallying calls for grandparents may be coming just at the moment when consequences of official neglect of wider families are starting to undermine their capacity to do so. For a third implication of our findings is that extended family support systems work most efficiently when burdens are spread fairly widely and thinly across a range of kin.

The activities which lead some commentators to declare that grandparents 'are doing more' these days may well represent in most cases the effect of *concentration* of kinship support into fewer hands – typically those of maternal kin following parenting breakdown. Where parents are together, two sets of interlocking kin groups co-operate to provide help. The survey data presented here show that where parents are together, kin in both descent lines become involved - in a reasonably balanced way. Case materials collected in the parallel qualitative study of BSA families (Arthur et al., 2002) reveal that in many families there are constant negotiations involved between family groups to ensure that some such parity is achieved, and that wide involvement in looking after grandchildren and their interests is generally seen as a good thing, not just for the children themselves but for all participants. What happens when parents are not living together is that such balance is virtually impossible to find. Most demands get focused on a few kin, and the total volume of family support may go down as they cannot carry a multiple load.

Our findings suggest that few if any parties benefit in these circumstances. Although the closeness of maternal grandparents to grandchildren may increase with greater contact when there is separation, levels of role satisfaction go down for all categories of kin. Maternal kin are doing too much. Paternal kin are often excluded. Again, this is confirmed in the qualitative study, which in addition nd that single mothers themselves do not enjoy their greater dependence on a [...] support group. Most of them try to achieve greater autonomy as quickly they can, in some cases through career development, but in many through ening their social network, by finding new partners and, via them, step-kin. Among ordinary families there does seem to be a keen awareness that extensive ship networks are the most reliable source of stability and personal security, through this become the foundation of wider community participation.

Thus policy makers and commentators may be looking to recruit grandparents step in as individual trouble-shooters to plug the childcare gap or become stitute parents. But the bottom-up aspect of current public interest and debate may be fuelled more by concerns about how ailing kinship networks can be forced, and broken community life repaired. At a popular level, discussion of changing role of grandparents inevitably seems to embrace other issues such the growing fragility of conjugal relationships and male abdication from family responsibilities. The essential connectedness of different aspects of family life may well be understood, and above all acknowledged, more readily on any busing estate in the realm than in the corridors of Whitehall.

We have ventured right to the edge of what the survey data can tell us. Some might feel beyond it. But that is because the glimpses of what is out there were so tempting. This study set out to establish, after a long dark age for family research which almost no materials were collected, some reliable indications of the broad features of grandparental relations in Britain today: a modern baseline against which future changes could be charted. That was what we felt was needed. Having done that and seen the outcomes we now hope that instead of just being seen as a study of a particular kinship tie, it may also be taken as a starting point – albeit quite limited in itself – for looking at changes in extended families in a much wider sense. For surely these are what are now being rediscovered.

'Grandparenting' is perhaps a relatively acceptable phenomenon to modernising statists precisely because they can if they wish interpret it simply as a relationship between individuals, rather than as evidence of the continuing relevance of kinship *groupings*. We do however now feel that it is far more than just an interpersonal tie – and that it may represent merely the tip of an iceberg of long-neglected extended family behaviour. There appears to be much of significance to the future wellbeing of our society that is on the move here, and which we can no longer afford to ignore.

APPENDIX A.

QUESTIONS ASKED IN GRANDPARENTING MODULE OF 1998 BRITISH SOCIAL ATTITUDES SURVEY[1]

[190-5] Can I ask you, which of these types of relatives do you have alive at the moment? Please include adoptive and step-relatives:
Son(s)/Daughter(s)
Parent(s)
Grandparent(s)
Grandchild(ren)
Great-grandparent(s)
Great-grandchild(ren)

[196] (For all with children but not grandparents or grandchildren) Can I just check how many of your child(ren), if any, are currently living in your household for at least two nights per week?

[197] (If any)   And do/does your child(ren) who live in your household have any grandparents alive at the moment?

(For all with grandchild) GROUP A
(How much do you agree or disagree with the following statements about your grandchildren?) [198-201]

[198] My grandchildren are a very rewarding part of my life

[199] Now my own children have grown up I want a life that is free from too many family duties

[200] I have often put myself out to help look after my grandchildren

[201] To help look after my grandchildren, I have had to cut down or give up my work

[202] How many grandchildren do you have, including step-grandchildren?

[203] *(For odd serial numbers only)*
Is there one grandchild you have more contact with nowadays than the others?

[204] (If no) Isn't there one grandchild you have a little more contact with nowadays than the other(s)?

[205] *(For even serial numbers only)*
I'd like to ask some questions about just one of your grandchildren. If you tell me their first names, then I can pick just one to ask about.
(For all with grandchild)

[228] Is (name of selected grandchild) your granddaughter, your grandson, your step-granddaughter or your step-grandson?

[229] Is (name of selected grandchild) your daughter's child your son's child, your daughter's step-child, your son's step-child, your step-daughter's child or your step-son's child?

[230] How old was ... last birthday?   [231]   or about how old...?

[232] Have you had any contact at all with him/her in the last two years?

[233] *(If no)* Can I ask how long is it since you last had any contact with ....?

[234] Some people would say they feel 'close' to their grandchildren. Others would say they do not feel particularly 'close'. What about you? Would you say you feel very close to ..., fairly close, not very close, or, not close at all?

[235] Does ...'s mother have a paid job at the moment?

[236] Who does ... live with at the moment?

---

[1] For full wording of questionnaire schedule, and percentage frequencies of all answers, see BSA98 report – Jowell et al, 1999, appendix III.

[237]   May I just check, does … live in the same household as you?

[238]   How often do you see …?

[239]   About how long would it take you to get to where … lives?

[240]   How often do you have contact with him/her by telephone?

[241]   And how often **in the past year** has .. spent time during the day with you, **without** his/her parents?

[242]   And how often **in the past year** has … stayed with you overnight, **without** his/her parents?

[243]   (Using this prompt card) please say how often, if at all, **in the past year**, you have given a present to, or received one from …?

[244]   And how often, if at all, **in the past year** have you and …. gone to a park or playground together without his/her parents?

[245]   (ditto)… gone out shopping, to the cinema, theatre, sports or other event together ….

[246]   (ditto) .. played indoor board or card games, or watched television or video together …

[247]   (ditto)…gone to visit relatives or friends together…

[248]   (ditto)…gone away at weekends or for holidays…

[249]   (ditto)…gone away at weekends or for holidays **with** his/her parents?
         (*Where selected grandchild aged 12 or under*)
         How often, if at all, in the past year have you done any of the following things for ….; including things to help your daughter or son?

[250]   … helped with baby-sitting or child-care **during the day**?

[251]   … helped with baby-sitting or child-care **in the evenings**?

[252]   … taken … to, or collected him/her from, nursery, play-group or school?

[253]   … cared for … in the home, during an illness or after an accident?

[254]   (*Where selected grandchild over 12*) How often, if at all, **in the past year** have you cared for … during an illness or after an accident?

[255]   At the moment, are you **yourself** providing **long-term** care for anyone which takes up a lot of your time? [256 - & who for]

[257]   Have you **ever** helped out …'s parent(s) with **money** for …, or not?

[258]   **In the past year**, have you helped out …'s parents with money for …?

[259]   Have you **ever directly** helped out … with money, or with regular pocket **money**, or not?

[260]   **In the past year**, have you helped out … **directly** with money?

[261]   (*Where grandchild 4 or more*) Some grandchildren, as they grow older, may need **advice** on things. Have you **ever** given … this sort of **advice**, or not?

[262]   **In the past year**, have you given … this sort of advice?

[263]   May I just check, are both …'s **own** parents still living?

[264]   And are …'s parents – together, separated, or divorced?

[265]   (*If not together*) How long ago was the (separation/divorce)?

[266]   (*If GC father dead*) How long ago did …'s father die?

[267]   (*If GC mother dead*) How long ago did …'s mother die?
         (*If GCs parents not together*) At the time of the (death/breakup)…

[268]   Did … stay with you for some of the time?

[269]   Did you have **more** contact with …?

[270]   Did you have **less** contact with…?

[271]   Did it become more difficult to keep in contact with …?

[272]   Were you not allowed to see …?

[273]   Grandparents and parents do not always agree on how best to bring up children. Please say which applies to you and …'s parents about ..:-
         We have agreed about almost everything
         We have agreed more often than not
         We have **dis**agreed more often than not
         We have **dis**agreed about almost everything
         Upbringing has not really been discussed

[274]   (*Where selected grandchild under 16*) When important decisions are being made that affect ..., **nowadays**, do you usually have a big say, some say, not a very big say, or no say at all?

[275]   (*Where selected grandchild 16 or over*) When important decisions were being made that affected ..., when he/she was younger did you feel you usually had a big say, *etc* ?

(For all with grandparents) <u>GROUP B</u>
(How much do you agree or disagree with the following statements about your grandparents?) [276-279]

[276]   My grandparents are an important part of my life

[277]   I wouldn't see my grandparents as often as I do if I didn't have to

[278]   My grandparents are not very interested in my life

[279]   I don't see as much of my grandparents as they would like

[280]   How many grandparents do you have alive, including step-grandparents?

[281]   (*For odd serial numbers only*)
Is there one grandparent you have more contact with nowadays than the others?

[282]   (If no) Isn't there one grandparent you have a little more contact with nowadays than the other(s)?

[283]   (*For even serial numbers only*)
I'd like to ask some questions about just one of your grandparents. If you tell me their first names if you know what they are or, if not, what you call each of them, then I can pick just one to ask about.
(*For all with grandparent*)

[297]   Is (name of selected grandparent) your grandmother, your grandfather, your step-grandmother or your step-grandfather?

[298]   Is (name of selected grandparent) your mother's parent, your father's parent, your mother's step-parent, your father's step-parent, your step-mother's parent or your step-father's parent?

[299]   How old was ... last birthday?   [300]   or **about** how old?

[301]   Have you had any contact **at all** with him/her in the last two years?

[302]   (If no) About how long is it since you last had any contact with ...?

[303]   Some people would say they feel 'close' to their grandparents. Others would say they do not feel particularly 'close'. What about you? Would you say you feel very close to (grandparent) etc as [234]

[304]   May I check, does ... live in the same household as you?

[305]   How often do you see ...?

[306]   About how long would it take you to get to where ... lives?

[307]   How often do you have any contact with him/her **by telephone**?

[308]   And how often **in the past year** have you spent time during the day with ... without your parents?

[309]   And how often **in the past year** have you stayed with ... overnight, **without** your parents?

[310]   (Using this prompt card) please say how often, if at all **in the past year**, you have given a present to, or received one from, ...?

[311]   And how often, if at all, **in the past year**, have you and ... gone out shopping, to the cinema, theatre, sports or other event together?

[312]   (ditto) .. played indoor board or card games, or watched television or a video together?

[313]   (ditto) .. gone to visit relatives or friends together?

[314]   (ditto) .. gone away at weekends or for holidays **without** your parents?

[315]   (ditto) .. gone away at weekends or for holidays **with** your parents?
How often, if at all, in the past year have you done any of the following things for ... without your mother or father, but including things done to help your mother or father?

[316]   .. helped ... with the shopping?

[317]   .. helped ... with household jobs, like cooking, washing or repairs, or with gardening?

[318]   .. taken … to, or collected him/her from, places he/she needed to go?

[319]   .. cared for … in the home, during an illness or after an accident?

[320]   At the moment, are you yourself providing long-term care for anyone which takes up a lot of your time? [321] .. & who for?

[322]   Has … **ever** directly helped you out with **money** or with regular pocket-money, or not?

[323]   **In the past year**, has … helped you out directly with money?

[324]   Some grandchildren as they grow older, may need advice on things. Has … ever given you this sort of **advice**, or not?

[325]   **In the past year**, has … given you this sort of advice?

[326]   May I just check, are both your own parents still living?

[327]   And are your own parents together, separated or divorced?

[328]   (*If not together*) How long ago was the (separation/divorce)

[329]   (*If father dead*) How long ago did your father die?

[330]   (*If mother dead*) How long ago did your mother die?

        (*If parents not together*) At the time of the (death/breakup)…

[331]   Did you stay with … for some of the time?

[332]   Did you have **more** contact with …?

[333]   Did you have **less** contact with …?

[334]   Did it become more difficult for you to keep in contact with …?

[335]   Were you not allowed to see …?

[336]   Parents and grandparents do not always agree on how best to bring up grandchildren. Please say which applies to … and your parents:-

        They have always agreed about almost everything

        They have agreed more often than not

        They have disagreed more often than not

        They have disagreed about almost everything

        Upbringing has not really been discussed

(For all with<u>out</u> grandchildren/grandparents, but <u>with</u> child(ren) with grandparent(s))
GROUP C

([338-369] = Questions for selecting particular child and grandparent)

[370]   Is … (selected grandparent) …'s (selected child) grandmother, his/her grandfather, his/her step-grandmother or his/her step-grandfather?

[371]   Is he/her on …'s mother's side, or his/her father's side?

[372]   How old was … last birthday?   [373} or about how old?

[374]   Has … had any contact **at all** with … in the last two years?

[375]   (If no) About how long is it since … had any contact with …?

[376]   Some grandchildren and grandparents would say they feel 'close'. Others would say they do not feel particularly 'close'. What about … and …? Would you say that they feel very close to each other, fairly close, not very close, or, not close at all?

[377]   Does …'s mother ('Do you?' if female) have a paid job at the moment?

[378]   Who does (child) live with at the moment? (Both parents or one …)

[379]   May I check, does (grandparent) live in the same household as you and (child)

[380]   How often does (child) see (grandparent)?

[381]   About how long would it take (child) to get where (grandparent) lives?

[382]   How often does (child) have any contact with (grandparent) by telephone?

[383]   And how often **in the past year** has (child) spent time during the day with (grandparent) without his/her parents?

[384]   And how often in the past year has (child) stayed with (grandparent) overnight, without his/her parents?

[385]   (Using this prompt card) please say how often, if at all, **in the past year**, (child) has given a present to, or received one from, (grandparent)?

[386]   And how often, if at all, in the past year, have ... and ... gone out shopping, to the cinema, theatre, sports of other event together without his/her parents?

[387]   (ditto) .. played indoor board or card games, or watched television or a video together without his/her parents?

[388]   (ditto) .. gone to visit relatives or friends together without his/her parents?

[389]   (ditto) .. gone away at weekends or for holidays together without his/her parents?

[390]   (ditto) .. gone away at weekends or for holidays together **with** his/her parents?

How often, if at all, **in the past year** has (child) done any of the following things for (grandparent) without his/her mother or father, but **including** things done to help his/her mother or father?

[391]   .. helped ... with the shopping?

[392]   .. helped ... with household jobs, like cooking, washing or repairs, or with gardening?

[393]   .. taken ... to, or collected him/her from, places he/she needed to go?

[394]   .. cared for ... in the home, during an illness or after an accident?

(Where selected child aged 12 or under)

How often, if at all, in the past year has (grandparent) done any of the following things for (child) including things to help (child's) parents?

[395]   ... helped with baby-sitting or child-care **during the day**?

[396]   ... helped with baby-sitting or child-care **in the evenings**?

[397]   ... taken ... to, or collected him/her from, nursery, play-group or school?

[398]   ... cared for ... in the home, during an illness or after an accident?

[399]   *(Where selected grandchild over 12)* How often, if at all, **in the past year** has (grandparent) cared for (child) during an illness or after an accident?

[400]   At the moment, is (grandparent) providing long-term care for anyone, that takes up a lot of his/her time?   [401 & who for]

[402]   Has (grandparent) **ever** helped you out with **money** for (child) or not?

[403]   In the past year, has (grandparent) helped you out with money for (child) ?

[404]   As far as you know, has (grandparent) ever directly helped (child) out with money, or with regular pocket money, or not?

[405]   In the past year, as far as you know, has (grandparent) helped (child) out directly with money?

[406]   Are you and (child's other parent) together, separated or divorced?

[407]   *(If not together)* How long ago was the (separation/divorce)?

[408]   (If widowed) How long ago did your (husband/wife/partner) die?

(If parents not together) At the time of the (break-up/death) ...

[409]   Did (child) stay with (grandparent) for some of the time?

[410]   Did (child) have **more** contact with (grandparent)?

[411]   Did (child) have **less** contact with (grandparent)?

[412]   Did it become more difficult for (child) to keep in contact with (grandparent)?

[413]   Was (child) **not** allowed to see (grandparent)?

[414]   Grandparents and parents do not always agree on how best to bring children up. Please say which applies best to you and (grandparent):- card as for [273]

[415]   *(Where child under 16)* When important decisions are being made that affect (child) nowadays, does (grandparent) usually have a big say, some say, not a very big say, or, no say at all?

[416]   *(Where child 16 or over)* When important decisions were being made that affected (child) when she/he was younger, did (grandparent) usually have ...(same response options)?

(For teenage grandchildren in YOUNG PEOPLE'S SOCIAL ATTITUDES survey) GROUP D

[47]   How much do you agree or disagree with each of these statements about you grandparents?

a   My grandparents are an important part of my life

b   I wouldn't see my grandparents as often as I do if I didn't have to c   My grandparents are not very interested in my life

[49]   How much do you agree or disagree with each of these statements about grandparents?
           (49.a – 49.e ---same propositions as general questionnaire A11, a-e, as given below)

[50]   Can I just check how many grandparents you have? (Grandparent selected [51-54]

[55]a   Is (grandparent) your grandmother, your grandfather, your step-grandmother, or, your step-grandfather?

[55]b   And is she/he your mother's parent, your father's parent, your mother's step-parent, your father's step-parent, your step-mother's parent, or, your step-father's parent?

[56]a   How old was (grandparent) last birthday, or are you not really sure?

[56]b   About how old do you think she/he is?

[57]a   Have you had **any** contact **at all** with her/him in the last **two** years?

[57]b   About how long is it since you last had any contact with (grandparent)?

[58]   Some people would say they feel 'close' to their grandparents. (Same as [303])

[59]   Does (grandparent) live with you?

[60]a   How often do you see (grandparent)

[60]b   And how often do you talk with her/him on the **telephone**?

[61]a   How often **in the past year** have you spent time during the day with (grandparent) **without** your parents?

[61]b   And how often, **in the past year**, have you stayed with (grandparent) overnight, **without** your parents?

[62]a   Has there ever been a particular time in your life when (grandparent) was very involved in looking after you?

[62]b   Why was that?

           (Question for all British Social Attitudes 1998 respondents)

[A.11]   How much do you agree or disagree with each of the following statements?

a   People today don't place enough value on the part grandparents play in family life

b   In most families, grandparents should be closely involved in deciding how their grandchildren are brought up

c   Grandparents have little to teach the grandchildren of today

d   Many parents today do not appreciate the help that grandparents give

e   Grandparents tend to interfere too much with the way their grandchildren are brought up

f   With so many working mothers, families need grandparents to help more and more

Appendix B.

Explaining Random and Most Contact streams

All respondents in the BSA sample were asked to say which categories of lineal relatives they had alive - son or daughter, parent(s), grandparent(s) grandchild(ren), great grandparent(s), great grandchild(ren). Those with a grandchild were put into a grandparents sub-sample (sometimes abbreviated in the report to 'GPs', sometimes labelled Group A) and subsequently they were asked to comment on their relationship with a selected grandchild. Those with a grandparent were placed in an (adult) grandchild sub-sample (GCs or Group B) and they were then asked about their relationship with a selected grandparent. Those without either grandchildren or grandparents, but with a dependent child living with them who did have a grandparent alive, were put in a 'linking parent' sub-sample (LP or Group C), and these respondents reported on the relationship between one of their children and one of that child's grandparents. Eleven respondents had both a grandchild and a grandparent alive. These were allocated to the grandparent group.

Of the 3,146 BSA respondents, 933 were thus enlisted as grandparents, 584 as adult grandchildren, and 674 as linking parents. It should be noted that these categories are mutually exclusive. This is to say that in some case, respondents who were identified as grandparents could also be grandchildren (n=9), but these respondents remained exclusively in the grandparent group. More importantly, grandchildren could also be linking parents (n=274, 47%), so that these grandchildren only replied to questions concerning their grandparents and not in the context of being a linking parents. Linking parents were however, neither grandchildren nor grandparents.

In addition to the main survey, BSA98 also surveyed young people living in the households of respondents. This resulted in a Young People sample of 11-17 year olds, of whom 88% had at least one grandparent alive. These respondents were defined by us as a 'teenage grandchild' sample, i.e. sample D.

Table B.1 Structure of the sample

A	B	C	D
GRANDPARENTS	**ADULT GRANDCHILDREN**	**LINKING PARENTS**	**TEENAGE GRANDCHILDREN**
answer questions about their relationship with a selected grandchild (*n=933*)	answer questions about their relationship with a selected grandparent (*n=584*)	answer questions about the relationship between one of their children and a selected grandparent (*n=674*)	answer questions about their relationship with a selected grandparent (*n=474*)

When designing the grandparenting survey, we decided that in order to be able to analyse grandparenting relationships fully and reliably we should concentrate on exploring the behaviour of sub-sample members regarding one relevant family member (or family relationship). Thus each member of the grandparent group, for example, would be asked in detail about their ties with a particular grandchild, each grandchild about one grandparent, and each linking parent about one grandchild/grandparent pair which they mediated. Of course, most respondents had more than one eligible relative. But it was not possible to ask detailed questions about each family member in turn, since this would have considerably extended the length of the interview. In designing the research procedure therefore, we had to find a way to select a relevant family member which would allow us to draw valid and reliable conclusions about that type of relationship in general.

There were different ways in which this selection could be made. We had to choose between these, and in the event we did not select all relationships in the same way. We decided that it was essential to pick some pairs of relatives at random - so that the data generated by them could be taken as directly representative of that relationship in the general population. Others however were identified on a most-contact basis, in order to give us a fuller set of findings relating to the most active and intensive relationships. It should be noted that most-contact could either result as an initiative of the respondent or by the identified role relationship, or by a combination of both.

To this end, all sub-sample members were assigned to one of two streams, on the basis of their serial number in the survey. For those respondents with an *even* serial number, a relevant family member was selected randomly by the interviewer from those available. If there was only one, this person was automatically selected. The other respondents, with *odd* serial numbers, were asked if there was a particular family member with whom they had more contact than others.

This second procedure led to a number of outcomes other than the simple identification of a most-contact pairing. Around one quarter of grandparent respondents with odd serial numbers had only one grandchild, and so had no choice to make. For analytic purposes these were no different to grandparents in the random stream with only one grandchild - and indeed could be effectively included with them. On top of this, some of the grandparents with more than one grandchildr pointed out that they always saw several as a group, and so could not really say that they had more contact with one of them. These cases were therefore transferred to the group with even serial numbers, and a *random* selection was made. The flow-diagram figure B.1 illustrates this.

Figure B.1 Selection procedure for streams of sample

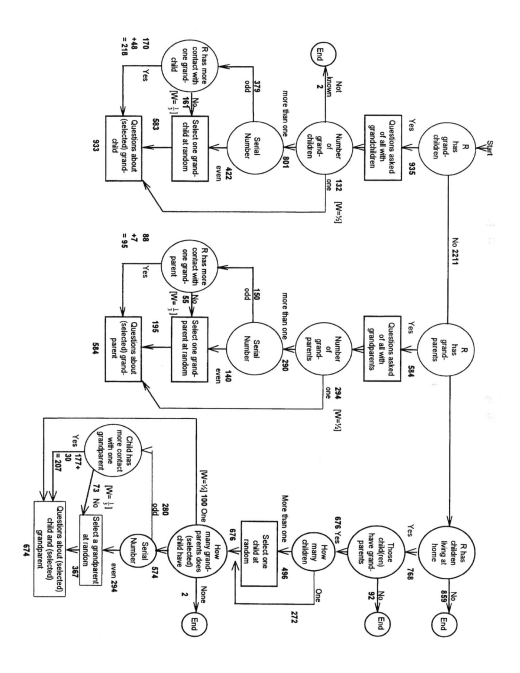

Grandparenting in Britain

Table B.2 summarises the outcome of this procedure.

Table B.2 Random and most contact streams of sample

A		B		C		D
GRANDPARENTS N= 933		**ADULT GRANDCHILDREN** N=584		**LINKING PARENTS** N=674		**TEENAGE GRANDCHILDREN**
Random *(n=715)*	Most contact *(n=350)*	Random *(n=489)*	Most contact *(n=389)*	Random *(n=467)*	Most contact *(n=307)*	(All random) *(n=474)*

Grandparents and grandchild weights

The procedure for identifying the selected lineal relative described above required weights to be applied separately to both streams (random and most-contact) within the three sub-samples (Groups A, B, and C). These weights correct for the different methods of selection used. In addition, these weights include the effect of the main sampling weight (WtFactor), which took into account the fact that not all the units covered in the survey had the same probability of selection (see Appendix 1 in Jowell et al., 1999). Table B.3 gives details of the different weights used in the survey.

Table B.3 Weighting procedure

Weight variable name	Group selected by weight	Unweighted sample size	Weighted sample size
WtFactor	**Questions asked about all respondents**	3146	3146
	Questions asked about grandchildren:		
WTGrchMo	- asked about most contact grandchild	350	284
WTGrchRa	- asked about random grandchild	715	542
	Questions asked about grandparents:		
WTGrpaMo	- asked about most contact grandparent	389	242
WTGrpaRa	- asked about random grandparent	489	305
	Questions asked about children and grandparent:		
WTParGMo	- asked about most contact grandparent	307	257
WTParGRa	- asked about random grandparent	467	368
YPWT	**Questions asked about Young Persons**	474	474

The teenage grandchildren were surveyed in a separate operation which did not involve splitting them into two streams with differential weighting. The weighting procedures in effect produced 7 different samples, each of which had to be treated as a separate unit of analysis. It is not possible, for example, to test for measures of association or to use any other statistical tests in comparing the responses of grandparents (Group A) with the responses of any other group, since each sample has its peculiar probability of selection characteristics. In other words, each sample is different, and combining two or more samples to form a single, random sample (the basic assumption for using inferential statistics) is not possible. As can be seen in table B.3, the weighting procedure reduces the size of each sample. Throughout the report, the base figures shown in the tables are always given for *unweighted* samples. Weights are applied for all figures in the tables unless otherwise stated.

This limitation of the data does not mean however, that responses of different groups cannot be compared. In many tables, we have presented data from the separate samples alongside each other so that comparisons can be made, particularly where this concerns those of grandparents in Group A and linking parents in Group C.

Use of different sample streams in the analysis

As a result of this selection procedure the random groups in each sub-sample ended up considerably larger than the most-contact. For the purpose of the original BSA chapter, we confined ourselves to analysing the random component when dealing with specific grandparent/grandchild ties. But for the present report we have also drawn on the most-contact sets of data as well.

Where the analysis is confined to one Group only, Pearson's chi-square statistic is used to test the hypothesis of no association of columns and rows in a crosstabulation. The statistic is only used where a) the total base for a column or row exceeds 20, or b) where no cell count is lower than 5. Where the statistic is not significant this is marked 'NS' in the note at the bottom of each table. For many of the tables presented in the text, the sample (or sub-sample) size remains small and therefore there are risks of Type 1 errors (concluding that there is a relationship where there is not) even where a significant result is obtained. Given this limitation of the data, we have opted to present a wide range of tables from all the Groups in order to obtain the best available descriptions of differences between variables within Groups and differences between similar variables across Groups.

APPENDIX C.

PROFILES OF SAMPLES AND GRANDPARENT/GRANDCHILD PAIRS

This section presents comparisons of the different streams within the grandparenting module **before** the applications of weights.

Group A Grandparents

Tables C.1 and C.2 which follow here show the ages of grandparents and selected grandchildren in Group A.

Table C.1 Age of grandparent
(unweighted data, column %)

Age of grandparent	Most contact (n=218)	One grandchild only (n=132)	Random selection (n=421)	Undifferentiated group (n=162)
30-39		2		
40-49	3	29	5	6
50-59	18	27	21	21
60-69	33	19	32	30
70-79	26	15	26	28
80+	20	8	15	15
Total	**100**	**100**	**100**	**100**

Read: 3% of grandparents in the 'most contact' group are aged 40-49 years compared with 29% of grandparents in the 'random' group, etc.

Table C.2 Age of grandchild selected by grandparents
(unweighted data, column %)

Age of grandchild	Most contact (n=218) Col %	One grandchild only (n=132) Col %	Random selection (n=421) Col %	Undifferentiated group (n=162) Col %
Under 6	27	62	27	30
6-13	33	22	39	38
14+	39	16	34	30
Not known	-	-	-	2
Total	**100**	**100**	**100**	**100**

The number of grandparents identified was 935, but two of these grandparents did not answer any of the questions on grandchildren (presumably because they did not know of their whereabouts). The base number of grandparents is therefore 933 respondents. The youngest grandparent identified was aged 37 years and the oldest grandparent was aged 99 years. Conversely, the youngest grandchild was aged less than 1 year and the oldest grandchild was aged 58 years.

Table C.1 shows that the majority of respondents in the 'most-contact' group (79%) were aged 60 years and above. A similar pattern is found also among the 'undifferentiated' group, where over two-thirds of grandparents were aged 60 years and above. In contrast, among the 'one grandchild' group, the majority (58%) are aged 60 years and below. As table C.2 indicates, the 'one grandchild' group have also selected a much younger grandchild than the other three groups.

This difference in the age of the selected grandchild between the four groups is also reflected in the mean age of the grandchild in the 4 groups, as is shown in table C.3 below.

Table C.3 Mean age of grandparent and selected grandchild

	Most contact (n=218)	One grandchild only (n=132)	Random selection (n=421)	Undifferentiated group (n=162)
Mean age of grandparent	69	67	57	67
Mean age of grandchild	14	7	14	11

Differences between these 4 groups on some of the key variables are presented in table C.4.

Table C.4 Four categories of grandchild selection
(unweighted data, column %, n=933)

Characteristics of grandchild	Most contact (n=218)	One GC (n=132)	Random (n=421)	Undifferentiat -ed (n=162)
Had contact in last 2 years *(*)*	100	94	96	94
Feels very close to grandchild *(**)*	81	79	64	62
G/child offspring of daughter *(NS)*	63	65	56	49
Granddaughter selected *(NS)*	55	52	47	46

Lives 15 mins away *(**)*	45	42	30	23
Has weekly physical contact *(**)*	45	46	25	22
Has weekly phone contact *(**)*	31	32	19	16
Plays games, watches TV weekly *(**)*	21	22	13	6
Goes on holiday yearly with parents *(NS)*	18	17	17	17
Goes on visits monthly without parents *(**)*	9	12	5	3
Goes holiday yearly without parents *(NS)*	9	7	7	9
Goes shopping weekly *(**)*	8	12	4	0
Goes to park weekly *(NS)*	6	10	5	3

*p=<.01
**p=<.001

Read (example): '45% of respondents whose serial number was odd and who have more contact with one of their grandchildren than with others live 15 mins away from that grandchild, compared with 42% of respondents who have one grandchild only, and 30% of respondents whose serial number is even and who have several grandchildren (for whom their 'selected' grandchild was randomly chosen by the interviewer), and 28% of respondents whose serial number was odd, had several grandchildren among whom they saw all of them equally'.

Table C.4 above shows higher rates of grandparental involvement among the 'most contact' and 'one-grandchild' groups than among the 'random' and 'undifferentiated' groups. In fact this latter group seems to have the lowest rate of involvement, suggesting that one of the reasons that grandparents did not see one grandchild more than another is that they are slightly less 'committed' group, although the similarities between all groups are equally as important as any differences. Table C.5 contains the mean ages of the GPs and their selected grandchild and the number of grandchildren identified.

Table C.5 Characteristics (means) of grandparents (weighted data)

	'Most contact' group		'Random' group	
	GM	**GF**	**GM**	**GF**
Age	64	65	65	64
Age of selected grandchild	12	11	12	9
Number of grandchildren	4.3	5.0	4.4	4.0

Group B Grandchildren

The base number of grandchild respondents was 584. The youngest grandparent identified was aged 54 years and the oldest grandparent was aged 97 years. Conversely, the youngest grandchild was of course, the youngest respondent in the survey (17), and the eldest grandchild was aged 47 years (mean age 28 years). Table C.6 gives mean figures for the age of grandchildren and their numbers of grandparents.

Table C.6 Characteristics (means) of grandchildren (n=584)

	'Most contact' group		'Random' group	
	Grandson	**Grandaughter**	**Grandson**	**Grandaughter**
Age	26	27	27	27
Number of grandparents	1.9	1.5	1.9	1.9
	* 29 missing cases		** 57 missing cases	

Differences between the four groups on some of the key variables are presented in table C.7.

Table C.7 Four categories of grandparent selection (unweighted data) (n=584)

Characteristics of grandchildren's relations with selected grandparent	'Most contact' group (n=95)	'One grandchild only' (n=294)	'Random' selection (n=140)	'Undifferentiated' group (n=55)
Had contact in last 2 years *(*)*	99	86	87	84
Given or received present in last year (NS)	95	88	89	74
Grandmother selected *(**)*	79	83	64	44
Matrilineal g/parent selected *(NS)*	60	63	60	65
Helped with jobs in past year (*)	51	26	33	30
Feels very close to grandparent *(**)*	44	30	28	37
Helped with shopping in past year (NS)	39	30	19	22
Accompanied somewhere in last year (NS)	39	32	22	18
Spend day together often without parents (**)	39	28	24	39
Has done activities together in last year (*)	39	25	26	18
Lives 15 mins away *(NS)*	35	25	25	26
Has weekly phone contact *(**)*	20	6	4	9
Looked after when ill in last year	18	11	9	15

(NS)				
Has stayed overnight in past year (NS)	17	18	15	9
Has weekly physical contact *(NS)*	15	9	10	6
Goes holiday yearly without parents *(*)*	11	2	4	2
Plays games, watches TV weekly *(*)*	10	7	1	6
Goes on holiday yearly with parents *(NS)*	9	4	5	9
Goes on visits monthly without parents *(NS)*	5	4	0	4
*p=<.01;**p=<.001				

Note: Grandchildren who have no contact with selected grandparent (n=66) and grandchildren who live with a grandparent(s) not included.

Group C Linking Parents

See flow diagram B.1 for selection of grandparent. The number of respondents answering questions on behalf of their children was 674. The youngest grandparent identified was aged 42 years and the oldest grandparent was aged 92 years. Conversely, the youngest grandchild identified was under 1 year old and the oldest grandchild was aged 34 years. The youngest parent (respondent) was aged 20 years and the oldest was aged 63 years.

Differences between the four groups on some of the key variables are presented in table C.8.

Table C.8 Four categories of grandparent selection, linking parents (unweighted data) (n=674)

Characteristics of grandchild	Most contact (n=204) %	One grandparent only (n=100) %	Random selection (n=290) %	Undifferentiated group (n=73) %
Had contact in last 2 years(**)	99	94	93	99
Feels very close to grandparent(**)	63	47	46	37
Grandparent of mother(ns)	70	59	59	56
Grandmother selected(***)	80	75	58	64
Give or receives presents monthly(**)	52	34	37	33
Lives 15 mins away(**)	50	45	34	40

Has weekly phone contact(*)	48	32	33	32
Spent day often without parents(***)	47	30	31	26
Has weekly physical contact(***)	43	24	23	19
Helped with chores in past year(ns)	42	33	35	32
Helped with shopping in last year(**)	39	31	28	29
Plays games, watches TV weekly(***)	28	5	28	12
Goes on holiday yearly with parents(ns)	28	11	21	22
Goes on visits monthly without parents(**)	23	12	11	5
Spent night often without parents(**)	19	7	11	11
Does activities together weekly(***)	11	2	4	1
Goes holiday yearly without parents(ns)	8	2	10	8
Helped with transport in last year(*)	8	15	4	8
Cared for when in last year(ns)	6	9	3	7

*p<.01; **p<.001;***p<.0001

DEMOGRAPHIC AND COMPARATIVE DATA

The place of grandparents within family generations

In Chapter 4 we showed how despite some minor changes and the possibility of further change in the future, in most respects the demographic features of grandparenting remained stable in the twentieth century. There is however, one important change which represents a radical departure from these trends. This is that grandparents today, unlike in the past, are no longer at the generational head of the family as a result of the gains in longevity that have been made during the past 40 years. Among respondents who were grandparents in the BSA 1998 survey, almost 1 in 4 (23%) had at least one parent still alive (see figure 4.2).

The dual effect of smaller family sizes and increased longevity has given rise to what some commentators refer to as a 'beanpole' type structure of family generations, with fewer members across several generations and a verticalisation of generational depth (Bengston and Achenbaum 1993). It is now no longer uncommon for four or five generational families to exist. As they age, grandparents in turn become *great-grandparents*, and the proportion of this latter group has increased dramatically within the population, such that over 40% of respondents aged 80 years and above in the BSA 1998 survey were great grandparents. Thus in the later stages of the life course, individuals occupy the role of grandparent and great-grandparent simultaneously. In the same way that older adults are spending an increasing amount of time in retirement, the time-span in which the grandparenting role is occupied can today account for up to 50% of an individual's life span.

The 'bean-pole' structure of the contemporary family is confirmed by the BSA 1998 survey data. All respondents in the survey were asked whether they had a parent, grandparent, child and grandchild alive. Five generational families are to be found in every age group from 18 to 69 years, as table D.1 shows.

In early adult life, over 80% of the population live within three or more generational families, most of which concern the triad of child/parent/grandparent. Towards the middle years of life, the proportions of one and two generational families begin to increase, but belonging to three or more generations is still the norm. This is the time when the diversity of family life is at its greatest - an individual may still be located at the bottom of the generational triad (child/parents/grandparents) as well as at the top (grandparents/parents/child). In the later stages of the life course, only the effects of childlessness and widowhood begin to alter this picture, with almost 1 in 5 of the population aged above 80 years having no ascending or descending generation members in their family. Nevertheless, grandparenthood remains the norm, and over 40% of the population aged 80 years and above are now in 4 generational families combining the dual role of great grandparent and grandparent.

Table D.1 Family generations (adults aged 18+)

Number of generations in respondent's family and his/her relative position	%
1 generation only	6.0
2 generations, respondent at head	11.3
2 generations, respondent at bottom	9.8
3 generations, respondent at head	11.3
3 generations, respondent in middle	17.3
3 generations, respondent at bottom	25.4
4 generations	18.6
5 & 6 generations	0.4
Base	*3146*

The effect of marriage patterns upon grandparenthood

One of the biggest changes affecting grandparenthood in the past 40 years stems from the increase in divorce and separation among the general population, together with a rise in the numbers of births outside of marriage. Before the 1960s, almost all grandparents would have been able to trace a direct family line between themselves and their grandchildren. The increase in divorce and separation rates since the 1960s has substantially changed lines of affiliation between grandparents and grandchildren. It is the generation of grandparents aged between 50 and 74 who are most likely to have step-grandchildren. Unlike the eldest generation of grandparents (those age above 75 years), this cohort is experiencing the effect of higher divorce and separation rates both within the cohort and in the descending generation of children. Since typically divorce and separation occur after several years of marriage, 'young' grandparents are less likely to experience step-grandchildren than the middle generation of grandparents. Figure D.1 shows the distribution of step-grandchildren in the survey. It should be noted that the graphic refers to the 'selected' grandchild of respondents, and therefore it does not show the existence of all step-grandchildren (on which data are not contained in the main survey, but where rates of the presence of step-grandchildren within families would have been higher).[1]

Figure D.1 Grandparents with a step-grandchild

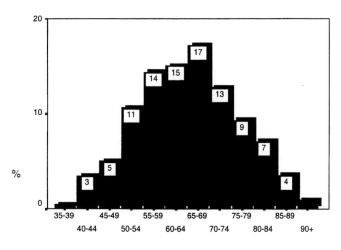

Age of grandparent

The second effect of marriage trends upon grandparenting is in the rise in the number of births outside marriage. One in four births now occur outside marriage, which in turn means that one in four 'new' grandparents have a different type of structural relationship with their grandchild than other grandparents. Of course, many of the unmarried parents of these young grandchildren are in some kind of informal relationship, but the rise in single parenthood, particularly among very young mothers, is a feature which has clearly altered the grandparenting role for those influenced by this trend. Among all parents in the survey who themselves had at least one parent alive, 6% are single parents (not married or not living together as married). These single parents are much more likely to be women (69% single mothers, 31% single fathers), and to be found between the ages of 20-24 years.

Households containing grandparents and grandchildren

Coresidence of grandparents and grandchildren in Britain has always been, and continues to be extremely rare. In the past, such living arrangements were a

---

[1] Data relating to the characteristics of grandparents and grandchildren are dependent upon the grandparent module survey methodology, i.e. questions relating to a 'selected grandchild' (see Appendix B).

consequence mostly of housing shortages, as Michael Young and Peter Willmott were to find in the 1950s. In the BSA 1998 survey, there are only 18 respondents who are grandparents and who have a grandchild living in their household (0.8%). The low number of cases makes it difficult to draw any conclusions concerning the reasons behind grandparent/grandchild coresidence. Nevertheless, two situations appear common. The first is where an adult grandchild lives with an elderly grandparent. These households, (with the exception of one three generational household in the survey), are two person/two generation households (i.e. an adult grandchild living with an elderly grandparent). The second situation, which is more common, concerns (with the exception of two cases) a grandparent living with a grandchild whose parents are divorced or separated, a living arrangement which unlike in Britain has become increasingly common in the USA (see below). Two types of household appear to be represented here. First those where the parent is not present, i.e. the grandparent appears to be permanently looking after a grandchild in the absence of the child's parents (n=4), and those where a single parent is present in the household, (n=7). Coresidence appears to be more frequent where the grandchild is the child of a daughter than that of son, reflecting the importance of the matrilineal line within British families (see chapter 6). All the parents of these coresiding grandchild and grandparents households were alive (i.e. the grandparent is not involved because of the death of one of the child's parents).

Ethnic diversity

It is well known that there exist wide variations in family formation and inter-generational relationships among different ethnic groups. In Britain, these relationships are further complicated by patterns of migrations history and the geographical separation of generations that often took place. Despite the BSA 1998 survey having asked respondents to identify their ethnicity, it is clear from the proportion of Black and Asian respondents in the survey as a whole (4.6%) that ethnic minorities are under-represented. Moreover, the mean age of Black and Asian respondents is approximately 10 years less than that of White respondents, and as a consequence there are fewer grandparents identified. Only 12 Black and Asian grandparents were identified, together with 25 grandparents who either refused to give their ethnicity or are of mixed origin. Despite these low figures, and notwithstanding the problems associated with an inclusive category of Black and Asian respondents, it is clear that some differences exist. First, no grandparent under the age of 40 years is to be found among the Black and Asian respondents in the survey. However, the mean age of grandparents tends to be lower among ethnic minority families (60 years for Black and Asian men compared with 65 years for White men, 56 years for

Black and Asian women compared with 64 years for White women). Moreover, it appears (again on the basis of the few cases in the data) that Asian grandmothers are among the youngest in the population, with a mean age of 55 years and that the age differentials between Asian grandmothers and grandfathers are higher than other ethnic groups (including White respondents).

British patterns of grandparenting in an international context

It is not only in Britain that there has been a renewed interest in the role of grandparenting. Here, we present three different demographic aspects of grandparenting which have recently preoccupied the USA, France and Spain in terms of responding to the issues raised. Each of these countries has recently focused on aspects of grandparenting with which we have been concerned throughout this report: the issue of grandparents as surrogate parents in cases of family breakdown in the USA; in France, the generational differences that are to be found both within and between different age groups of grandparents, parents, and grandchildren and the effect that different styles of parenting have upon the three generational family; and in Spain, the role of grandparents in providing child care for working mothers.

The basic demographic trends discussed throughout the report which are changing the role of grandparenting apply equally to all post-industrial societies. In the USA however, one of the main issues (unlike in Britain or France) is the increase in the number of children who are coresident with grandparents - an increase from 3% of children aged under 18 years living in a grandparent maintained home in 1970 to 5.5% in 1997 (Bryson and Casper 1999). Moreover this increase has taken place both in situations where the grandchild's parents are present and where they are absent, although recently the greatest increase is where there is no parent present - the 'skipped generation'. The evidence concerning whether single mothers are returning to their parent's household is less clear (Uhlenberg, 1999). These demographic trends have been attributed to a wide range of social ills, including drug abuse, teenage pregnancy, mental illness, AIDS, crime, child abuse and the incarceration of parents. Clearly, many American grandparents appear to be assuming parental responsibility in situations where their own children are either not able or willing to fulfil their parental obligations. As we have noted in this report, the possibility of British grandparents playing a similar role has come under increasing discussion recently.

In the USA, this upsurge in grandparent/grandchild coresidence has raised many issues concerning the rights of grandparents with respect to their grandchildren. Both the grandparents and grandchildren in these households are disadvantaged in many ways. The grandparents are often comparatively young and unemployed and a high proportion are from Black families, although Bryson and Casper conclude that Black families are not experiencing significantly greater economic hardships than other Black families where coresidence does not take place. In addition, these young grandparents have themselves experienced high rates of divorce and family separation, so that single grandparents caring for a grandchild is not uncommon, and it is this form of household that experiences the most severe forms of poverty. The most stable form of living arrangement for grandchild/grandparent coresidence is a marred grandparent household, and recent research suggests that adolescent grandchildren growing up in a household with both their grandparents can in educational terms be compared favourably with adolescents living with both parents (Uhlenberg, 1999).

The preoccupation in France (where, as in Britain, coresidence between grandparents and grandchildren is rare and not on the increase) is from a different perspective. A recent publication (Attias-Donfut and Segalen, 1998) drawing on data from several sources, has emphasised the arrival of the first of the baby-boomer generation into grandparenthood along with the values and behaviour particular to this cohort. This generation of 'middle' or 'pivot' grandparents (so defined because they have at least one parent and one adult child alive) represent a generation with more individualistic aspirations than their predecessors. Compared with the eldest generation of grandparents, they have more leisure time, are more affluent, and some would argue less likely to be locked into family life. In focusing on these young grandparents, the French study demonstrates how these generational effects have changed but not undermined the role of grandparenting. The 'emotional distance' for example, between mothers and daughters, would appear to be closer than in the past, and the study claims that grandfathers too, are playing a more active role than previously.

Our third example of grandparenting styles is that of Spain. Compared with the USA and France, Spain represents a country which, in social welfare terms, is still very much in a transitional phase. The past 10 years have seen a large increase in the numbers of women aged between 30 and 40 years in the labour market, and most of these women are working full time (Tenaillon and Dupland, 1999). For the majority of grandparents, traditional gender roles remain firmly intact - older women both expect and express satisfaction in playing a large part in the daily parenting activities of their grandchildren. Working mothers, regardless of social class, are keen to use this valuable resource which allows them to work full-time and not to incur financial child care costs. Moreover, they know that 'Mum' is best, since as a recent survey has shown, while only 21% of working mothers agreed that mothers should not be in paid employment, 48% believe that it is in the best interests of the child to have a mother at home. These dissonant values are resolved through the grandmother. Living near to each other is therefore a strategy that many older women and their daughters engage in from their respective 'self' interests. However, this structural pattern of family life appears threatened if the future behaviour of current mothers when they in turn become grandmothers is line with their current beliefs. Today's working mothers are emphatic that they will not replicate their own mother's role as a grandmother with a heavy involvement of child care in their grandchildren. The cycle of intergenerational assistance, where the older generation gives more than the younger generation appears to be closing in without their being alternatives (such as a generous system of external child care facilities) in place.

Summary

- The proportion of grandparents in the population did not change substantially during the twentieth century. Future patterns will be determined by trends in childlessness among women. The majority of adults over the age of 55 years are grandparents.
- Current cohorts of grandmothers appear to be achieving grandparenthood at an earlier age than their predecessors or than for future generations of women. Repeating the patterns of parenthood, grandparenthood is achieved earlier for women than for men.
- Grandparents are no longer at the generational head of the family, as an increasing number have at least one parent still alive.
- Grandparents have fewer grandchildren than in the past. Most grandparents have on average 4 to 5 grandchildren.
- Lines of affiliation between grandparents and grandchildren (the presence of 'step-grandchildren') are much less likely to be direct than in the past. The proportion of grandparents who have a step-grandchild is particularly high among grandparents aged 50-74 years.
- Coresidence between grandparents and grandchildren is extremely rare.
- Lower social class groups have a higher proportion of young grandparents than middle or higher social class groups, together with a greater number of grandchildren.
- Grandparenthood appears to be achieved at an earlier age among ethnic minority families than in White families.

APPENDIX E.

MULTIVARIATE ANALYSES

Data presented in the report are mainly in the form of crosstabulations. Organising data in this way has many advantages, not least because percentages are easily understood. However, there are also disadvantages, in so far as it is often difficult to see how three variables interact, and virtually impossible to examine four or more variables within a single (or even several) tables.

Logistic regression is a form of multivariate analysis that allows several categorical variables to be simultaneously examined. This statistical technique is an extension of linear parametric methods used where data are continuous, the most common method being ordinary least square regression and analysis of variance. Logistic regression is appropriate where the response variable is dichotomous.

In this section, we use logistic regression to examine the effect of several independent variables from Group A (randomly selected) grandparents on two dichotomous response variables – seeing a grandchild weekly, and being involved in extensive childcare. For both of these response variables, only grandchildren aged under 13 are included in the model. For the second response variable, only grandmothers are included in the model. Extensive childcare is defined as those grandmothers who help with baby-sitting or childcare once a week or more often, *and* whose grandchild often spends time with them during the day without his/her parents, *and* whose grandchild often stays overnight without his/her parents.

The proportions of grandparents and grandmothers who are respectively engaged in these two activities are shown in table E.1. This indicates that rates for seeing a grandchild aged under 13 weekly are higher than those where the grandchild's age is not restricted (see table 3.3, where the rate is 30% for all Group A randomly selected grandparents, grandchild age unrestricted). The highest rates for seeing a grandchild weekly are where the travelling time between grandparent and grandchild is less than 30 minutes, and the lowest rates are where this distance is greater than 30 minutes – where there is practically no weekly face-to-face contact. Significant associations are found for age and sex of grandparent, social class of grandparent, employment status of grandparent, educational level of grandparent, marital status of grandparent, employment status of grandchild's mother and lineage links. No associations

Grandparenting in Britain

Table E.1 Response variables in logistic regression analyses

	% of grandparents who:- See grandchild weekly		% of grandmothers who:- Involved in extensive childcare	
	Unweighted	Weighted	Unweighted	Weighted
Women	**47.6**	43.2		
Men	**34.7**	33.8		
Under 70	**46.1**	**43.2**	**15.6**	17.4
70+	**23.3**	**12.8**	**4.2**	4.5
GC <5	48.3	44.5	10.1	12.0
GC 5+	37.5	34.6	16.9	19.4
Couple	43.4	39.6	16.7	17.0
Separated	43.5	40.7	14.5	17.4
Widowed	37.4	34.4	6.6	11.1
Child at home	48.9	46.1	**24.5**	**27.8**
No child at home	41.1	36.5	**11.7**	**11.8**
Salariat	**30.1**	**22.7**	7.4	6.5
Intermediate	**44.3**	**43.9**	15.1	20.5
Working class	**49.4**	**47.2**	16.5	18.3
Working	**49.0**	**48.1**	12.4	13.0
Unemployed	**44.1**	**46.2**	18.5	25.0
Retired	**33.2**	**27.1**	11.2	12.1
Housewife	**53.7**	**44.8**	20.8	25.9
Works full-time	**41.9**	**44.4**	**3.4**	**4.9**
Works part-time	**64.7**	**58.5**	**21.3**	**22.9**
Medium income	40.9	38.8	10.7	15.6
Low income	44.7	40.0	17.4	16.5
Qualification	**34.3**	**46.8**	**9.3**	**11.1**
No qualification	**51.0**	**32.8**	**18.1**	**20.9**
GCs parents together	**39.7**	37.8	**10.6**	**9.9**
GCs parents apart	**52.7**	45.3	**22.1**	**26.6**
GC mum ft job	39.5	**30.3**	16.9	**13.2**
GC mum pt job	47.0	**48.1**	18.0	**26.3**
GC mum not working	41.1	**36.0**	9.1	**15.9**
GC by daughter	**50.7**	**45.6**	**18.8**	**20.0**
GC by son	**30.7**	**30.4**	**6.9**	**11.8**
GC < 30 min	**62.9**	**61.1**	**20.6**	**25.2**
GC > 30 min	**4.8**	**4.5**	**0.9**	**1.4**
Base	*533*	*533*	*317*	*317*

Note: Bold figures *p*<0.05.

are found for the age of the grandchild, whether the GP still has one of their own children still living in their home, and income levels.

For extensive childcare (where grandmothers only are concerned) distance is still a strongly associated variable – where the travelling time is over 30 minutes virtually no grandmothers are involved in childcare. But at distances of less than 30 minutes, the rates suggest that other factors determine childcare. Rates are notably higher when the grandmother herself still has a dependent child in the home, when the grandmother has no educational qualifications, where the grandchild's parents are separated, where the grandchild's mother is working part-time and where the lineage link is through a daughter.

These trends reflect some of the main findings contained in the report – the polarisation of involvement following separation of the grandchild's parents, the interaction of sex and lineage, and the association of childcare by grandmothers where the mother of the grandchild is working part-time. The logistic regression analyses presented below help us to assess the importance of individual explanatory variables (as shown in table E.1) on seeing grandchild weekly and grandmothers doing extensive childcare. Table E.2 shows the coding used for these explanatory variables.

Table E.2 Categorical Variables Codings for Logistic Regressions

GRCHMJOB "Does the grandchild's mother have a job, and if so, is she working full-time or part-time?"	1 Yes, full-time 2 Yes, part-time 3 No
MARSTAT1 "Marital status of grandparent"	1 couple 2 separated 3 widowed
CLASS1 "Social class of grandparent"	1 salariat 2 intermediate 3 working class
DISTAN 'Travelling time between grandparent and grandchild'	1 <30 mins 2 over 30 mins
GCAGE 'Age of grandchild'	1 under 5 2 5+
CHLHOME1 1 'Does grandparent have their own child at home?'	0 No 1 Yes
INCOME 'Self-rated income is 'high' or 'low'	1 Higher 2 Lower
LINE 'Grandchild related via a daughter or a son	1 via daughter 2 via son

SEPAR 'Grandchild's parents together or apart	1 together
	2 apart
EDUCAT 'Does grandparent have a qualification?'	0 qualification
	1 no qualification
RSEX Sex of grandparent	1 Male
	2 Female
HOURS: Working hours of grandparent	1 Full-time
	2 Part-time
	3 Not working

Table E.3 shows that in the full model, distance, lineage, educational qualifications and grandparents age and grandparent sex are the variables with a significant effect on seeing a grandchild weekly, and of these distance is by far the most important. If a grandchild lives within 30 minutes as opposed to more than 30 minutes travelling time, the odds of seeing a grandchild weekly increase by a factor of 34, *when other variables are controlled*. In other words, having a grandchild living close-by will generally mean that weekly, face-to-face contact takes place - whatever the characteristics of the grandparent, the grandchild, or the grandchild's parents. The other significant variables show that older grandparents, grandfathers, and grandparents who have an educational qualification are *less* likely to have weekly contact.

Table E.3 Full logistic regression model for seeing a grandchild aged under 13 several times a week

	B	S.E.	Wald	df	Sig.	Exp(B)
RSEX(1)	**-,731**	**,257**	**8,125**	**1**	**,004**	**,481**
GCAGE(1)	,336	,260	1,666	1	,197	1,399
MARSTAT1			3,084	2	,214	
MARSTAT1(1)	,491	,351	1,959	1	,162	1,634
MARSTAT1(2)	-,002	,461	,000	1	,997	,998
CHLHOME1(1)	,404	,317	1,618	1	,203	1,497
CLASS1			,781	2	,677	
CLASS1(1)	-,188	,336	,311	1	,577	,829
CLASS1(2)	,086	,280	,094	1	,759	1,090
INCOME(1)	,170	,256	,440	1	,507	1,185
RAGE	**-,034**	**,016**	**4,393**	**1**	**,036**	**,967**
EDUCAT(1)	**-,650**	**,265**	**6,023**	**1**	**,014**	**,522**
SEPAR(1)	-,039	,306	,016	1	,898	,962
GRCHMJOB			3,060	2	,217	

GRCHMJOB(1)	,366	,318	1,328	1	,249	1,442
GRCHMJOB(2)	,441	,265	2,768	1	,096	1,555
LINE(1)	**,848**	**,239**	**12,608**	**1**	**,000**	**2,336**
DISTAN(1)	**3,527**	**,382**	**85,448**	**1**	**,000**	**34,007**
Constant	-1,992	1,127	3,124	1	,077	,136

Note: bold figures $p<0.05$

In table E.4, only grandchildren living within 30 minutes travelling are entered into the same regression model. The significant variables remain the same – a 'young' maternal grandmother with no educational qualifications is the profile that emerges for the most regular contact with grandchildren.

Table E.4 Full logistic regression model for seeing a grandchild aged under 13 several times a week where travelling time is within 30 minutes

	B	S.E.	Wald	df	Sig.	Exp(B)
RSEX(1)	**-,771**	**,271**	**8,121**	**1**	**,004**	**,462**
GCAGE(1)	,270	,277	,951	1	,329	1,310
MARSTAT1			4,033	2	,133	
MARSTAT1(1)	,452	,366	1,524	1	,217	1,571
MARSTAT1(2)	-,258	,481	,288	1	,592	,773
CHLHOME1(1)	,300	,331	,823	1	,364	1,350
CLASS1			,598	2	,742	
CLASS1(1)	-,149	,358	,174	1	,677	,862
CLASS1(2)	,106	,294	,130	1	,719	1,112
INCOME(1)	,143	,270	,281	1	,596	1,154
RAGE	**-,036**	**,017**	**4,320**	**1**	**,038**	**,965**
EDUCAT(1)	**-,629**	**,284**	**4,886**	**1**	**,027**	**,533**
SEPAR(1)	,141	,320	,194	1	,660	1,151
GRCHMJOB			2,538	2	,281	
GRCHMJOB(1)	,462	,343	1,817	1	,178	1,587
GRCHMJOB(2)	,359	,278	1,669	1	,196	1,432
LINE(1)	**,847**	**,253**	**11,226**	**1**	**,001**	**2,332**
Constant	1,719	1,135	2,294	1	,130	5,579

Note: bold figures $p<0.05$

The remaining two tables show the full logistic regression models for grandmothers doing extensive childcare, firstly where there is no restriction on distance (table E.5) and secondly (E.6) where the grandchild lives within 30 minutes travelling time.

Table E.5 Full logistic regression model for GRANDMOTHERS DOING EXTENSIVE CHILDCARE for grandchild aged under 13 several times a week

	B	S.E.	Wald	df	Sig.	Exp(B)
GCAGE(1)	**-,934**	**,448**	**4,339**	**1**	**,037**	**,393**
MARSTAT1			3,141	2	,208	
MARSTAT1(1)	,985	,586	2,822	1	,093	2,677
MARSTAT1(2)	,493	,779	,400	1	,527	1,637
CHLHOME1(1)	**-1,054**	**,482**	**4,784**	**1**	**,029**	**,348**
CLASS1			,556	2	,757	
CLASS1(1)	,513	,693	,548	1	,459	1,671
CLASS1(2)	,163	,447	,133	1	,715	1,177
INCOME(1)	-,342	,415	,678	1	,410	,710
RAGE	-,038	,031	1,529	1	,216	,962
EDUCAT(1)	-,387	,439	,778	1	,378	,679
SEPAR(1)	-,367	,474	,601	1	,438	,693
GRCHMJOB			4,884	2	,087	
GRCHMJOB(1)	1,009	,571	3,125	1	,077	2,743
GRCHMJOB(2)	**1,016**	**,490**	**4,298**	**1**	**,038**	**2,762**
LINE(1)	**1,030**	**,462**	**4,973**	**1**	**,026**	**2,801**
DISTAN(1)	**3,262**	**1,090**	**8,961**	**1**	**,003**	**26,099**
HOURS			7,566	2	,023	
HOURS(1)	**-2,458**	**,895**	**7,540**	**1**	**,006**	**,086**
HOURS(2)	-,504	,530	,906	1	,341	,604
Constant	-2,532	2,194	1,331	1	,249	,080

Note: bold figures $p<0.05$.

Table E.5 shows that distance is again the most important criterion for doing extensive childcare. Lineage also has an important effect, showing the contribution of maternal grandmothers. Both the working status of the grandchild's mother (increase among part-time workers) and the grandmother (reduction when working full-time) have a significant effect.

Another significant variable is where grandmothers themselves still have a child at home. Unfortunately, we know little about the characteristics of this child, but some clues as to the profile of the grandmother who is extensively involved in childcare are found in the final table, where only grandmothers who live within 30 minutes are included in the model.

Table E.6 Full logistic regression model for GRANDMOTHERS DOING EXTENSIVE CHILDCARE for grandchild aged under 13 several times a week

	B	S.E.	Wald	df	Sig.	Exp(B)
GCAGE(1)	-,892	,458	3,791	1	,052	,410
MARSTAT1			2,905	2	,234	
MARSTAT1(1)	,961	,591	2,647	1	,104	2,615
MARSTAT1(2)	,502	,789	,405	1	,525	1,652
CHLHOME1(1)	**-1,150**	**,492**	**5,464**	**1**	**,019**	**,317**
CLASS1			,625	2	,732	
CLASS1(1)	,553	,708	,609	1	,435	1,739
CLASS1(2)	,079	,455	,030	1	,861	1,083
INCOME(1)	-,404	,425	,902	1	,342	,668
RAGE	-,038	,033	1,331	1	,249	,963
EDUCAT(1)	-,272	,444	,374	1	,541	,762
SEPAR(1)	-,418	,485	,742	1	,389	,659
GRCHMJOB			4,843	2	,089	
GRCHMJOB(1)	1,118	,589	3,610	1	,057	3,060
GRCHMJOB(2)	**,986**	**,502**	**3,859**	**1**	**,049**	**2,680**
LINE(1)	**,996**	**,468**	**4,526**	**1**	**,033**	**2,708**
HOURS			7,872	2	,020	
HOURS(1)	**-2,560**	**,920**	**7,748**	**1**	**,005**	**,077**
HOURS(2)	-,660	,552	1,432	1	,232	,517
Constant	,874	2,152	,165	1	,685	2,395

Note: bold figures $p<0.05$.

Table E.6 shows the probability of an increase in extensive childcare for part-time working mothers in the maternal line and a decrease when the grandmother is working full-time (compared to part-time or when not working). These findings confirm the main trends presented in chapter 8.

APPENDIX F.

FREQUENCY VARIABLE LABELS AND DERIVED VARIABLES

For ease of presentation we have adopted a similar frequency wording format for all tables in the report. The original wording of frequency variables differed according to two types of variable, which are reproduced here.

FREQUENCY VARIABLE LABELS (Questionnaire)

Type 1 (*See* and *telephone*)

1	Daily
2	At least several times a week
3	At least once a week
4	At least once a fortnight
5	At least once a month
6	Several times a year
7	Less often
8	Never

Type 2 (*Activities* and *childcare*)

1	Once a week or more often
2	Several times a month
3	Every month or so
4	Every six months
5	Once in the past year
6	Never in the past year

Type 3 (*Stay, advice, money*)

1	Often
2	Occasionally
3	Not in the past year
4	Never

FREQUENCY VARIABLE LABELS (Tables in report)

The wording of frequency variables in the tables throughout the report also follows the format reproduced below:

"Several times a week" = Type 1 (1 + 2, plus child living in household).

"Less than once a month" = Type 1 (6+7+8, plus no contact in last 2 years)

"Weekly or more" Type 2 (1)

"Several times a month" = Type 2 (1 + 2)

"At least monthly' = Type 2 (1 + 2 + 3)

DERIVED VARIABLES

The report contains a number of derived variables. SPSS syntax for the construction of these variables is shown here, listed according to chapter where first adopted.

Chapter 2

Collapsed social class variable

missing values rghgrp (lowest thru -1) (8,9).

compute class1=rghgrp.

recode class1 (2,3,4=2) (5=3) (-1=9)./*routine non-manual, petty bourgeoisie, foremen and supervisors
exe.

missing values class1 ().

variable labels class1='Social class of respondent'.
value labels class1 1 'salariat' 2 'intermediate' 3 'working class' 9 'DK'.

Chapter 3

Variable for contact after separation (con2)

compute con2=0.

do if (grchparl=1).
    do if (grchpams=2 or grchpams=3).

```
        do if (grchpdv3=1 or grchpdv4=1 or grchpdv5=1).
        compute con2=1.                        /*less contact at separation
        else if (grchpdv2=1).
        compute con2=4.                        /*more contact
        else.
        compute con2=3.                        /*same contact
        end if.
    else if (grchpams=1).
    compute con2=2.                            /*parents together
    end if.
end if.
exe.
```

value labels con2 1 'less' 3 'same' 2 'together' 4 'more contact' 0 'orphan'.

missing values con2 (0).

Chapter 5

Variables for household composition

```
vector h (10).
vector a=p2rel2 to p11rel2.
loop #i=1 to 10.
        do if (a(#i)=2).
        compute h(#i)=1.
        end if.
end loop.
exe.
```

```
compute chlhome = sum(h1,h2,h3,h4,h5,h6,h7,h8,h9,h10) .
recode childliv chlhome  (sysmis=91)  .
recode chlhome
(1 thru 9=1)  (91=0) into  chlhome1 .
exe.
```

****.

compute couple=0.

```
vector j (10).
vector a=p2rel2 to p11rel2.
loop #i=1 to 10.
        do if (a(#i)=1).
        compute j(#i)=1.
        end if.
end loop.
exe.
```

compute couple = sum(j1,j2,j3,j4,j5,j6,j7,j8,j9,j10) .

```
recode couple (sysmis=91).
exe.

variable labels couple 'has partner'.

compute couple1=0.

do if (couple=1) & (chlhome=91 & relsonda=2).
        compute couple1=1.
        end if.
exe.

variable labels couple1 'childless couple'.

compute enest=0.

do if (relsonda=1 & chlhome1=0 & gp=0).
        compute enest=1.
        end if.
exe.

variable labels enest 'empty nest parents'.

compute loner=0.
exe.

do if (p2rel2=0 & relsonda=2).
        compute loner=1.
        end if.
exe.

variable labels loner 'lives alone & no children'.

compute gphh1=0.

do if (gp=1).
do if (p2rel2=1 & househld le 2).
        compute gphh1=1.
        else if (househld=1).
        compute gphh1=2.
        else.
        compute gphh1=3.
        end if.
end if.
exe.

variable labels gphh1 'grandparent hhold'.
value labels gphh1 1 'couple only' 2 'lives alone' 3 'other'.

compute hhld=0.

do if (gp=0).
        do if (loner=1).
```

```
              compute hhld=1.
              else if (couple1=1).
              compute hhld=2.
              else if (chlhome1=1).
              compute hhld=3.
              else if (enest=1).
              compute hhld=4.
              end if.
else if (gp=1).
              do if (gphh1=1).
              compute hhld=5.
              else if (gphh1=2).
              compute hhld=6.
              else.
              compute hhld=7.
              end if.
end if.
exe.
```

recode hhld (0=8).
exe.

variable labels hhld 'household type'.
value labels hhld 1 'childless loner' 2 'childless couple' 3 'couple with child' 4 'empty nest' 5 'gparent couple' 6 'gparent loner' 7 'gparent other' 8 'other'.

********correct for single parents****************.

compute hhld1=hhld.

if (hhld=3) & (marstat=3 or marstat=5) hhld1=9.
exe.

variable labels hhld1 'household type'.
value labels hhld1 1 'childless loner' 2 'childless couple' 3 'couple with child' 4 'empty nest' 5 'gparent couple' 6 'gparent loner' 7 'gparent other' 8 'other' 9 'single parent'.

recode hhld1 (9=4) (4=5) (5=6) (6=7) (7=8) (8=9).
exe.

value labels hhld1 1 'childless loner' 2 'childless couple' 3 'couple with child' 4 'single parent' 5 'empty nest' 6 'gparent couple'
                7 'gparent loner' 8 'gparent other' 9 'other'.

compute hhld2=hhld1.

recode hhld2 (2=1) (6=5) (8,9=7).
exe.

variable labels hhld2 'household composition'.
value labels hhld2 1 'childless' 3 'couple with child' 4 'single parent' 5 'empty nest' 7 'other'.

********Determine grandparent household composition*************.

```
***********Identify couple only households************.

compute couple=0.

vector a=p2rel2 to p11rel2.
loop #i=1 to 10.
do if (a(#i)=1) & househld=2.
compute couple=1.
end if.
end loop.
exe.


************identify dependent children in household****************.

**determine whether there is a child and age of child in the
***household****.

vector ychld (10).
vector a=p2rel2 to p11rel2.
vector b=p2age to p11age.
loop #i= 1 to 10.
do if (a(#i)=2) & (b(#i)<18).
+  compute ychld(#i)=b(#i).
+  end if.
end loop.
exe.

***********.

count
  depchild = ychld1 ychld10 ychld2 ychld3 ychld4 ychld5 ychld6 ychld7 ychld8
  ychld9  (0 thru highest)  .


recode depchild (1 thru highest=1).


**determine whether there is a child and age of child in the
***household****.

vector ochld (10).
vector a=p2rel2 to p11rel2.
vector b=p2age to p11age.
loop #i= 1 to 10.
do if (a(#i)=2) & (b(#i)>17).
+  compute ochld(#i)=b(#i).
+  end if.
end loop.
exe.

***********.
```

```
count
  child = ochld1 ochld10 ochld2 ochld3 ochld4 ochld5 ochld6 ochld7 ochld8
  ochld9  (0 thru highest) .

recode child (1 thru highest=1).


***************************************************************.
*********compute grandchild in household*****************.

compute gchhld=0.

vector a=p2rel2 to p11rel2.
loop #i=1 to 10.
do if (a(#i)=3).
compute gchhld=1.
end if.
end loop.
exe.

**********************************************************.
************create grandparent household variable********.

compute gphhold=0.


do if (househld=1).
compute gphhold=1.            /*gp loners
else if (couple=1).
compute gphhold=2.            /*gp couples
else if (depchild=1).
compute gphhold=3.            /*gp with dependent child two generations
else if (child=1).
compute gphhold=4.            /*gp with non dependent child
else if (gchhld=1).
compute gphhold=5.            /*gchild in household
else.
compute gphhold=6.            /*other
end if.
exe.

variable labels gphhold 'type of grandparent household'.
value labels gphhold 1 'loner' 2 'couple' 3 'dep child' 4 'adult child' 5 'gp with gc' 6 'other'.

********************.
*********correct for all grandchildren**********************.

if (gchhld=1) gphhold=5.
exe.
```

Chapter 7

Activity Index.

```
do repeat r=act1 to act9.
compute r=0.
end repeat.
exe.

if (grchputo=1) act1=1.
if (grchday=1) act2=1.
if (grchstay=1) act3=1.
if (grchvist>0 & grchvist<6) act4=1.
if (grchcar1>0 & grchcar1<4) act5=1.
if (grchmond=1) & (grchmodf=1 or grchmodf=2) act6=1.
if (grchadv=1 or grchadv=2) act7=1.
if (grchstwk=1 or grchstwk=2) act8=1.
if (grchcar2>0 & grchcar2>4) act9=1.
if (grchesco>0 & grchesco>4) act9=1.
if (grchill>0 & grchill>4) act9=1.
exe.

compute act=sum(act1 to act9).

compute supgran=act.

recode supgran (0 thru 1=1) (,4=2) (5 thru highest=3).
exe.

variable labels supgran 'Level of activity'.
value labels supgran 1 'low' 2 'medium' 3 'high'.
```

Chapter 12

Living arrangements variables

a.   **Grandparents' living arrangements** (for tables 12.1/12.2)

```
compute livarr=0.
execute.

do if (rsex=2).
   do if (p2rel=0 & married=3).
   compute livarr=2.              /*widow living alone
   else if (p2rel=0).
   compute livarr=1.              /*other GM living alone
   else.
   compute livarr=3.              /*GM not living alone
   end if.
else if (rsex=1).
   do if (p2rel=0 & married=3).
   compute livarr=5.              /*widower living alone
   else if (p2rel=0).
```

```
        compute livarr=4.          /*other GF living alone
        else.
        compute livarr=6.          /*GF not living alone
        end if.
   end if.
   execute.
```

value labels livarr 1 'GM alone' 2 'widow alone' 3 'GM not alone' 4 'GF alone' 5 'widower alone' 6 'GF not alone'.

compute reside=livarr.
exe.

recode reside (2=1) (1=2) (6=4) (4=5).
exe.

value labels reside 2 'GM alone' 1 'widow alone' 3 'GM not alone' 5 'GF alone' 4 'GF not alone'.

b. **General sample living arrangements** (for tables 12.6/12.7)
Variable defined in the following way.:-

'Trad'=If the respondent is married and living in the same household OR the respondent is widowed.

'Neo-Con'=Excluding any of the above respondents, those respondents who are living together as married OR any respondent who does not have a child.

'Unconv'=those respondents who have a child and are not living with a spouse or partner.

Syntax:-

compute resconj=0.
execute.

do if (marstat=1 & p2rel=1) or (marstat=4).
compute resconj=1.
else if (marstat=2 & p2rel=1) or (relsonda>1).
compute resconj=2.
else if (relsonda=1 & p2rel ne 1).
compute resconj=3.
end if.
execute.

variable labels resconj 'Residential and conjugal status'.
value labels resconj 1 'traditional' 2 'neo-conventional' 3 'unconventional'.

REFERENCES

Allen, I. and Dowling, S.B. (1999) 'Teenage mothers: decisions and outcomes', in Wertheimer, A. and McRae, S., *Family and Household Change in Britain*, Oxford: Oxford Brookes University.

Anderson, M. (1972) *Family Structure in Nineteenth Century Lancashire*, Cambridge: Cambridge University Press.

Arber, S. and Attias-Donfut, C. (2000) *The Myth of Generational Conflict*, London: Routledge.

Arber, S. and Ginn, J. (1995) *Connecting gender and ageing*, Buckingham: Open University Press.

Armitage, B. and Babb, P. (1996) 'Population Review: (4) Trends in fertility', in *Population Trends*, No. 84, Summer 1996.

Arthur, S., Snape, D. and Dench, G. (2002) *The moral economy of grandparenting*, London: National Centre for Social Research.

Askham, J., Barry, C., Grundy, E., Hancock, R., and Tinker, A., (1992) *Life after Sixty: a profile of Britain's older population*, London: Age Concern Institute of Gerontology.

Attias-Donfut, C. and Segalen, M. (1998), *Grands-Parents: La famille à travers les générations*, Paris: Odile Jacob.

Barnes, J. A. (1973) 'Genitor: genetrix: nature: culture', in Goody, J. (ed.) *The character of kinship*, Cambridge: University Press.

Barrett, M. and McIntosh, M. (1982) *The Anti-social Family*, London: Verso/New Left Books.

Batchelor, J., Dimmock, B. and Smith, D. (1994), *Understanding stepfamilies*, London: Stepfamily publications.

Bengtson, V. and Robertson, J.F. (eds.) (1985) *Grandparenthood*, Beverly Hills, CA.: Sage.

Bengtson, V.L. and Achenbaum, W.A. (eds.) (1993) *The changing contract across generations*, New York: de Gruyter.

Berthoud, R. and Gershuny, J. (eds.) (2000) *Seven years in the lives of British Families*, Bristol : Policy Press.

Bornat, J., Dimmock, B., Jones, D. and Peace, S. (1999a) 'Generational ties in the "New Family" ', in Silva, E.B. and Smart, C., *The New Family*, London: Sage.

Bornat, J., Dimmock, B., Jones, D. and Peace, S. (1999b) 'Stepfamilies and older people: evaluating the implications of family change for an ageing population', *Ageing and Society* 19.

Bryson, K. and Casper, L.M. (1999) *Co-resident grandparents and grandchildren*, Washington: US Census Bureau.

Casper, L. M and Bryson, K. R. (eds.) (1998) *Co-resident Grandparents and Their Grandchildren*, Washington D.C.: Grandparent Maintained Families Population Division, U.S. Bureau of the Census, Washington, D.C., March 1998, Population Division Working Paper No. 26.

Chalfie, D. (1994) *Going it alone: A closer look at grandparents parenting grandchildren*, Washington D.C.: American Association of Retired Persons.

Cherlin, H.J. and Furstenberg, F.F. Jr. (1988) 'Styles and Strategies of Grandparenting', in Binstock, R.H. and George, L.K. (eds.), *Handbook of Ageing and the Social Sciences*, New York: Van Nostrand Reinhold.

Council of the European Commission (2002) Cion doc. No. 588/02, *Increasing labour-force participation and promoting active ageing*, Brussels: European Commission.

Cox, C.B. (ed.) (2000) *To Grandmother's House we Go and Stay*, Boulder: Springer Publ. Co.

CSO (Central Statistical Office) (1995) *Social Trends 26*, London: HMSO

CSO (1997) *Social Trends 28*, London: HMSO

Dalley, G. (1996) *Ideologies of caring*, London: Macmillan.

Dench, G. (1996) *The place of men in changing family cultures*, London: Institute of Community Studies.

Dench, G. (1997) 'Listening to the elders', Report to Joseph Rowntree Reform Trust.

Dench, G. (ed.) (2000) *Grandmothers of the Revolution*, London: Hera Trust.

Dench, G. and Ogg, J. (2000) 'Grands-parents par la fille, grands-parents par le fils', in Attias-Donfut, C. and Segalen, M. (eds.) *Le Siecle des Grands-Parents*, Paris: Autrement.

Dench, G., Ogg, J. and Thomson, K. (1999) 'The role of grandparenting', in Jowell, R., Curtice, J., Park, A., and Thomson, K., (eds.) *British Social Attitudes, the 16th report*, Aldershot: Ashgate.

Douglas, G and Lowe, N. (1990) 'Grandparents and the legal process', *Journal of Social Welfare Law*, 2: 98-106.

Drew, L.A. and Smith, P.K. (1999) 'The impact of parental separation/divorce on grandparent-grandchild relationships', *International Journal of Aging and Human Development*, Vol. 48(3) 191-216.

Elliott, F.R. (1996) *Gender, family and society*, Basingstoke: Macmillan.

Evans, G. (2000) "The working class and New Labour: a parting of the ways?" in Jowell, R. et al., (eds.) *British Social Attitudes, the 17th Report*, London: Sage.

Furstenberg, F. F. and Spanier, G. (1984) *Recycling the family: remarriage after divorce*, Beverley Hills, Ca: Sage.

Gardiner, J. (1997) *Gender, Care and Economics*, Basingstoke: Macmillan.

Hagestad, G. (1985) 'Continuity and connectedness', in Bengtson, V.L. and Robertson, J.F. (eds.) *Grandparenthood*, Beverley Hills, Ca: Sage.

Hansard (1998) House of Lords debate on 'The Role of Grandparents', 24th March, London: HMSO.

Haskey, J. (1996) 'The proportion of married couples who divorce: past patterns and current prospects', *Population Trends*, 83: 28-36.

Hibbert, C. (1987) *The English: A Social History 1066-1945*, London: Harper Collins.

Hirshorn, B.A. (1998) 'Grandparents as caregivers' in Szinovacz, M. E. *Handbook on grandparenthood*, Westport: Greenwood.

Home Office, (2000) *Supporting families: a consultation document*, London: HMSO.

Hrdy, S. B. (1999) *Mother Nature*, London: Chatto & Windus.

Johnson, C.L. and Barer, B.M. (1987) 'Marital instability and the changing kinship networks of grandparents, *The Gerontologist*, 27, 330-335.

Johnson, C.L. (1998) 'Effects of adult children's divorce on grandparenthood', in Szinovacz, M. E. *Handbook on grandparenthood*, Westport: Greenwood.

Jowell, R., Curtice, J., Park, A., and Thomson, K., (eds.) (1999) *British Social Attitudes, the 16th report*, Aldershot: Ashgate.

Kerr, M. (1960) *The people of Ship Street*, London: Routledge & Kegan Paul.

Kiernan, K E. (1992) 'The Impact of Family Disruption in Childhood on Transitions Made in Young Adult Life', *Population Studies* 46: 213-234.

Kiernan, K.E. (1999) 'Childbearing outside marriage in Western Europe', *Population Trends*, December.

Kornhaber, A. (1996) *Contemporary Grandparenting*, Thousand Oaks: Sage.

Kosberg, J. (Ed.) (1992) *Family Care of the Elderly*. Newbury Park, CA: Sage.

Kotlikoff, L. J. (1992) *Generational Accounting - Knowing Who Pays, and When, for What we Spend*, New York: Free Press.

Land, H. (2002) 'Spheres of care in the UK: separate and unequal', *Critical Social Policy*, 22.1.

Laslett, P. (1977) *Family Life and Illicit Love in Earlier Generations*. Cambridge: Cambridge University Press.

Lewis, J and Meredith, B. (1988) *Daughters who care*, London: Routledge.

McAllister, F. and Clarke, L. (1998) *Choosing childlessness*, London: Family Policy Studies Centre.

McFarlane, A. (1978) *The Origins of Individualism in England*. Cambridge: Cambridge University Press.

Maccoby, E. and Jacklyn, N. (1966) *The Psychology Of Sex Differences*, Stanford: University Press.

Marsh, C. and Arber, S. (1992) (eds.) *Families and Households: Divisions and Change*. London: Macmillan.

Martin, J. and Roberts, C. (1984) *Women and Employment: A lifetime perspective*. London: HMSO.

Mead, M. (1949) *Male and Female: a study of the sexes in a changing world*, New York: Morrow.

Midwinter, E. (1992) *Citizenship: from ageism to participation*, London: Carnegie United Kingdom Trust.

Minkler, M. and Estes, C. (1994) *Critical gerontology*, New York: Baywood Press.

Minkler, M. and Roe, K. (1993) *Grandmothers as caregivers*, Newbury Park, Ca: Sage.

Morgan, D. (1996) *Family connections*, Cambridge: Polity.

Mulgan, G. and Wilkinson, H. (1995) *Freedom's children*, London: Demos.

Neate, P. (2000) 'Where were you in the Revolution, Granny?' in Dench, G. (ed.) *Grandmothers of the Revolution*, London: Hera.

Nelson, H.L. (ed.) (1997) *Feminism and Families*, London: Routledge.

Nelson, J. (2000) 'Contemplating Grandmotherhood', in Dench, G. (ed.) *Grandmothers of the Revolution*, London: Hera.

Ni Bhrolchain, M. (1993) 'Recent fertility differentials in Britain', *Studies on Medical Population Subjects*, 55: 95-109, London: HMSO.

Ogg, J. (2001) 'Transitions and Pathways to Living Alone: changes in living arrangements amongst older people', unpublished PhD thesis, Keele University.

ONS (Office for National Statistics) (1998) *Living in Britain. Results from the 1996 General Household Survey*. London: HMSO.

ONS (1999) Annual update: Births and Conceptions 1998, *Population Trends* 98, HMSO

ONS (2001) Demographic statistics available on ONS Website.

OPCS (Office of Population Censuses and Surveys) (1993) *1991 Census: Persons aged 60 and over in Great Britain*, London: HMSO.

Orr, D. (2000) 'We can't rely on grandparents for cheap child care', *The Independent*, Feb. 15.

Orwell, G. (1937) *The road to Wigan pier*, London: Gollancz.

Peace, S. (1990) (ed.) *Researching Social Gerontology*, London: Sage.

Phillipson, C. (1996) 'Intergenerational conflict and the welfare state', in Walker, A. (ed.) *The new generational contract*, London: University College Press.

Pitcher, D. (1999) *When grandparents care*, Plymouth: Plymouth City Council.

Platt, J. (1971) *Social Research in Bethnal Green: An evaluation of the work of the Institute of Community Studies*, London: Macmillan.

Rogers, L. (1999) *Sexing the Brain.* London: Weidenfield and Nicolson.

Rossi, A.S. (ed.) (1983) *Gender and the Life Course*, New York: Aldine Publishing Company.

Rossi, A.S. and Rossi, P. (1990) *Of Human Bonding: parent-child relationships across the life course*, Hawthorn, New York: Aldine & Gruyter.

Rosser, C. and Harris, C. (1965) *The Family and Social Change: a study of family and kinship in a South Wales town*, London: Routledge & Kegan Paul.

Secker, S. (2001) *For the sake of the children*, London: Families Need Fathers.

Sheldon, J.H. (1948) *The Social Medicine of Old Age: Report of an Inquiry in Wolverhampton.* Oxford: Oxford University Press.

Simpson, B. (1995) 'Bringing the 'unclear' family into focus', Man (NS) 29, 831-851.

Stacey, J. (1991) *Brave new families*, New York: Basic Books.

Szinovacz, M.E. (1998a) 'Grandparents today: a demographic profile', *The Gerontologist*, 38: 37-52.

Szinovacz, M.E. (ed.) (1998b) *Handbook on grandparenthood*, Westport: Greenwood.

Tenaillon, S. and Dupland, N. (1999) Le rôle des grands-parents, *Retraite et Sociéte*, 28, 63-83.

Thompson, P., Itzin, C. and Abendstern, M. (1991) *I don't feel old*, Oxford: Oxford University Press.

Thompson, P. (1999) 'The role of grandparents when parents part or die', *Ageing & Society*, 19: 471-503.

Thomson, D. (1989) 'The Welfare State and Generation Conflict: Winners and Losers', in Johnson, P., Conrad, C. and Thomson, D. (eds.) *Workers versus Pensioners: Intergenerational Justice in an Aging World*, Manchester: Manchester University Press.

Thomson, K. (1995) 'Working mothers: choice or circumstance?' in Jowell, R., Curtice, J., Park, A., Brook, L. and Arendt, D. (eds.), *British Social Attitudes: the 12th Report*, Aldershot: Dartmouth.

Townsend, P. (1957) *The Family Life of Old People*, London: Routledge and Kegan Paul.

Troll, L. (1985) 'The contingencies of grandparenting', in Bengtsen, V.L. and Robertson, J.F. (eds.) *Grandparenthood*, Beverley Hills, Ca: Sage.

Tunaley, J.R. (1998) 'Grandparents and the family: support versus interference', *Proceedings of the British Psychological Society*, 7: 78.

Uhlenberg, P. (1999) 'Grandparents with parental care of their grandchildren', paper given at conference *'Les solidarites entre les generations: le role des grands-parents'*, organised by the Caisse Nationale d'Assurance Vieillesse, Paris, 29th Sept. 1999: summary given in *Retraite et Societe*, no. 28.

Uhlenberg, P. and Hammil, B.G. (1998) Frequency of grandparent contact with grandchild sets: six factors that make a difference, *Gerontologist*, 38(3), 276-285.

Uhlenberg, P. and Kirby, J. B. (1998) 'Grandparenthood over time: historical and demographic trends,' in M Szinovacz (ed.) *Handbook on Grandparenthood*, Westport: Greenwood.

Wall, R. (1984) 'Residential isolation of the elderly : a comparison over time', *Ageing and Society*, 4(4), 483-504.

Wall, R. (1992) 'Relationships Between the Generations in British Families Past and Present', in Marsh, C. and Arber, S. (eds.) *Families and Households.* London: Macmillan.

Wall, R. (1995) 'Elderly persons and members of their households in England and Wales form pre-industrial times to the present', in Kertzer, D. I. and Laslett, P. (eds.) *Aging in the Past, Demography, Society and Old Age*, London: University of California Press.

Wenger, C. (1984) *The supportive network*, London: Allen & Unwin.

Willmott, P. and Young, M (1960) *Family and Class in a London Suburb*, London: Routledge & Kegan Paul.

Wilson, G. (1987) 'Women's work: the role of grandparents in intergenerational transfers', *Sociological Review*, 354: 703-720.

Winterson, J. (2002) 'Whatever the changes in our outlook and lifestyles, a mother is still the heart of a home', *Guardian*, 12th March, 2002.

Young, M. (1977) 'Towards a new concordance', *New Society*, 17th November.

Young, M. (1997) 'The three pillars of the new family', *Philosophical Transactions of the Royal Society of London,* 352:1857-9.

Young, M. and Willmott, P. (1957) *Family and Kinship in East London*, London: Routledge and Kegan Paul.

INDEX

Note on authors:

Geoff Dench and Jim Ogg are both research fellows at the *Institute of Community Studies* in London and at *University College, London*.

Geoff Dench has been involved in research on family relations for the last ten years, and has previously written *Transforming Men* and edited *Rewriting the Sexual Contract*, both published by *Transaction*. Before that his research was mainly on ethnic relations, in which he wrote *Maltese in London*, and *Minorities in the Open Society*, both published by *Routledge & Kegan Paul*. Until recently he was professor of sociology at *Middlesex University*.

Jim Ogg was formerly a research fellow at the *Centre for Social Gerontology* at *Keele University*, and co-author of *The Family and Community Life of Older People* (*Routledge*, 2001) plus many articles and papers on the life of the elderly. He is also currently working in Paris at the *Caisse Nationale d'Assurance Vieillesse* on a number of European projects relating to family life and older people.